The Bloody Covenant

The Bloody Covenant

CROWN AND KIRK IN CONFLICT

RONALD IRELAND

The History Press

This story of the past is for Annabelle, Sophie, Alexander and Matthew,
who are the future

First published 2010

The History Press
The Mill, Brimscombe Port
Stroud, Gloucestershire, GL5 2QG
www.thehistorypress.co.uk

British Library Cataloguing in Publication Data.
A catalogue record for this book is available from the British Library.

ISBN 978 0 7524 5258 6

Typesetting and origination by The History Press
Printed in India by Nutech Print Services

Contents

Illustrations

13. The Martyrs Cross, Grassmarket, Edinburgh. (*Photograph by the author*)
14. Covenanters' Prison, Greyfriars Kirkyard, Edinburgh. (*Photograph by the author*)

The quotations noted from *The Passing of the Stewarts* are © Agnes Mure MacKenzie, 1937, reproduced by permission of Chambers Harrap Publishers Ltd.

Chronology

1517   Martin Luther – Declaration Against Indulgences, Wittenberg.

1528   Patrick Hamilton burned at St Andrews. James V commences personal rule.

1537   James V marries Madeleine of France, daughter of Francis I, who dies nine months later.

1538   James V marries Mary of Guise.

1542   Birth of Princess Mary on 8 December. Death of James V on 14 December.

1543   Treaty of Greenwich. March: reading of the Bible in Scots sanctioned by Parliament.

1544   The 'Rough Wooing'.

1545   The theologian, George Wishart, returns to Scotland; translates 'The First Helvetic Confession' into Scots; commences preaching campaign. First appearance of John Knox as supporter of Wishart at Haddington. Wishart burned at the stake at St Andrews. Destruction of Border Abbeys by the English.

1546   Murder of Cardinal Beaton. Knox taken prisoner by French at St Andrews.

1547   Death of Henry VIII.

1548   Infant Mary, Queen of Scots reaches France on 13 August.

1555   John Knox returns to Scotland.

1556   Knox returns to Geneva; writes *First Blast of the Trumpet against the Monstrous Regiment of Women*.

1557   The 'Lords of the Congregation' sign the 'First Covenant'.

1558   Mary Queen of Scots marries the Dauphin of France 24 April.

1559   Knox returns to Scotland; preaches a sermon at Perth portraying the Church of Rome as idolatrous and sparks a wave of violence and destruction against church property. Mary, Queen of Scots becomes Queen of France on the death of her father-in-law, Henri II.

1560   Death of Mary of Guise in June. The Scottish Estates pass an Act in August
       endorsing Knox's 'Confession of Faith' and Acts removing the authority of
       the Pope in Scotland. Francis II of France dies on 5 December and Mary
       becomes Queen Dowager of France.

1561   Mary Queen of Scots returns to Scotland, reaching Leith on 19 August. One
       week later Knox condemns the Mass in a sermon in St Giles, Edinburgh and
       is summoned by Mary to Holyrood. There follows a series of interviews.

1563   Mary undertakes a progress throughout the south of Scotland.

1565   Marriage of Mary and Henry Stuart, Lord Darnley, in July.

1566   Son, James, born to Mary on 15 June.

1567   Murder of Darnley on 10 February. Mary marries Bothwell in May.
       Bothwell defeated at Carberry Hill. Mary captured by Protestant Lords
       and moved to Loch Leven Castle. Signs Deed of Abdication on 24 July.
       Earl of Moray appointed Regent. Infant James crowned King of Scots at
       Church of the Holy Rude, Stirling on 29 July.

1568   Mary escapes from Loch Leven Castle on 2 May. Defeated at Langside on
       13 May, flees to Dundrennan Abbey and leaves Scotland on 16 May.

1571   Archbishops appointed to St Andrews and Glasgow.

1574   Andrew Melville returns to Scotland.

1578   James VI commences active reign.

1581   Melville produces the *Second Book of Discipline*. The 'Negative Confession'
       accepted by James.

1584   The Scottish Parliament introduces the 'Black Acts' on 22 May, introduc-
       ing the principle that the King is Head of the Church.

1587   Mary Queen of Scots executed at Fotheringay Castle in February.

1590   James VI addresses General Assembly on 4 August.

1592   Act of Parliament endorses *Second Book of Discipline*.

1600   Charles Stuart, later Charles I, born at Dunfirmline.

1603   Death of Elizabeth I on 24 March. James VI proclaimed James I of England
       and Ireland.

1606   James summons Andrew Melville and seven other Scottish divines
       to London. Melville is imprisoned in the Tower. Meeting at Perth, the
       Scottish Parliament passes an Act restoring the position of bishops. James
       commands a 'Convention' to meet at Linlithgow in December. Bishops to
       be permanent moderators of Presbyteries and provincial Synods.

1610   Courts of High Commission established under jurisdiction of each bishop
       – changes endorsed by General Assembly.

1611   Publication of King James Bible.

1612   Changes endorsed by Scottish Parliament.

1617   James returns to Scotland for short visit.

1625   James VI & I dies on 27 March. Prince Charles proclaimed King of Scots
       and King of England and Ireland; marries Henrietta Maria, daughter of

Henri IV of France. John Spottiswoode, Archbishop of Glasgow and four bishops become members of Scottish Privy Council. Privy Council passes an Act of Revocation.

1633 Charles visits Scotland and is crowned King of Scots in Edinburgh.

1634 New Court of High Commission created by Charles.

1635 Archbishop Spottiswoode appointed Chancellor. Charles orders the introduction of a Book of Canons, naming him as Head of the Church and requiring the use of the English Prayer Book.

1637 At a service in St Giles, Edinburgh, new liturgy introduced on 23 July. A riot follows. Representatives of the nobility, lairds, the towns and the Kirk establish 'The Tables'. Text of the 'National Covenant' drafted by Alexander Houston and Archibald Johnston.

1638 The National Covenant signed in the Kirkyard of Greyfriars, Edinburgh, on 8 February. General Assembly meets in Glasgow Cathedral in November and demands an Assembly and Parliament free of the absolute control of the King.

1639 Charles gathers army at Berwick. Covenanter army, led by Alexander Leslie, camps at Duns Law. Charles concedes Covenanters' main demands provided, Tables are disbanded and army stands down. Pacification of Berwick signed on 18 June. John Stuart, 1st Earl of Traquair appointed Lord High Commissioner. General Assembly meets late in year and endorses all the decisions of 1638 Assembly.

1640 Covenanting army led by General Leslie leaves Edinburgh and crosses the Tweed on 21 August and takes Newcastle by 30 August. Charles summons Parliament in England and then meets Scots Commissioners at Ripon, where Scots halt their advance and agree substantial subsistence payment.

1641 English Parliament concludes terms of agreement and Scottish army returns to Scotland. Charles goes north and arrives at Holyrood Palace on 14 August and opens Scottish Parliament the following week. Only those who have signed the Covenant can attend.

1642 Westminster Assembly set up by English Parliament in July. Charles raises standard at Nottingham on 22 August. Start of Civil War. Negotiations between the General Assembly and English Parliament lead to the Solemn League and Covenant.

1643 The Estates (Scottish Parliament) ratify the Solemn League and Covenant on 17 August and General Assembly adds its approval. Scottish Commissioners and members of both houses of English Parliament meet to sign the Westminster Confession.

1644 Scottish army led by the Earl of Leven (Alexander Leslie) crosses the border and joins the English Parliamentary army, led by Oliver Cromwell, in defeating the Royalist army at Marston Moor on 2 July. Scots march south as far as Hereford and besiege Newark on their return. Charles appears at their camp and siege is lifted. Charles joins Scots on return north to Newcastle. English Parliament demands removal of Scots from England. Charles arrested by English Parliamentary army. Solemn League and Covenant at an end.

1645 Montrose destroys Covenanting forces at Inverlochy. Montrose defeated at Battle of Philiphaugh by Covenanting army led by David Leslie.

1648 The 'Wiggamore Raid'. Estates pass the Act of Classes.

1649 The trial of Charles I commences on 20 January. Execution of Charles I on 30 January.

1650 Montrose defeated and captured at Carbisdale and executed in Edinburgh on 21 May. Charles II signs Covenants at Breda on 1 May and arrives in Scotland later that month. Battle of Dunbar, 3 September. Covenanters defeated by Cromwell.

1651 Charles II crowned King of Scots at Scone on 1 January. Battle of Worcester. Charles II defeated and flees into exile.

1653 General Assembly closed by Cromwellian troops in July. Oliver Cromwell appointed Lord Protector of Commonwealth of England, Scotland and Ireland on 16 December.

1657 Cromwell offered kingship. Declines and becomes Lord Protector again on 26 June.

1658 Cromwell dies on 3 September.

1659 The Rump Parliament revived.

1660 General Monk returns from Scotland to London. Convention meets at Westminster and recognises Charles as King. The Declaration of Breda brought to London on 1 May. Charles proclaimed King on 8 May and a few days later as King of Scots in Edinburgh.

1661 Executions of Marquis of Argyll on 27 May and Reverend James Guthrie on 1 June. Charles writes to Scottish Privy Council in September confirming his intention to reintroduce bishops and this is ratified by the Estates.

1662 Scots Parliament meets in Edinburgh in January and abandons the Solemn League and Covenant, and later confirms the return to Episcopacy.

1665 The Great Plague in London.

1666 The Great Fire of London, 2 September. Sir James Turner captured by Covenanters at Dalry on 13 November. Battle of Rullion Green, 28 November. Execution of Hugh McKail, 22 December.

1667 Act of Pardon and Indemnity, October.

1668 Attempt to murder Archbishop Sharpe in July.

1669 Indulgence issued on 25 July. Failed attempt by Lauderdale to introduce a scheme for union.

1670 Field conventicle held at Hill of Beith in June. First violent confrontation between Covenanters and authorities. Conventicle Act outlaws field conventicles.

1672   Start of Dutch War.

1673   English Parliament introduces the Test Act in March. Conventicle Act extended in July for further three years.

1674   Proclamation makes it the duty of heritors and employers to prevent attendance at conventicles.

1675   Letters of Intercommuning issued against non-Indulged clergy.

1677   1674 Proclamation renewed.

1678   8,000 Highlanders sent to south-west in spring. The Popish Plot.

1679   James Graham of Claverhouse appointed Sheriff Depute of Dumfries and Annandale in March. Archbishop Sharpe murdered at Magnus Muir on 3 May. Party of Whigs fix a declaration and testimony to the market cross of Rutherglen on 29 May. Battle of Drumclog on 1 June. Claverhouse defeated by Covenanters. Battle of Bothwell Brig on 22 June. Covenanters routed by Monmouth.

1680   Richard Cameron returns to Scotland. Party led by Cameron and Cargill pin a declaration on the market cross of Sanquhar on 22 June. Cameron killed at Airds Moss in July. Hackston executed in Edinburgh on 30 July.

1681   Cargill executed in Edinburgh on 27 July. The Test Act introduced in Scotland in August.

1682   At a conventicle at Talla Linn, James Renwick is chosen for the ministry.

1684   A royal proclamation in May names those charged with rebellion, among them James Nicol. Ambush at Enterkin Pass on 29 July. Three of the perpetrators hanged in Edinburgh on 5 August, watched by James Nicol who is apprehended. James Nicol hanged on 27 August. Renwick publishes *An Apological Declaration and Admonitory Vindication* in October.

1685   Charles II dies on 5 February. James, Duke of York proclaimed James VII & II, King of Scots on 10 February.

1686   Election of Town Councils suspended.

1688   Execution of James Renwick in Edinburgh on 17 February. Indulgence issued in April in England. Bishops protest. Son born to James VII & II on 11 June. James VII & II flees to France on 23 December.

1689   Estates meet as a 'Convention' in March. Estates issue a declaration on 11 April, including a 'Claim of Right'. William III (of Orange) and Mary II proclaimed as joint sovereigns from Mercat Cross of Edinburgh.

1690   Estates meet and on 25 April pass an Act removing royal supremacy from church affairs. On 26 May, Estates declare the Westminster Confession of Faith to be the only doctrinal source of the new Kirk of Scotland. Presbyterian courts restored.

1692   First General Assembly of restored Kirk called by King William which expels all Episcopalians.

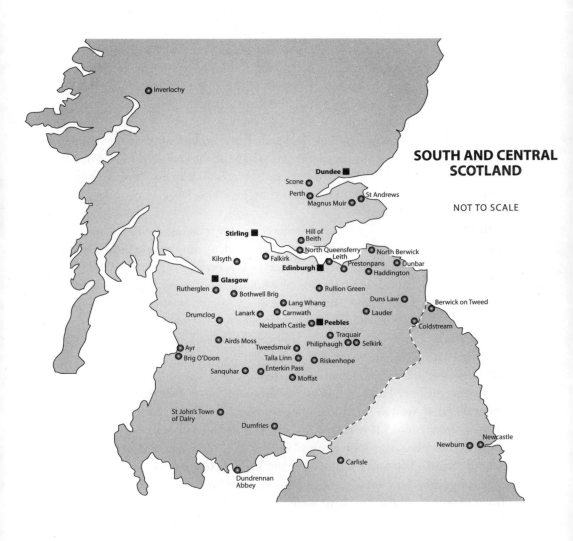

Inverlochy

SOUTH AND CENTRAL
SCOTLAND

NOT TO SCALE

Dundee

Scone
Perth
Magnus Muir
St Andrews

Hill of
Beith
Stirling
North Queensferry
Leith
North Berwick
Kilsyth
Falkirk
Edinburgh
Prestonpans
Dunbar
Haddington
Glasgow
Rutherglen
Rullion Green
Bothwell Brig
Duns Law
Lang Whang
Drumclog
Lanark
Carnwath
Lauder
Berwick on Tweed
Neidpath Castle
Peebles
Coldstream
Airds Moss
Traquair
Ayr
Tweedsmuir
Philiphaugh
Selkirk
Brig O'Doon
Talla Linn
Riskenhope
Sanquhar
Enterkin Pass
Moffat

St John's Town
of Dalry
Dumfries
Newcastle
Newburn
Carlisle
Dundrennan
Abbey

Introduction

This book was initially intended to be the story of the Covenanting tradition as it affected a Scottish burgh and, in particular, one of its inhabitants. In the event it has turned out to be the much wider story of the Scottish Reformation, not only as it affected that town and its people, but also the Scottish nation as a whole.

In 2004 Richard Holloway, the former Episcopal Bishop of Edinburgh, presented a series of programmes called *The Sword and the Cross*, outlining the history of Christianity in Scotland. The third of those programmes covered the seventeenth century. This included the time of the Covenanters and what became known as the 'the Killing Times', which reached a climax in 1684. That date struck a chord with me. As an active member of the Old Parish Church of Peebles, I was reminded of the four chalices which are in the possession of the congregation and which were gifted and dedicated some time after the month of July in 1684. It occurred to me that it was odd that this should have happened at a time when, although Episcopacy was still the order of the day, it was increasingly under threat from Presbyterianism. The four donors of the chalices are clearly identified, but no explanation remains as to why the gifts should have been made at that time. I decided to investigate further. Early in that investigation it became clear that the records for the period 1679 to 1692, which might have provided an explanation, no longer existed apart from a brief reference in the records of the Town Council of Peebles, which in July 1684 confirmed its decision to be the donor of one of the chalices. It was a mystery worthy of further research.

Very early in that investigation, I chanced upon a reference in a book called *Scottish Covenanter Stories* by Dane Love. This recorded that, in August 1684, James Nicol, a merchant burgess of Peebles, had been hanged in the Grassmarket of Edinburgh for Covenanting activities. This must have happened at about the same time as the dedication of the four chalices. Here was a strange coincidence indeed which set me off on a rather different trail. It was the starting point, but it seemed to me that those events could not be understood without exploring earlier events, which eventually culminated in the 'Killing Times' and which dominated the political and religious life of Scotland over almost two centuries.

The story of the Reformation in Scotland is a long and complicated one. There is a widespread misconception that it started and ended with John Knox, but he is only part of the story. In reality, the Reformation spanned a period of more than 165 years, until the Church of Scotland was finally established in 1690 in the Presbyterian form in which it exists today. Knox, although a significant and dominating figure, was not the first Scottish reformer (that accolade lies with George Wishart), nor was he the last, and many others, such as Andrew Melville, Alexander Henderson and James Guthrie, were also to play a prominent part.

In writing this book I have attempted to draw together three differing strands. First there is the story of the Scottish Reformation and its effect on the religious and political life of the country. In attempting to set this out I have used *A History of Scotland* by J.D. Mackie, first published in 1964, as a primary source. Although perhaps not the most detailed study of Scotland's history, it provides a broad sweep encompassing the essentials of that story in a way that is both readable and easily understood by the ordinary layman, among whom I certainly count myself.

More particularly for the period 1638 to 1684 I have used as my guide *The Passing of the Stewarts* by Agnes Mure MacKenzie, published in 1937. She is a historian largely forgotten today, but someone who writes in a style that combines a wide knowledge of her subject with a light touch and yet with much insight. Where appropriate I have also used information taken from many other historical works, which are listed at the end of the book. In relation to the part that covers the period of the association of John Stuart, Earl of Traquair with King Charles I, I have had access to the Traquair House archive.

The second strand relates to the Royal Burgh of Peebles, its life and times during the period covered and how that related to the wider Scottish scene. We tend to absorb the story of the past in a broad sweep. It is the great events and the actions of powerful men and women that command our attention. Just as today there is another dimension, so in times past there is also the story of how those events and the actions of those men and women affected ordinary folk, living ordinary lives in ordinary communities. Great events are remembered as taking place in great cities or at the very least in places whose names are part of the folklore of Scotland: Bannockburn; Flodden; Culloden; Stirling and Edinburgh Castles and the like, but they are only part of the story of Scotland.

Many of the events and life that I have included relating to Peebles, could doubtless be mirrored in many another Scottish burghs of the time. Although these events may seem trivial and certainly parochial, I have included them because its life and times can arguably be seen to represent contemporary life as it affected the ordinary people and their local leaders throughout Scotland. For example, in the decades leading up to the Reformation, the corruption of the

Church of Rome filtered down through every level of society and this is amply demonstrated by the experience of Peebles. There were those times when national events directly affected the lives of ordinary people: the violence of the Border Raids by the followers of Henry VIII; the signing of the National Covenant and the Cromwellian invasion and occupation. Then there were those national events which seem to have passed by without comment, when the ordinary concerns of the town and its rulers, in the shape of the Town Council, focused on local issues and problems. There was, however, a degree of oversight at a national level and indeed, up to the Union of the Crowns the monarch commonly dispensed justice in person, and in the earlier part of the book I have shown how this was often the case in Peebles. The Town Council was always powerful, but after the departure of James VI to London, it dominated everyday life. This was a time when modern communications were lacking and when hearsay and rumour enjoyed a prominence which modern mass media renders irrelevant. Although not necessarily isolated from central affairs, in an age that lacked the nationally codified law and policing present today, the Council were judge and jury, regulator of prices and the conduct of trade and every aspect of life in the town. It decided who might live there. In this, the Town Council of Peebles was no different from any Town Council of the day, and I have introduced a number of incidents and events to illustrate how parochial events may have mirrored the wider conduct of life during the period concerned.

A constant theme throughout the book is the question of loyalty to the Crown, and also the impact of the ever-changing religious order. These were issues that engaged the attention of both great and lesser mortals. Peebles was a strategically important town lying fairly close to the capital, Edinburgh, and not far from the centre and influence of government. At the same time, particularly during the period of high Covenanting activity, it must have been influenced by that activity, much of it occurring on its doorstep. Thus Peebles is not the main theme, but it is a reflection of it.

Peebles was, in a very real sense, a 'Royal' burgh and was frequently visited by Scottish Kings and Queens and their courts, most notably by Alexander III and then by the succession of Stewart monarchs, starting with James I and going up to the departure of James VI to London in 1603 at the Union of the Crowns. I have used as my main local sources extracts from the Records of the Royal Burgh and the Kirk Session, as these have been collected first by Rev. Robert Renwick, at the end of the nineteenth century, and later by Dr Clement Gunn, in the early part of the twentieth. In addition, I have had assistance from the works of Robert and William Chambers in the nineteenth century and by J. Walter Buchan in the twentieth.

The final strand relates to the person of James Nicol, the 'Martyr of Peebles'. There were many Covenanting martyrs. Many are names well known. Little is known of James Nicol and what *is* known is largely forgotten. That he was a real man of flesh and blood is without doubt. His name emerges, fleetingly, from the records and histories of Peebles, only to retreat again into the shadows of time. There is a brief mention here, an odd reference there; the suggestion that perhaps he kept a diary. What does remain is a written testimony attributed to him, written, or possibly dictated, just before his death. This appears in a book entitled *A Cloud of Witnesses* published in Edinburgh in 1871 and is based upon a much earlier publication, which in turn dates from not many years after he died. The testimony is almost certainly authentic and, while giving away little by way of background, it says something of the character of the man: a character of courage and conviction, attributes which were ultimately to cause him to suffer the direst of penalties. His testimony alone makes his part in the story worthy of inclusion. What is certain is that he lived through a period of fast-moving events, changing circumstances and changing loyalties; a time when the questions of religious practice, faith and belief were the cause of struggle, persecution and bloodshed on an unimaginable scale.

In some chapters, especially during the period covering the life of James Nicol, I have used the present tense as a device to give a sharper focus to the events portrayed. In those chapters, while I have used my own imagination to a degree, the basic facts and the descriptions of the life of the town and buildings are based on facts gleaned from the various sources to which I have referred. In 'The Great Conventicle', I owe something to the work of Scott and Stevenson, each of whom has given a vivid, if fictional, description of these large gatherings. I have included the testimony of James Nicol virtually verbatim as it speaks far more eloquently than any words of mine could.

One of the difficulties in attempting to write a clear and coherent account of the evolution of the Covenanting cause is that there are numerous movements, factions and parties that crop up throughout the period, each with its own particular identity. The term 'Covenanter' seems clear enough and in essence covers all those who sought adherence to the principles of the National Covenant of 1638, but within that broad definition there are a multitude of groupings, each with its own title and *raison d'etre*. Thus in the earliest days it encompassed much of the body politic of Scotland, but in time divisions arose, separating 'Engagers' from 'Protesters', who then evolved into 'Remonstrants' and 'Resolutioners', and so on through 'Whigs' to 'Cameronians' and 'United Societies'. In an attempt to shed light on all these groupings and also some of the contemporary political institutions, I have included a 'Glossary of Political and Religious Factions' and I have there given an explanation for each in the order in which they arise.

I make no pretensions to being an academic historian. Rather I write as an amateur, albeit a passionately interested one. As such I have tried to write the book in a way which makes it readable and of interest to a wide audience. I hope that those who do read it may find it enjoyable as a story (and what is history if not a story?), but also informative about a period in the life of Scotland largely overlooked today. It is a period which covers a critical time in the development of religious and political authority; a period which, after much strife, was to lead on in due course to the quieter waters of the eighteenth century and the great period of the Scottish Enlightenment.

I am indebted to a number of people for their advice and assistance in producing this book. My thanks are due to Dane Love for pointing me towards the testimony of James Nicol, for allowing me to use extracts from his own published work and for his constructive comments on the original text; to Bill Goodburn, Elizabeth Forrest and Margaret Houston, for proof reading and making helpful comments and suggestions; Catherine Maxwell-Stuart for allowing me access to the Stewart Family archive and for permission to include the portrait of the 1st Earl of Traquair and the holograph letter of Charles I as illustrations; Margaret Fox for assistance in accessing those documents; Rosemary Hannay and Chris Sawers of Tweeddale Museum for their help with some of the illustrations; the Kirk Session of Peebles Old Parish Church of Scotland for permission to photograph the 1684 communion cups; Elizabeth Benson for permission to include a photograph of 'The Seige of Neidpath' by Jack Roney; Alastair MacFarlane for photographs and Ian Ronaldson for outlining the map and help and advice about printing.

    Last, but not least, special thanks are due to my long-suffering wife Margaret, who has supported me throughout this venture, tolerating my silences and tetchiness during the long months of composition; for her helpful comments and suggestions and not least for guiding my sometimes wayward grammar.

Ronald Ireland
Peebles

Prologue

27 August 1684 dawned brightly upon Edinburgh, sunshine permeating the pall of reek that seemed an almost permanent feature of the old Scottish capital. It was as warm and bright as any day in late August can be. The citizens and visitors to the town, a motley collection of the highest and lowest in society, thrown together by the close-packed streets and closes, were about their normal business. Those who moved about picked their way carefully through the straw and mire and general garbage that were a feature, and which made the old town something of a cesspit. Dwellers in the high 'Lands', which rose on either side of the High Street and elsewhere, discharged the detritus of their dwellings casually into the street below, with little regard and less concern for anyone walking on the street, be they lord or beggar. By mid-morning the taverns were alive with raucous activity, the better of them already filled with the legal cognoscenti, lords and lairds, and others for whom the capital and its taverns were the focus of their lives. Claret flowed, oiling the wheels of government and justice.

At about three o'clock on that Wednesday afternoon, a horse-drawn cart, carrying its driver and four others, emerged from the Tolbooth prison and made its way through the filth and mire of the winding streets. Two of the occupants of the cart were bound and sat dishevelled, sullen and silent. Both held their heads high and in their faces was a hint of pride and steely determination. Occasionally, their glance strayed to the faces of those who stopped to watch their passing, some from street level and some hanging out of the high windows of the Lands above, seeking a better view. Behind them stood two guards, muskets at the ready. The destination for these five, for a brief time joined together, was the Grassmarket, lying at the foot of the louring Castle Rock and Edinburgh's place of execution. Some of those who watched their journey jeered and laughed in the way that people do when presented with any undignified spectacle. Some cheered and gave vent to their feelings of approval for what they deemed to be the rightful despatch of the two condemned men, about to receive their just deserts, but others looked on with the silence of pity and a sense of the injustice of the thing.

As was usual on such occasions, the Grassmarket, a relatively large open space in the constricted town, was filled with an expectant crowd of onlookers. Perhaps the crowd was not as large here as at other such gatherings, for these occasions were now all too commonplace and the novelty was greatly diminished. The cart passed between the towering lands of the High Street and the Land Market and then descended the steep incline of the West Bow, which led down into the Grassmarket itself. At its approach the beat of a drum started, a constant, monotonous beat, echoing from the surrounding walls and rock face. The crowd, watchful and silent, turned towards the approaching cart, necks craning for a first view of the principal participants in the unfolding drama. Some of the jostling throng were openly derisive, but many stood in sympathetic silence. In those days the good folk of Edinburgh expressed their views with little sound.

Reaching the scaffold platform, the condemned men were hustled unceremoniously up the waiting steps. Both men knelt briefly in a prayer of thanksgiving for past life and hope for their future salvation in the true House of God and then awaited their fate; for these two were Covenanters, and for that crime against King and country they were about to die. Both climbed the waiting ladders unaided and for a moment paused, heads held high, committing themselves to God's mercy, which they doubted not. The hangman did his duty, with a swift twist of the ladder, and after but a few minutes the tightening ropes squeezed the last remnants of life from the bodies of William Young and James Nicol. Soon they hung silent, gently swaying, lifeless in the warm August air.

James Nicol was fifty-one years of age and a merchant burgess of the Royal Burgh of Peebles.

A few weeks earlier, on the Sunday following the Lammas Fair, an altogether different event took place in the ancient Border town of Peebles. It was a celebration. A religious celebration. A celebration of the ascendancy of Episcopacy over Presbyterianism; the two rights which had created a vacillating Church order since the final eclipse of the Church of Rome, some 125 years previously.

The town was in festive mood and quite a crowd had gathered to witness the procession of clergy and town dignitaries from the Burgh Tolbooth to the Cross Kirk, then the Parish Church of the burgh. The entrance to the Tolbooth was flanked by the halberdiers in their scarlet coats and black hats, each holding a long pike. Behind them, in the courtyard of the civic centre of the town, the procession was assembling, with not a little jostling and considerable noise, as each person sought to ensure his proper station and position.

At last the procession was ready to move off and, amid the cheers of most of the assembled crowd, the halberdiers led the way, turning westwards into the High Street, followed by the town drummers and fifers. Then came the beadle with his staff of office, leading the clergy in ascending order of superiority, the minor clergy preceding the minister of the parish, the Reverend John Hay, and lastly, magnificent in his brilliant robes, Arthur Rose, Lord Archbishop of Glasgow and loyal servant of King Charles II. Behind him came the provost, bailies and members of the Town Council, seventeen in all, each in his official robes, each aware of his own importance and wearing that self-satisfied expression so typical of town dignitaries. Behind them came the members of the Guildry, representing the trade and craftsmen of the town. Not everyone who watched the procession did so with pleasure. Not all were enthusiastic supporters of Episcopacy, although in those days it was best not to let such lack of support be seen or known.

As the procession wended its way down the High Street towards the West Port, many of the crowd at the Tolbooth, rather than attempting to follow, made their way to the Cross Kirk by a shorter route, some by way of Cunzie Nook into the Northgait, and some taking the slightly shorter route down the Deans Wynd to the gate through the town wall at the Trie Brig, and then across the bridge itself and up the Kirkgait to the church. In the meantime, the procession itself had passed the old Chapel of St Mary and through the West Port, turning north towards the Auld Toun across the Peebles Brig, with the remnants of the Castle of Peebles on their left. Then up the Hie Gait through the Auld Toun, turning north again into the Lychgait and then east into the road or gait that ran between the Hie and the Cross kirks. By the time the procession reached the Cross Kirk a goodly crowd was already there, and it was with some difficulty that the halberdiers forced their way to the door, then standing aside in order to let the great and the good of Church and Royal Burgh enter the church building, which was already well filled.

The service followed the now established Episcopal form. The centre point was to be the dedication of four silver chalices, two donated in memory of former local gentlemen of note, one by the present incumbent of the parish and the fourth by the Town Council of the Royal Burgh. Together the donation of these chalices represented a demonstration of loyalty to King Charles II and the Episcopal structure of reformed religion demanded by him. The chalices having been duly dedicated with appropriate ceremony by the Lord Archbishop of Glasgow, the service was brought to a close. Once more the procession re-formed to return to the Tolbooth, this time by way of the Kirkgait, the Trie Brig, the Northgait and Cunzie Nook, no doubt for further celebration of the day with suitable refreshment.

From his distant vantage point at the top of the Kirklands, James Nicol looked down on the loyal representatives of Episcopacy emerging from the church – and spat on the ground in disgust – 'Priests of Ba'al!'*

---

*and he said unto him that was over the vestry, Bring forth vestments for all the worshippers of Ba'al. And he brought them forth vestments.

2 Kings 10:22

In 1684 the execution of a seemingly ordinary and humble man, who refused to acknowledge the King as Head of the Church, and a Church which demonstrated its subservience to that same King, epitomised the point at which the great ecclesiastical debate had reached. It was theology against politics and, as so often in history, for the moment at least, it was politics and the power of the State in the person of the King that prevailed, dictating the government of the Kirk and destroying those of a different mind. These are events that happened within six years of the final victory of Presbyterianism, but they show that the religious conflict of the seventeenth century, even in its death throes, reached down into the very heart of Scottish society.

The road from Rome to Kirk was a long one. The whole process started with the Reformation, in Scotland Calvinist and Presbyterian. The initial battle was to destroy the power of the Pope of Rome. That battle was effectively won in 1560 with the establishment of the Presbyterian order. In England, in somewhat different circumstances, it was to continue into the seventeenth century and beyond. There the Elizabethan age saw a fierce campaign to stamp out the remnants of Catholicism, not least because of the political threat it posed to the Crown. In Scotland, what followed the victory of Presbyterianism developed into a struggle between the Crown and the people, with successive monarchs seeking to fill the vacuum which the destruction of Papal power had created. It is perhaps one of the great ironies of history that 'the people' finally prevailed because of the attempt by a foolish King, James VII & II, to restore the influence of the Church of Rome.

The Catholic Church had long represented power and material wealth. It made Kings and Queens and, when displeased, used the sledgehammer of excommunication to un-make them. Its prelates filled the great offices of State. English Episcopacy, which replaced it, was created out of the marital problems of a belligerent and megalomaniac King, Henry VIII. It can be seen as something of an anachronism, with its liturgical roots still in the Roman Catholic tradition, but with its power in the hands of the monarch. Its structure had great attractions for those who followed him. James VI & I had long flirted with a form of Episcopacy for the Kirk in Scotland, although he would have seen this as far removed from Papal supremacy. For a time he struggled to impose it, but supreme pragmatist that he was, he was wise enough to recognise the limits of what he could achieve, which was a Kirk largely Presbyterian but with Episcopal overtones. With the Union of the Crowns in 1603, he saw, first hand, the attractions of Episcopacy. This was a spur for him to impose them again on his northern kingdom. The attractions were as much political as theological, bringing with them the unification of Church and State under one supreme head; but once again pragmatism resulted in his settling for an uneasy compromise.

For his son, Charles I, there would be no compromise. For him the Divine Right of Kings, which his father had espoused but had applied within practical limits, was an absolute, incapable of compromise. In seeking to impose Episcopacy in Scotland, a country where the Reformed Order was strongly Calvinist Presbyterian, Charles found himself faced with a strength of opposition which he failed to recognise, far less understand. It was opposition from a nation that for centuries had shown a sense of fierce national independence. Within it were factions of an even more radically independent mind, most notably the Covenanters. At first this was largely a national movement, supported by the broad body politic of Scotland, but in time evolving into a faction that espoused fanatical Biblical fundamentalism, which it sought to defend to the death.

No nation is an entirely homogeneous unit and certainly not Scotland, where independence of thought has long been a tradition. No doubt because of the nature of the country, with its diverse structure and the need to provide defence against aggressors both local and from further afield, there grew up a culture of mutual defence within local communities. Thus in the Highlands the system of clans evolved and in the Lowlands there grew up burghs, many of which received special royal recognition.

The Royal Burghs of Scotland are numerous and have had a significant part to play in the structure of government, at least since the fourteenth century. By the fifteenth century Scotland had a Parliament, different from that of England, but representative of the whole nation. This was the Estates, to be precise the Three Estates, the Lords Spiritual (the Church), Temporal (the landed magnates and lairds), and the Common Weal (the representatives of the counties and burghs), all presided over by the monarch. Much of the power in the land had been in the hands of the great magnates, their power derived from their ownership or overlordship of geographical areas. Over the centuries these magnates were a source of conflict, particularly in the fourteenth and fifteenth centuries, but as the power and influence of the Crown grew, so too did the influence of the Church and the counties and burghs. As well as being effectively self-governing units, represented in the Estates, the burghs, or at least the major ones, were centres where the monarch personally dispensed justice and from which he might raise a militia, as there was no standing army in Scotland, at least not until the reign of James VII & II. Peebles, one of the oldest Royal Burghs in Scotland, shared many features with other Royal Burghs, but it also had a strategic place as a stepping off point for control of the Borders and as a defence against English invasion, up to the sixteenth century. It was also an important ecclesiastical centre until the Reformation. In the seventeenth century it lay on the very edge of the regions that saw most of the later Covenanting activity.

For centuries Kings of Scotland supported the Catholic tradition. Then as the shockwaves from the Reformation spread out across Europe, the power of the people, led by dynamic preachers like Wishart and Knox, began to break down the power and influence of the Pope. The ordinary folk, as well as the great of the land, became part of a power struggle for minds and loyalties; first a struggle for religious belief and then a struggle for power over and governance of the Church. Those were two distinct struggles, but in understanding the second it is necessary to understand the first, and in understanding both it is helpful to see how this affected not only the national scene, but how it affected a much smaller part of the nation, a Royal Burgh, which had an independent life of its own. In understanding the place of a Royal Burgh, there needs to be some understanding of its antecedents, its evolution and in particular where it stood in relation to the Scottish Crown, the Kirk and those who sought to amend it. Peebles and its long history provide a rich source.

Those events of 1684, looked at in isolation, may not seem significant, but they represent two extremes of a conflict which had raged across Scotland for 150 years. Rome was not built in a day and neither was the Kirk of Scotland.

PART I

I

———ɷɷɷ———

A Town of Kings

The town of Peebles lies some 25 miles south of the capital city of Edinburgh, at the foot of the long, broad valley of Eddleston Water where it joins the River Tweed. It stands astride the confluence of these two waters as it has done for centuries past. Today it is a flourishing and picturesque former market town, with more than a hint of by-gone days. Climb Venlaw Hill, which lies close by on the north-east, and from that viewpoint look down into the centre of the town. Before you lies a medieval town with its High Street on an elevated central spur, running alongside the River Tweed on its southern flank, from the former Castle Hill, now occupied by the Old Parish Church, to the Eastgate. To the north and south of the High Street, narrow vennels run down to the Eddleston Water and to the banks of the River Tweed, which is spanned by a medieval bridge. Two further bridges, although modern, cross Eddleston Water as bridges have done for centuries. Although most of the buildings originate from the eighteenth century or later, this ancient townscape has remained basically unchanged for more than 500 years.

Peebles is a much more ancient place than even these signs suggest. There has been a settlement there at least since Roman times. It is one of Scotland's oldest burghs – its Burgh Charter was possibly granted by David I, King of Scots, some-time before AD 1153. This has often been disputed, some authorities suggesting that the Charter was granted by David II. Dr Pennecuik[1] suggests that the town was created a Royal Burgh in the thirteenth century by Alexander III, but later writers support the earlier date. Whatever the truth of the matter, it is likely that the status of Peebles as a place of regular visitation by Kings of Scots was recognised by the succession of monarchs following David I. It does not frequently feature in major works of Scottish History, yet throughout the centuries it has had its moments. On 9 May 1261, Alexander III, King of Scots, established a religious house here. It was the only religious foundation by a King, who was arguably one of the great Kings of Scotland. It was under his rule that Scotland became a national entity, largely as we know it today. The foundation was further added to in 1493 by the ill-fated James III, with much encouragement from his wife Margaret of Denmark, when a monastery was built around it. This seems to have been a major religious institution and became the Conventual Monastery of the Order of Trinity Friars, and probably provided a comfortable place of residence for the King and his successors on their visits to Peebles. The remnants can still be seen today within the grounds of the Cross Kirk, although it is likely that the whole complex of buildings would have extended far beyond the limits of the present boundary walls.

In medieval times Peebles was situated at the western edge of the great Forest of Ettrick, which stretched south and east over much of the area beyond the Tweed. The forest was the frequent hideaway of William Wallace during the years of his struggle to regain the independence of Scotland from the ravages of Edward I, and it was at Peebles that the feud between Robert Bruce, later to become a great King of Scots, and John Comyn reached a crisis. Wallace had been heavily defeated by Edward at Falkirk in 1298 and thereafter escaped to France, taking less of a direct part in the continuing resistance. Bruce, then Earl of Carrick, and John the 'Red' Comyn, were appointed Guardians of Scotland in his absence. Each represented one of the two great families claiming the Scottish Crown. Together they had led an unsuccessful attempt to dislodge the English from Roxburgh Castle, and with the leading Scottish lords and their forces, they had returned to Peebles to re-group and plan their continuing strategy. There was a great deal of frustration and ill-feeling amongst them and, according to a report by an English spy, there was a disagreement between Sir David Graham and Wallace's brother about lands that belonged to William Wallace. As the report records: 'At this the two knights gave lie to each other and drew their daggers. And since Sir David Graham was of Sir John Comyn's following, it was reported to the Earl of Buchan and John Comyn that a fight had broken out without their knowing it; and John Comyn leaped at the Earl of Carrick and seized him by the throat and the Earl of Buchan turned on the Bishop of St Andrews, declaring that treason and *lese majeste* were being plotted.' Bruce was nearly killed, but somehow, after the altercation, the two protagonists came to an agreement that Comyn would support Bruce's claim to the throne and that Bruce, in turn, would grant his lands to Comyn. It was Comyn who failed to keep the bargain and not long after, in a further altercation, in the Church of the Greyfriars in Dumfries, Bruce killed Comyn. This was a crime which led to his excommunication, but nevertheless paved his way to the Scottish throne.

It was doubtless the proximity to Ettrick Forest, with its wealth of every type of wild animal available to hunt, which endeared Peebles as a place of lodging to the long line of Stewart Kings and Queens.

That the town of Peebles has been a Royal Residence, is very evident, from
the walls, ports, and other remains of regal security: several decayed buildings & etc. still retain the names of their possessors in office; as the Dean's
house, Usher's wynd, Borthwick's walls, King's house, Castle hill, King's
orchards & etc.

> Captain Armstrong, Peebles, 1775[2]

Peebles would appear to have been often used as a hunting residence by our
Scottish Kings. Money would seem to have been coined in it; an house still
retaining the name Cuinzee Nook.[3]

> Agricultural Survey of Peeblesshire, 1802[4]

James I is reputed to have known the town well and the phrase 'Peebles at the
play' is certainly attributed to him, although the origins are disputed. It appears in
two completely different poems. Probably the one truly attributable to James I is
'Christis Kirk of the Greene'.

> Wes nevir in Scotland hard or seen
> Sic dansing nor deray
> Nouthir at Falkland on the grene
> Nor Pebillis at the play.[5]

The other poem which uses the phrase is also attributed to James I by William
Tytler[6], who claims that it was written by the King during one of his visits to
Peebles when he stayed at St Leonard's Well, a hospice some one and a half miles
downstream of Peebles. However, it seems more likely to have been written at
a later date, possibly during the reign of James V, and whether by that King's or
indeed any King's hand is also in some doubt. In any event, it is a lengthy poem,
which is called 'Peebles at the Play' with some twenty-six stanzas, but the following extracts give the flavour of it:

> At Beltane, when ilk body bounds
> To Peebles to the play,
> To hear the singing and the sounds,
> Their solace, sooth to say
> By firth and forest forth they found,
> They graithit them full gay;
> God wait that wald they do that stound,
> For it was their feast-day,
> They said,
> Of Peebles at the Play.

All the wenches of the west
Were up ere the cock crew;
For reeling there might nae man rest,
For garray nor for glew.

The poem then goes on to mention a number of places where some of the revellers are to be found:

Hope, Cailye, and Cardrona,
Gatherit out thick-fald,
With 'Hey and Howe, rohumbelow,'
The young folk were full bald.
The bagpipe blew, and out they threw
Out of the towns untald;
Lord, sic ane schout was them amang,
When they ower the wald,
There wets,
At Peebles at the Play.

There is a description of a tavern where, inevitably, there is a quarrel and a fight. (Not much has changed!)

They thrang out of the door at ance
Withouten ony reddin;
Gilbert in ane gutter glayde,
He gat nae better beddin.
There was not ane of them that day
Wad do ane other's biddin;
Thereby lay three-and-thirty-some,
O draff,
At Peebles at the Play.

The twenty-sixth stanza brings the poem finally to a close:

By this the sun was setting fast,
And near done was the day:
There men might hear shookin of chafts
When that they went their way;
Had there been made of the sang,
Mair suld I to you say;
At Beltane, when ilk body bounds
To Peebles to the play.[7]

Opinions differ as to what might have constituted the 'Play' of Peebles. It would probably have been held on the day of a fair. Possibly there would have been some competitive events and these were most likely to have been archery and horse racing, although it has been suggested that there might also have been some form of football game. Certainly, if the quoted poem is anything to go by, it was a day of celebration, fun and conviviality.

Fairs and plays apart, there is a charming story told by Robert Chambers in his *Picture of Scotland*, which again confirms the presence and hunting fervour of the Scottish monarchs. The King, unnamed, but possibly Alexander III, and some of his nobles were one day engaged in hawking along the banks of the Tweed, a short distance to the east of Peebles. In pursuit of its prey the hawk flew across the Tweed, but as the river was in flood, the King and his retinue were unable to follow the bird, and to make matters worse, they were unable to recall it. This particular bird seems to have been a special favourite of the King, who was much distressed by its impending loss. However, their predicament was solved unexpectedly by a local farmer. This man was an ancestor of the Horsburgh family (although that was not his name at the time). He was ploughing land on the other side of the river and as he knew the depth and flow of the river, whose banks he had cultivated for many seasons, he unhitched his plough and with one of his horses he came across the river and returned the hawk and its prey to the King. For this service the King, as a token of his gratitude, instantly granted him all the lands north of the Tweed which could be seen from his plough. Tradition adds that as he was crossing the river the King, anxiously watching, called out 'horse bruik weel', by which he meant 'may the horse carry you well against the current'. From that time on, the lands and their new owner became known as 'Horsbruik', and in time this became 'Horsburgh'. The remnants of Horsburgh Castle can still be seen today, close to the main Peebles/Galashiels road, just after the entrance to Glentress, and the surrounding lands still retain the name.[8]

Peebles was a favourite place for the Stewart Kings and Dr Gunn records that all the Stewart sovereigns (up to the Union of the Crowns in 1603) worshipped in the Cross Kirk. The regular presence of the Scottish monarchs is recalled in the names of parts of the town: 'Kings Meadows', 'Kingsland', 'Kingsmuir' and 'Kings Orchard', which are still extant today.

At least six registered State documents under the hand of James IV are recorded as issued at Peebles and doubtless he was not an infrequent visitor, in pursuit of his enlightened policy of showing himself to all his people, be they in the Highlands, the Lowlands or the Borders. A King of Scots indeed. The descendants who followed him, at least until the Union of the Crowns of Scotland and England in 1603, seem to have had a special affinity for their Royal Burgh and its people, as the records of the subsequent period show.

2

'The Guidman O' Ballengeich'

British historians have generally not been kind to the Stewart monarchs, concentrating on their weaknesses and failing to recognise their virtues. Weaknesses they had aplenty, and most of their reigns ended to some degree a failure, but then what modern statesman, and for that matter stateswoman, has not similarly ended their career in decline or at least outstayed their welcome?

The problem for the Stewarts was that so often their accession was as a minor and this allowed the great lords and magnates a freedom, which they might not otherwise have had, to run amuck and abrogate power to themselves, often in bloody conflict with their rivals. That rivalry was centred upon control, if not actual possession of the child monarch. Strangely, however, although still trying to retain influence, the rights and power of the monarch were recognised when the age of personal rule[1] was reached. It is fair to say that upon achieving personal rule the young Stewart monarchs usually succeeded in taking control, imposing royal authority and reducing the power of the great magnates once again. Naturally this was hardly popular with the magnates stripped of their former power and this inevitably sowed the seeds of later failure. The Stewart Kings, youthful as they may have been, were no shrinking violets. Certainly this was true of James I: kidnapped as a child and kept in virtual captivity at the English Court for twenty years, before returning to Scotland to rule what was by then a very unruly nation. By force of will and not a little military strength, he subjugated his dissident lords with some ferocity. The backlash was inevitable and ultimately it was the subjugated lords who gained the upper hand, although they had to resort to murder to do so.

His son, James II, succeeded to the throne as a six-year-old and for a number of years was a pawn in the power struggle between the magnates, vying with each other to keep his person under their control and investing themselves with royal power and authority. This was the time when the power of the great Douglas family was at its zenith. There is an old children's bedtime rhyme:

Hush thee, hush thee, do not fret thee,
The Black Douglas will not get thee.

When he reached the time of his personal rule, James II showed himself to be no
mean King. His crushing of the House of Douglas was ruthless and brutal, and his
treatment of those who had plotted the downfall of his father was no less severe.
No doubt he too might have suffered a backlash, had an exploding fire piece at
the siege of Roxburgh Castle not ended his life.

Once again Scotland had a boy King. James III was ten years old when his
father was killed and, although following the assumption of his personal rule
much progress was made in the good governance of Scotland, his reign ended
in his failure to control the magnates, unhappy with the imposition of a state of
order in the land. Rebellion was the result and his life was ended at the hands
of the rebels. Even the reign of his charismatic son James IV, who succeeded his
father at the age of fifteen, and was both successful and dominant in his control
and enhancement of the nation state and its culture, is clouded by the tragic failure of Flodden.

Perhaps of all the Stewart Kings, history has dealt most harshly with James V.
He was one and a half years old at the time of his father's death, but at the early age
of twenty-nine turned his face to the wall and died at Falkland on 14 December
1542, following the humiliation of the Scottish army by the English at Solway
Moss. Yet his reign was not all failure. His personal rule began when he was thirteen years of age, and soon after he set out to impose his will over the once more
troublesome Douglases, the Highlands and Islands and, not least, the Borders.
In the early years, James seems to have been popular with the ordinary folk, the
Common Weal. His concern for the people is shown by the creation, with his
full support, of the Court of Session, which has remained as the final arbiter of
Scottish law ever since. To this court, during his reign, were brought a number
of civil cases by poor tenants against oppressive lairds. It is also demonstrated by
his visits to the Borders in most years of his reign, to personally preside at justice
ayres, where again, ordinary folk might seek redress for ills inflicted upon them by
their own kind or those of rank above them. It was probably not without reason
that he was known as the 'poor man's king'.

A more romanticised version of his role as a champion of the people is found
in the stories of 'the Guidman O' Ballengeich', the unknown gentleman of
noble birth, who went about in disguise visiting the poor in their humble hovels
and distributing his largesse to them. The more cynical view is that such visitations had more to do with his sexual appetite; however much the poor may have
benefited, James's contribution to the increasing population of Scotland was not
exactly insignificant. Like his father, he was a Renaissance King, well educated
and with personal knowledge of the great royal courts of Europe. He spent
many months at the French Court of Francis I, before wedding his daughter,

Madeleine. No doubt it was at that court that he learned of the great world of the arts and architecture. Madeleine died only nine months after she was brought to Scotland by her new husband. The palace, which he subsequently built within Stirling Castle, is still recognised as one of the finest examples of Renaissance architecture in Britain, as is the Palace of Linlithgow and its magnificent fountain, which he built for his new bride, Mary of Guise. The hunting lodge he built at Falkland is a further Renaissance gem inspired by him. He seems to have had a particular affection for Peebles and its surrounding forests, to judge by his many recorded and perhaps many more unrecorded visits to the Royal Burgh.

His personal rule commenced in 1524 and his first recorded visit to Peebles was in August 1525, when he stayed in the town together with his Lords and Council. Probably they, or at least the principal among them, enjoyed the hospitality of the minister and brethren of the Cross Kirk. Wherever it may have been, on the evidence of the food and drink purchased and consumed they must have been a sizeable company – 157 loaves of bread, 1 bullock, ¼ calf, 17 sheep, 72 poultry, 9 capons, 8 plovers and large quantities of barley, eggs, pears, apples, butter and mustard, not to mention 46 gallons of ale were needed to sustain them. The next day they moved on to Selkirk. James was back again the following year from 17–19 July, at a time when he was still under the forcible fostering and tutelage of the Earl of Angus and the Douglas family. He made his escape from the Douglases' clutches in 1528 and from then on, although still only eighteen years old, he was able to be very much his own man.

The household accounts for the spring of 1529 disclose the first of several expeditions aimed at re-asserting royal authority in the Borders. James was at Peebles on 20 and 22 April. The Border country had long been lawless and difficult to control. It was populated by many extended families or clans who were constantly feuding and despoiling each others' property. During the minority of James, after a period of relative stability during the reign of his father, James IV, lawlessness had gone unchecked. The great magnates who might have maintained some control were more concerned by the pursuit of their own interests, which centred on the struggle for power and for control of the boy King. Consequently, little attention was paid to the feuding of minor Border lairds and the whole area had descended into a state of virtual anarchy.

The clans, principal among them being the Kerrs, Scotts, Elliots, Armstrongs, Littles and Irvines, were a law unto themselves. They generally lived in fortified tower houses and they regarded their lands and the surrounding countryside as their personal fiefdom and owed no allegiance to any higher authority. There remain a number of these towers in a virtually complete state and the traces of many others can still be seen scattered throughout the area. From the fastness and safety of their tower fortresses they marauded far and wide, with no respect for the rights, property and possessions of others. Whatever they could pillage and carry away was theirs to have. These were the Border Reivers, romanticised in the legends and folklore of the Border Ballads, but in truth they were no better than gangland thugs, with little regard for the rights or the lives of their compatriots. It was said that marauding and the destruction of the property of their neighbours was regarded as nothing other than normal, and thereby treated in much the same way that a fair or any other social event might be treated by more civilised citizens.

One such was Cockburn of Henderland. The Forest of Ettrick stretched over a vast area south of the Tweed including the valleys of Ettrick and Yarrow, and Henderland lay on the southern slopes of the hills which dipped down to the banks of Megget Water, close to where it emerges into St Mary's Loch. The whole of the surrounding countryside at that time was heavily wooded, although now it is almost bare of trees. It is said that it harboured some of the largest stags in all of Scotland.

Henderland Tower was typical of its type, set on a prominent site, with the main tower occupied by the clan chief or laird, and with the lesser dwellings of retainers and clan members close by.[2] There is a story that in 1529, at the time James V assumed personal rule, the Laird of Henderland was one Parys Cockburn. Typical of his peers, he was possessed of natural qualities of courage allied to a degree of honour, but these characteristics were offset by an inborn disregard for the rule of law, which saw warring with neighbours and a total disregard for their property as the normal way of life. Enterprise was seen by such as Cockburn as not so much a matter of applying skills in trade or husbandry, as in setting forth to scour the countryside for what could be taken by stealth or force. If there was honour, it was honour among thieves. These raids were frequently undertaken under cover of darkness and any luckless neighbour unfortunate enough to leave cattle or sheep unattended was likely to have them removed unceremoniously, to be driven back to Henderland and their crops despoiled. In this Cockburn was no better or worse than any of his kind and such activity created a constant ebb and flow of stealing and counter-stealing, revenge and counter-revenge. As with any modern-day yob, any act of vandalism was pleasure in itself.

In the Minstrelsy of the Scottish Borders there is the 'Ballad of the Border Widow'. This is thought to be the story of the final demise of Cockburn of Henderland. The story[3] goes that Parys Cockburn had decided to make a raid on his near neighbour, Adam Scott of Tushielaw, another Border tower not many miles distant from Henderland. Cockburn was married to Marjory Scott, who unlike many of her contemporary chatelaines, was of a gentle persuasion and much opposed to her husband's lawless, reiving habits. There is an older Border legend that tells that when the larder was bare the laird's wife would bring to the dining table a silver salver with a pair of spurs on it. This was a sign that the master of the house should go out and about to replenish the empty larder by whatever means he had at his disposal. But this was not Marjory Cockburn's style.

On the occasion in question Marjory had got wind of preparations for the raid to
Tushielaw. She did what she could to stop Parys. She had recalled an old prophesy
of Merlin the Wizard:

> On Cockburn's elm, on Henderland Lee,
> a Cockburn laird shall hangit be.

She had also heard some word that the King was about to unleash his wrath
against the Border chiefs and that he might be close by. Parys brushed aside her
concerns and continued his preparations with the rest of his retinue. At about
midnight, the reiving band set out for Tushielaw. It was a wild and stormy night,
but, quite undaunted, Cockburn led his men through the darkened hills and glens
in high good humour.

Some two hours later, there was a disturbance at the gate of the tower. Lady
Cockburn was awoken by the noise and was not a little surprised to find a former
family servant by the name of Ralph ushered into her presence. Out of breath,
he had ridden hard from Peebles, some 15 miles distant, by way of Manor and
Redsikehead to warn that the King, with a group of nobles and armed retainers,
was at Peebles and was about to set out for Liddesdale on a mission of vengeance
against those petty Border chiefs who had been foremost in marauding and reiving. In addition to his nobles and soldiery, a hangman was in the party, with his
rope prepared to hang the ringleaders from the buttresses of their own fortresses.
Cockburn of Henderland was to be first on the list. Ralph gave a reminder of
Merlin's prophesy. Marjory immediately despatched Ralph towards Tushielaw, in
the hope that he could catch up with Cockburn and his party and persuade
them not to return to Henderland, but seek refuge, over the border if necessary.
At the same time she sent Thomas, the only remaining servant other than the
gatekeeper, to head towards Peebles and to give advance warning of the approach
of the King's party.

Towards dawn Thomas returned. The King and his avenging horde were on
their way having crossed the high ground beyond Manorhead and were even
now descending towards Megget. They would be at Henderland within the hour.
Thomas was now ordered to ride at once to Tushielaw to give a second warning
to Cockburn and confirmation of the King's approach. Marjory had not long to
wait before she heard the unmistakeable sound of men and horses approaching
from the direction of Peebles, as the grey light of dawn turned towards daylight.
Soon the flares of many torches were visible, winding their way through the trees
and down the hill towards Henderland itself. In a few moments the blast of a
trumpet was heard together with the stamping and champing of the restless feet
of many horses. The voice of a herald rang out, demanding in the name of James,
King of Scots, that the gate be opened. Marjory, perhaps in the hope that she
might plead for her erring Lord, commanded the gate to be opened and the

principal part of the cavalcade entered the courtyard to form a circle round the young King. A large group of soldiers fully armed remained outside. The King immediately demanded of the gatekeeper where his master might be. After some persuasion (for if nothing else Border chiefs commanded the loyalty of their servants), and not least due to the sight of the rope and noose, which the hangman had strung over one of the buttresses, the frightened gatekeeper told the King that Cockburn had left around midnight on a raid to Tushielaw. This, he assured the King, was an act of retaliation for a raid made by Adam Scott, its laird, on Henderland, not many weeks beforehand, when twenty head of cattle had been taken and many of Cockburn's men injured. It was one of many such raids in Ettrick and Liddesdale, although his master was by no means party to them all and only responded like for like.

Whether on account of ignorance, although well warned, or arrogance, naivety or total disregard for any higher authority, his mission to Tushielaw completed, Cockburn ignored the pleas of Marjory's messengers to flee to the south, and set off back to Henderland. Perhaps he thought he could convince this young King of the rightness of his cause and actions, and of his overriding loyalty to the Crown. He was wrong. Whatever pleas or supplications he may have made, James had been determined to make an example of him from the outset. Upon his return home, where James awaited him, he was immediately seized and unceremoniously hanged from the buttress of his own house.

It is said that as preparation for his execution was made, Marjory fled from the castle to the nearby woods. From the distance she could hear the sound mounting as the climax approached, and then falling again, indicating that all was now done. Sometime later, as she heard the departing sounds of the cavalcade heading towards Tushielaw to mete out similar justice to Adam Scott, she returned to the tower and, as she entered the gate, there before her was the inert body of her husband hanging from the buttress. So Parys Cockburn was not hanged from the elm tree, as prophesied, but, in a final twist to the story, during the storm of the previous night many trees had fallen. Standing alone among them, unharmed, was the great elm of the prophesy. It is also said that Marjory never recovered from the horror of that day and died three years later of a broken heart. To this day there is a gravestone in Henderland churchyard that bears the caption, 'Here lie Perys of Cockburn, and his wife Marjory'.

A somewhat different version of the story has it that James did indeed set out from Peebles on his first mission to quell the Borders, in the spring or possibly the autumn of 1529. In March of that year, the Lords of the Council announced that justice ayres would be held in Lauder, Jedburgh, Selkirk and Peebles. So as to bring some semblance of order to the region, various local magnates were given the responsibility for the conduct of law and order. This system was simple. If they failed to maintain order and punish wrongdoers, they themselves would be punished by warding or, in the last resort, forfeiture of property. Thus, on

25 June at Peebles, Patrick Hepburn, 3rd Earl of Bothwell, gave a bond for good rule in Liddesdale. It seems that about this time, or shortly after, Cockburn of Henderland (although named in the records as William, not Parys as in folk-lore) and Adam Scott of Tushielaw were apprehended and taken to Edinburgh. The following year they were charged with various offences and executed by beheading. Whatever the truth of these differing versions, there is no doubt that at an early age (he was still only nineteen years old) James made it clear who was master in Scotland.

Following the justice ayres of 25 June, James and his party left to hunt at Cramalt and Meggetland in Ettrick Forest, not far from Henderland. This became a favourite hunting venue and was an added attraction to the pleasures of Peebles nearby. Cramalt itself seems to have been an established royal hunting lodge. It must have remained in existence into the eighteenth century as it was seen by Dr Pennecuik[4] as the following description shows:

> The water of Meggit hath its furdest spring from a part of the famous Loch Skeen, and is the only water in Tweeddale, that pays no tribute to Tweed; but runs from south-east, some five miles, and ends its course in the St Mary Loch, and from there, with Yarrow, watereth the woods and banks of the Forrest – Upon the head of this water is to be seen, first, a house deservedly called Dead-for-cald, Wintrop-burn; Meggit-Knows; the Crammel, which seems to have been an old hunting-house of our kings, for I saw in the hall thereof a very large Hart's-horn upon the wall for a clock-pinn; the like whereof I observed in several other country men's houses in that desart and solitary place, where both Hart and Hynd, Dae and Rae have been frequent and numerous of old.

Thereafter James returned and rode from Peebles to Edinburgh on 1 July. That visit is marked by letters given under his 'privie sele at Peblis' when he confirmed the grant of a house of religion in Dunbar and its revenues to the minister and brethren of the Cross Kirk 'quhair ane pairt of the verray croce that our Salvatour was crucifyit on is honorit and kepit'.[5] This, no doubt, is some recompense for the frequently enjoyed hospitality of the said minister and brethren.

The affairs of State and pursuit of the pleasures of the chase were very much intertwined. Like his father, James IV, James V's reign demanded that he be a peripatetic monarch, in days when the only way to communicate with distant subjects and to address the problems of the day was by personal visitation. That Peebles was the subject of such frequent visits is due to a combination of circum-stances. Not only was it a pleasant place, with loyal and agreeable townsfolk, but also its geographical location, a day's ride from Edinburgh, made it a convenient stepping off point for excursions into the wilder and more distant Border lands. Its location on the edge of the Forest of Ettrick, with its unrivalled hunting, was a bonus.

Together with his Lords and Council, James again rode to Peebles from Linlithgow on 2 July and was at the town the following day. From there he rode to Douglas Water on 4 July and returned to Peebles on 13 July. He was at Cramalt hunting on the 15th and back in Peebles on the 18th, before returning to Linlithgow on the 20th. This was during a period when Linlithgow rather than Edinburgh was the centre of State business on account of fear of the plague, which seems to have been rife in the capital at that time. It is noted that in September 1539, the Lords of the Council, meeting in Peebles, agreed that their next meeting should be held in Edinburgh 'geif it be clene of the pest', failing which, it was to be held in Linlithgow.

He returned to Peebles some six weeks later, on 14 September and, after hunting at Cramalt on the 15th, he was back in Peebles on the 16th and 17th. While most visits combined the pleasures of hunting with State administration, some continued to be part of the drive to pacify the Border clans. Most notorious of these were the Armstrongs. They were something more than common Border reivers and set themselves up as lords and masters of much of the area of Liddesdale and more besides. They recognised no authority other than their own, and certainly not that of the King. This was something that James could not tolerate. The story of his pursuit, capture and destruction of the chief of the clan, Johnnie Armstrong of Gilnockie, and his cohorts is, again, the stuff of Border legend, but suffice it to say that it was from Peebles in July 1530 that James and his followers set out on the expedition that would finally bring him control of the southern Borderlands of his kingdom.

Regular visits to the Royal Burgh continued, although later records are more sparse. James's interest and affection for it is confirmed by his renewal, on 27 November 1539, of royal protection for the citizens, and by letters issued under his Privy Seal on 12 October 1541 confirming the market privileges of the burgh. There are Crown Charters labelled 'Peblis 10 July 1542'. Towards the end of November 1542 James visited Peebles and spent the night in the burgh among the folk he clearly regarded as his loyal burgesses. This was to be his last visit. The immediately preceding years had been a time of illness and disappointment. In April 1541 both his young sons had died, leaving no heir to the throne. He had become embroiled in a war with his English neighbour and uncle, the arrogant and avaricious Henry VIII. His attempts to muster a Scottish force to oppose him were largely a failure; a failure which culminated in the ignominious defeat of the Solway Moss, which finally broke his spirit. On 8 December a daughter, Mary, was born to his wife, Mary of Guise, and a few days later, on 14 December, only three weeks after his sojourn in Peebles, James V died at Falkland. Whether or not he uttered the words 'it came with a Lass and will pass with a lass' as he turned his face to the wall is a matter for conjecture. What is without doubt is that the ending of his reign ushered in a period of strife centred on religious belief.

It was during the reign of James V that an event took place which was to send shock waves throughout Europe and, in due course, Scotland, including Peebles. On 31 October 1517, a German Augustinian friar named Martin Luther pinned a declaration against Indulgences to the door of the Schlosskirchen of Wittenberg. It was the start of the Reformation. It was to be the cause of the downfall of his daughter Mary, his great-grandson Charles I, and his great-great-grandson James VII & II. In time it would set Scot against Scot in a bloodbath which came to be known as 'the Killing Times'.

The folk of Peebles were kinder to the memory of James V, the 'poor man's king', than later historians. When, in 1543, the Parish Church of St Andrew was made into a collegiate church, it was ordained that one of those to be remembered in the services was 'James Fifth, our dearest father, of good memory'.

3

≈ɷɷ≈

A Rough Wooing

On the death of James V, Mary, the daughter who succeeded him, was an infant at only one week old.

Mary, Queen of Scots is perhaps the most widely known of all the monarchs of Scotland, if not for all the right reasons. Her story is legendary. Her childhood upbringing at the court of King Henri II of France and his Queen, the formidable Catherine de Medici; her marriage to the Dauphin and her brief time as Queen of France as well as Scotland; her return to Scotland as a beautiful, elegant and charming eighteen-year-old, with all the joy, pageantry and bright hope for the future which that return seemed to signify; her many confrontations with the fanatical and certainly not subservient John Knox; the murder of her secretary David Rizzio in Holyrood Palace; the murder of her pathetic and dissolute husband, Henry, Lord Darnley at Kirk O'Field; her infatuation with James Hepburn, Earl of Bothwell; her ride across the length of the Borders in order to be at his side to tend to his battle wounds; her capture after the Battle of Carberry and subsequent incarceration and escape from Loch Leven Castle; her flight to Galloway and Dundrennan Abbey before crossing the Solway Firth into, as she thought, safe refuge in England; her years of confinement at the hands of her cousin Elizabeth; the battle of minds between the two Queens which occupied those years, and her final demise beneath the headsman's axe at Fotheringay, perhaps a martyr for her religion and almost certainly the victim of an outrageous and illegal act by the Queen of England. More significantly, her reign marked a period of profound political and ecclesiastical change in the life of the Scottish people.

The earliest years of her reign were, for the people of Peebles, a time of humiliation, deprivation and some terror. It took her grand uncle, Henry VIII of England, arguably one of the least attractive characters in British history, little time before seeking to coerce the people of Scotland into acceptance of his claim to the overlordship and domination of his northern neighbour. It started, not entirely unreasonably, with his proposal that his son and heir, Edward, and Mary should be joined in marriage, thus uniting the two kingdoms. The response he received from the Queen Dowager, Mary of Guise, and the Scottish Lords was not encouraging. The Scots had entered into a treaty in 1543,[1] which would have ended the conflict that had sullied the final years of the reign of James V, and which provided for the marriage of Mary to Prince Edward when she reached the age of eleven. However, Henry prevaricated in ratifying the treaty and this gave the Scots time to reconsider the serious implications that it would have brought. Whatever advantages the treaty might have held for Scotland, it was inevitable that the proposed marriage would, at long last, confirm English domination, and this prospect was less than palatable. At the same time ties with France were being strengthened, mainly due to the influence of the Queen Mother's family, the Guises, who were becoming a powerful force at the court of King Henri II of France. Better the Auld Alliance than English hegemony. Henry responded with his usual lack of subtle diplomacy. The proposal became a demand and a demand which he sought to bolster by sending the Earl of Hertford north with an order to enter Scotland and to lay it waste by fire and sword. Peebles was to feel his ire, a 'rough wooing' indeed. Not long after the accession of the baby Queen Mary, twelve Border towns were robbed and damaged by raiders from Liddesdale, acting on the orders of the English Warden of the Marches. The Warden's specific instructions had been to venture as far as Peebles, which he noted was some 28 miles within Scotland.

A greater conflict broke out in 1544, with English raiders rampaging across the border. One such raid was led by Lord Evers and Sir Brian Latoun, and it has been suggested that as many as 192 towns, ferm touns including churches and bastel houses,[2] were burned or destroyed, while 400 Scots were killed, more than 800 taken prisoner and nearly 1,000 cattle and 12,000 sheep were reived.[a] Whether or not this raid affected Peebles is unknown, but it does seem likely that the burgh and its surrounding shire felt the effect of the marauding English; effects which even town walls, the fortified houses of the local lairds and the bastel houses of the townsfolk were unable to withstand.

Following the appointment of the Earl of Angus as Lieutenant of the Borders, a detachment of his army assembled at Peebles. It was reported to the English Warden of the Middle Marches that the Earls of Angus, Glencairn and Cassels, with a troupe of men from the west, were encamped in the town for two nights. This is likely to have included a contingent of Peebles' men through the influence of the local laird, Lord Hay of Yester, who was a kinsman of the Earl of Angus. The departure of this force was reported to the Warden of the West March by a spy, identified as Robert Scot of Wamphray. The Earl of Angus had been instructed by the Governor General, James Hamilton, 2nd Earl of Arran, to make for Coldingham in the Merse and 'they lap onne Sunday night at ane of the clok and rayd furth of Pebles ane thowsand men by carriages'.[3] This does seem to be the start of a counter-offensive, which culminated in a heavy defeat of the English invaders at Ancrum Moor in February 1545, where the Peeblesshire contingent of Lord Hay played its part. This caused the invaders to retreat beyond the border for some time, but revenge was not long in coming. Later that year a further incursion by the Earl of Hertford saw the burning and destruction of the abbeys of Kelso, Jedburgh, Dryburgh and Melrose, never to be rebuilt. Nor did it end there. Although the detestable Henry VIII died in January 1547, this did not bring a halt to English avarice and aggression. However, in March of that year there was a brief respite, which allowed the Scottish Privy Council to attempt to re-establish its own authority over the Borders, as they had been disrupted by English marauding, a situation that had also encouraged a descent into lawlessness and a reversion to theft and reiving by the Border clans. An army, under the command of the Governor General Arran, was therefore commanded to assemble at Peebles with sufficient provisions for twenty days, with a view to bringing the area back under control. Its further purpose was to prepare for a major incursion by the English. Word had reached Scotland of an impending invasion by land and sea with the stated intention of laying waste to the countryside by burning and wreaking death and destruction on an already fearful population.

The expected invasion by forces led by the Earl of Hertford duly arrived, and on 10 September ('Black Friday') the Scots, under the leadership of the weak Earl of Arran, suffered a severe defeat at Pinkie Heuch in East Lothian. Lord Hay, who had succeeded his father as Lord Yester in 1543, was taken prisoner and as commander of part of the force that included the Peebles contingent, it is likely that some of the Peebles men suffered similarly. However, at the same time it appears that the townsfolk of Peebles, at a safe distance from the battle, were showing some support for the English, and continued to do so for about fifteen weeks thereafter, until saner influences prevailed. For this treacherous and almost treasonable behaviour, a fine of £200 was imposed on the burgh, which seems modest in the circumstances. In mitigation, it can perhaps be said that the people of the town and their leaders had merely adopted a pragmatic approach, for the Earl of Somerset (formerly the Earl of Hertford), the Lord Protector of the English realm and Regent for the young King Edward VI, had effectively occupied most of the east of Scotland with headquarters at Haddington. Thus, the whole area was at the mercy of the English and, in submitting to them, the burgh probably had little choice. For Peebles worse was to come. The continued threat from England gave the Queen Dowager, Mary of Guise, the opportunity to strengthen the already strong ties with France. Although the Earl of Arran was nominally Regent of Scotland, he was weak and ineffectual. His total failure at Pinkie had further weakened his position and, in practice, it was the Queen Dowager who exercised the major influence over the Privy Council. The English attack had a particular danger for her. England was, for the present at least, nominally Protestant and while the Reformation was stirring in Scotland, and

Protestantism had its adherents, the country remained predominantly Catholic, a situation that Mary was determined to preserve. In response to her appeals, the French sent a fleet and a large contingent of soldiers to Leith with the intent of assisting the Scots in dislodging the English from the large area of south-east Scotland that they effectively occupied.

How aware or affected the child Queen Mary was by this warfare is difficult to say. In the aftermath of the Battle of Pinkie she had been taken with some of her companions to the safety of the island Priory of Inchmahome on the Lake of Menteith. Subsequently she was moved to the safer haven of Dumbarton Castle. However, the English policy of seeking to unite the Scottish and English Crowns in such a heavy-handed and uncompromising way merely produced a totally adverse effect, and was thwarted when the Scottish Parliament finally decided that enough was enough. No doubt aided by the French party of the Queen Dowager and influenced by her powerful French relations, the Guises, it was decided that Mary should be betrothed to the Dauphin, the heir to the French throne. In July 1548 a formal treaty was entered into which provided for French troops to be sent to bolster the beleaguered Scottish forces in exchange for the hand of the Queen of Scots. For her continuing safety, education and enlightenment as the future Queen of France, as well as of Scotland, the French King Henri II insisted that Mary should be brought to France and live under his benign and fatherly eye at the French court. The French sent a fleet of ships to Scotland by way of the Irish Sea. So it was that Mary left Dumbarton and set sail for France, the fleet again taking the route through the Irish Sea. After days of storms and rough seas, avoiding marauding English ships, the fleet reached France and Mary landed at Roscoff on 13 August 1548.

It is impossible to imagine what the five-year-old Queen felt as she left that day for an unknown country, leaving behind her mother, Mary of Guise, who had been her close companion, guide and guardian since birth. True, she had with her the 'Four Marys' Beaton, Seton, Livingstone and Fleming, who had been her companions in Scotland, but although she had some knowledge of French from her mother, Scots was her first tongue and she knew nothing of the country to which she was bound. Yet the next thirteen years were for Mary perhaps the happiest of her life, secure in the hands of a powerful and stable regime, solidly in the sphere of the Church of Rome. For Peebles and Scotland things would be somewhat different.

The departure of Mary, although it signified the end to any question of an English marriage, by no means deterred the English from pursuing their campaign of carnage and destruction. It is true that much of this was encouraged by a deep divide in the Scottish body politic, and that divide was centred on religion. The kingdom of England, now firmly Protestant and severed from the Church of Rome, wished to ensure that its northern neighbour was also separated from the Catholic Church. The raiding and marauding continued unabated and although in due course the combined Scottish and French forces succeeded in finally driving the English invaders back beyond the border, this was not before the English made a final attempt to implement a scorched-earth campaign throughout the area. Peebles did not escape. The town, which was virtually unprotected, was to suffer near catastrophic destruction in 1549. This was no random attack. In July of that year, one of the English commanders, Sir Thomas Halcroft, wrote: 'I trust your grace shall hear that we will burn Peebles, and other things which we never burned, to welcome Monsier de Termes to the country.'[4] A less confident Halcroft wrote again on 25 September to the effect that mounted forces under Buccleuch were at Selkirk and Peebles, and this seems to have been a temporary deterrent; but not for long, and in November or December there was a major attack. There is no direct record of the attack, but later records give some indication of the damage that must have resulted. The East Wark, which was then a fortified steeple at the eastern approach to the town, was destroyed and considerable damage was done to the buildings in the Northgait and Briggait. The Church of St Andrew was badly damaged and never thereafter rebuilt,[5] while the Cross Kirk also suffered. The town's Rood Mill, situated near the Castle, also suffered major damage with the result that the records show the rent as falling into arrears for some years afterwards, presumably because it had been rendered inoperable and remained so. It was also of no doubt that at this time the old Castle of Peebles reached its final demise. There is certainly no record of its having been used after that date.

The ordinary citizens suffered much material and financial hardship, and in the subsequent years there are many references in property dispositions to sales of fire-damaged properties, which the owners had to dispose of in their dilapidated state. In March 1550 there is reference to a couple being forced to sell their damaged property: 'a burned land of theirs' sold 'in their great need and necessity'.[6] In April of the same year there is reference to 'a property lying on the north side of the Briggait and the east side of the Almshouse … as then being burned by our auld enemies of England, it being sold on account of its owners great necessity and need for a certain sum of money in gold and silver'.[7] In May, George Paterson and his wife Christian Smyth 'passed their land burned by our auld enemies of England lying in the Northgait, and sold the same in their great necessity and need'.[8]

It is difficult to imagine the horror of such a raid. There were no permanent defences or town wall at that time. Indeed, it was not until 1569 that a protective perimeter wall was built as a permanent fortification, although some buildings would have been individually fortified. This was a defenceless town, largely populated by unarmed citizens, living in houses that were mainly built of timber with thatched roofs and thus tinder boxes. The mounted attacking force, even if no more than 100–200 strong, would have presented a formidable and fearsome spectacle as it relentlessly approached the East Wark and then charged through the town, throwing lighted torches of tar onto the thatched roofs. Townsfolk could only cower back in fear, trying often ineffectively to protect their little ones from flailing horse hooves. How many died or suffered injury is not known, but it is unlikely that all escaped unharmed. This was terror intended to instil fear and, like all acts of terror, it was the defenceless and innocent who suffered.

Chapter Note

a. stolen.

———❧❧❧———

4

Reformation

There is a tendency to think of the Reformation in Scotland as largely the work of John Knox. Certainly he was a towering and dominant figure, but his contribution spanned no more than thirty years in a process which, from beginning to end, lasted for more than 170 years, from its birth on the day in 1517 when Luther pinned his Declaration Against Indulgences to the door of a church in Wittenberg, until 1690, when the Church of Scotland in the form recognised today was established.

In Scotland the Reformation had two distinct phases. The first was the struggle between the established Catholic Church of Rome and Protestantism, and the second was the later struggle between Episcopacy and Presbyterianism, which dominated the seventeenth century. The thirteen years during which Mary Stuart was absent from Scotland and at the court of France saw the culmination of the first phase.

Although Martin Luther can rightly be seen as the catalyst which finally set the Reformation in motion, there had long been stirrings of discontent with the conduct of the Church, its hierarchy and even its humbler servants. In England, in the fourteenth century, the philosopher and theologian John Wycliffe spoke out against the materialism of the Church. In turn, he inspired John Huss, who instigated a reform movement in Bohemia at the beginning of the fifteenth century and was burned as a heretic at Prague for his trouble. Heresy also reared its head in Scotland when James Resby, an Englishman and follower of Wycliffe, was burned at Perth in 1407, and in 1433 Paul Craw, a follower of Huss, found his way to Scotland where he too suffered death by burning after openly preaching Hussite doctrine.

It seems that the deteriorating condition of the Church was universal across Europe. Materialism and personal aggrandisement had pushed aside pastoral care. The malaise spread all the way down from the heights of the Papacy to the lowest levels of the priesthood and clergy. The Papacy reached its nadir in the person of Rodrigo Borgia who was elected Pope Alexander VI in 1492, although to describe his as an 'election' is euphemistic. Many of those who voted for him did so only as a result of bribery or other forms of inducement. Alexander represented the complete triumph of temporal over spiritual power. He was acquisitive, dishonest, morally corrupt and far from celibate. His son was the infamous Cesare Borgia, while his daughter was the notorious Lucretia Borgia. The man who succeeded him to the throne of St Peter in 1503 was Guiliano de Rovere, who ruled as Julius II. Perhaps less morally corrupt, he was a man of iron will. His vision of the Church saw material wealth as the symbol of spiritual power, which should be displayed for all to see. It was he who commissioned the rebuilding of St Peter's Basilica into the form in which it stands today, and who commanded Michaelangelo to paint the ceiling of the Sistine Chapel. He believed that the Church should be politically dominant and that its power should be enforced by military conflict. He personally led his troops in battle to the defeat of the State of Venice and to the limitation of the power and expansion of France. Just as significant as his military and political power was his creation of a huge fortune for the Papal coffers.

The third Pope in this critical period was Giovanni de Medici, who ruled as Leo X from 1513 until 1521. He was the son of the great Florentine leader Lorenzo the Magnificent and, although he was intelligent and highly educated, he allowed himself to succumb to personal indulgence and the pleasures of the flesh, in the course of which he managed to largely dissipate the fortune gathered by Julius II. He totally failed to understand the implications of the reforms sought by Luther and rewarded him with excommunication in 1520, something he would live to regret.

Due to the fact that the material wealth of the Church throughout Europe had become so blatant, particularly during the reign of these three Popes, it was a target for temporal rulers. Hard-pressed emperors, monarchs and princes from Scotland to Bohemia, saw the Church as a source of much-needed finance for their wars and personal indulgence and as a ready source of taxation. The result was that the Church in turn sought ever increasingly to maintain its enviable financial position. At every level there was a price to be paid for the services of the Holy Church. Even the humblest peasant seeking to have a prayer or prayers said for a departed loved one might only have this in exchange for payment in cash or in kind. The sale of Indulgences had become commonplace. The fragments of the 'True Cross' that were spread throughout Europe were so numerous that, assembled together, they might have made a forest of crosses. The combined sum that these fragments could have realised would certainly put a smile on the faces of the custodians of the Papal coffers. Comfort and plenty in the 'hereafter' could be assured, if the price was right. It was the promotion of these sales by Leo X that finally propelled Luther into action. In addition, there was wide-

spread moral corruption. The princes of the Church lived like great magnates
and matched them in wealth and power. They disregarded the rule of celibacy.
In Scotland Cardinal Beaton had eight children who he recognised, and possibly
many more that remained in anonymity. Little wonder that the lower ranks of the
clergy were equally lax in view of the example of their superiors. Vows of chastity
were ignored and, while the marriage of an ordained priest was punishable by
death, concubinage was regarded as an acceptable substitute.

Good living among the clergy was the order of the day, and those in Peebles
seem to have been no exception. An old verse poem of unknown authorship,
thought to have been written during the reign of James III, gives a snapshot. It is
known as 'the Tailes of the Thrie Priestis of Peblis' and relates to the meeting of
three priests in a hostelry in Peebles, where they spend an evening of couthy conviviality, during the course of which each of the priests, Maister Johne, Maister
Archebald and Sir William, tell a tale of politics and morality, these being full of
references to the current state of the country. The opening lines of the poem are:[1]

In Peblis toun sum tyme, as I hard tell,
The foremost day of Februare, befell
Thrie priestis went unto collatioun[a],
Into ane privie place of the said toun.
Whair that they sat richt soft and unfute-sair[b];
Thay luifit na rangold[c] nor repair[d]
And gif I sall the suith[e] reckin and say,
I traist it was upon Sanct Brydis day.
Whair that thay sat full easilie and soft;
With monie lowd lauchter apoun loft.
And wit ye weil, thir thrie meid gude cheir;
To thame thair was na dainties than too deir;
with thrie caponis on a speit with creis[f],
with monie other sundrie meis[g].
And thame to serve thay had nocht bot ane boy;
Fra companie thai keipit thame sae coy.
Thai lufit nocht with ladry[h] nor with lown[i]
Nor with trumpouris[j] to travel throw the town,
Bot with themeself quhat thai wald tell or crak[k];
Umquhyle sadlie; umqhuyle jangle[l] and jak[m];
Thus sat thir thrie beside ane felloun[n] fyre,
Quhil thair capons war roistit lim and lyre.
Befoir them was sone set a Roundel bricht,
And with ane clene claith, fielie dicht[o],
It was ouirset; and breid was laid.
The eldest than began the grace, and said,

And blissit be the breid with Benedicite,
With Dominus Amen, sa mot I thee.

The first priest's tale starts after they had begun their meal and they had 'drunken about a quarte'. It poses the question why the wealth of merchants is never passed on to the third generation and is always squandered by the second generation; while another tale questions why the clergy are no longer able to work miraculous cures in the way that seemed to have been common in the early church. It suggests the reason is that the clergy no longer observe purity of living, knowledge, or spiritual graces:

Sic wickedness this world is within,
… that symonie[P] is countit now na sin.

From top to bottom, the Church seemed to be concerned with money and materialism and to have little regard for its true purpose. Correspondence between the Scottish hierarchy and the Pope in Rome dealt almost exclusively with money matters and, in particular, the enjoyment of benefices. Rarely, if ever, did it deal with spiritual affairs. In Peebles the same attitudes seem to have prevailed. The church records are littered with examples that relate to material matters and there is little reference to questions of pastoral care or the conduct of worship. Robert Chambers[2] comments:

It may here be mentioned, that the burgesses of Peebles were as liberal, in proportion to their means, to the clergy of the Catholic church, as any of their contemporaries. Their donations of houses and rents for sawl-heill, or soul welfare, during the fifteenth century, were very numerous; one of them is in the following terms:- 'On the 12th day of February 1473, William of Peebles, burgess of that ilk', resigned his 'foreland, under and aboon, by and on the Conyhe [maison de coin, the corner house – the place is now called Cunyie Neuk], neist the North Gate, to Sanct Lenard's hospital, for his sawl, his wyff's sawl, his bairnis sawlls, and for all the sawlls that the said William had ony gud wrangously of, in bying or selling, or ony enterchangyng'.

At the beginning of the fifteenth century, in addition to the Church of St Andrew and the Cross Kirk, there were also the Chapel of St Mary in the High Gait and the Chapel of the Hospice of Saints Lawrence and Leonard at Eshiels. In each of these were a number of altars. In the case of St Andrew there were as many as eleven. The clergy were numerous and, as well as the local hierarchy, clergy would be assigned to each individual altar and benefited from the revenues with which each was endowed. These endowments usually arose from land or property, granted or gifted in former years and were a source of considerable revenue. According to Dr Gunn:[3]

the wealth of the church, even in a burgh like Peebles was enormous. There was hardly a piece of land or a tenement which did not pay something to the revenues of the Church. Besides which the Church possessed much property herself. All the altarages were endowed, some more, others less: and their incomes were constantly increasing. As Magistrates were officially patrons of most of them, it has been seen how Burgess fees went toward the upkeep of the Altars and the Services of the Parish Church.

How many clergy there actually were in the town is not recorded, but what with Trinity Friars and the army of altar chaplains and others, it must have been a considerable number. As Dr Gunn goes on to comment:

A.D. 1543. The clergy in Peebles formed a sufficiently numerous body to be a caste or a cult by themselves. Their residences and lands in the Old Town rendered that locality the ecclesiastical quarter. The position of the Parish Church and of the Cross Church, connected with each other by the Cross road, added to the tone of the neighbourhood; and constant intercourse between both the Churches and the New Town across Eddlestone Water was ensured over two bridges. Night and morning the church bell rang to Matins and Evensong; and the smaller bell summoned the devout to the other altar services throughout the day. The Church dominated the town intellectually as well as spiritually. Almost all scholarship was confined to the clergymen … In municipal matters it was the same; the Town Clerk had to be a priest, as priests almost alone knew how to write. What an influence the Church could exert upon the burgh through this official! The notaries were priests also; hence the accretion to the Church of annual rents, legacies, and bequests from pious burghers. The town clock was wound by a priest. The Church was so wealthy that there was hardly a property or piece of land in the parish which did not pay an annual charge to the Church, or actually belonged wholly to it: and this enormous aggrandisement of the ages formed a potent factor in the downfall of the Church; for all those who clamoured for reform were not actuated by a love of truth and purity of doctrine; there were others who groaned under the burdens and extractions borne by their lands as annual charges to the Church.[4]

By the sixteenth century financial pressures on the Church generally, and the personal greed and indulgence of the clergy, resulted in many of the properties and land from which the endowments were derived being sold or alienated for cash. For example, on 15 June 1554, 'Sir John Bullo, Chaplain of St Martin's altar in the Church of St Andrew, passed waste land on the north side of Briggait pertaining to him in patrimony by virtue of Recognition, led thereupon by the late Sir Gilbert, Chaplain of St Martin, predecessor of Sir John. And there Sir John resigned the property in the hands of a Bailie, who gave sasine to Thomas

Hoppringle. The feu duty payable to the chaplain being 10s.'[5] Or again on 23 October 1554: 'Sir Thomas Purves, Chaplain of Our lady Altar in the College Kirk of St Andro, passed to a land of the late John Gledstanes of Cocklaw, on the north side of Hie Gait, and resigned all right to the land by delivering earth and stone in the hands of the Bailie James Robeson. Sasine given to Walter Gledstanes. Annual of 7s payable to the chaplain.'[6]

It did not take long for the ripples from Luther's defiant action to spread out across Europe and, in due course, they reached Scotland. Within a few years books expanding Lutheran doctrine found their way to Scotland, and in 1525 the Scottish Parliament introduced an Act banning the importation of any such books. This was re-enacted in 1535. In 1525 Patrick Hamilton, who had been titular Abbot of Fearn, returned to Scotland following a period of study at the great continental centres of learning, including Paris and Louvain. There he was attracted to the teachings of Luther and became a dedicated follower. On his return, Hamilton proceeded to preach this new gospel, based on the Lutheran concept of 'Justification by Faith'. This was extreme heresy in the eyes of the Holy Church, which in Scotland exercised a dominating influence upon the body politic, and in 1528 Hamilton was declared heretic and burned at St Andrews. This produced a wave of revulsion and public sympathy.

The year 1528 was also when James V commenced his personal rule. How far James approved of such heavy-handed action is difficult to say. There is no doubt that as time went by he became increasingly aware of the shortcomings and laxity of the clergy and the increasing antipathy of the ordinary folk towards them. In January 1540 a play called the *Interlude* by Sir David Lindsay of the Mount was performed at Linlithgow Palace in front of the King and Queen and the whole court. In a later revised version this play became known as *Ane Satyre of the Thrie Estaites*. Lindsay had been the boyhood tutor of James. He was a prominent figure at court in his capacity as Lord Lyon, King of Arms. No doubt because of his close personal relationship with James he may have been allowed more latitude than most in the exercise of his opinions. The *Satyre* is a devastating critique of the corrupt state of the nation, and an indictment of the Lords Spiritual and Temporal. In particular, Lindsay directed his fire at the treatment of the poor and the Common Weal. The following extract[7] gives a flavour of the play. It is part of a conversation between a pauper and a character called Diligence.

> PAUPER: We had three kye, that were both fat and fair,
> None tidier in the town of Ayr.
> My father was so weak of blood and bone,
> That he died, wherefore my mother made great moan:
> Then she died within a day or two;
> And then began my povertie and woe.
> Our good grey mare was battening on the field,

And our landlord took her for his hyreild^q.
The vicar took the best cow by the head
Incontinent, when my father was dead.
And when the vicar heard tell how my mother
Was dead, off hand he took to him another!
Then Meg, my wife, did mourn both eve and morrow,
Till at the last she died for very sorrow:
And when the vicar heard tell my wife was dead,
The third cow he cleiket by the head!
Thair upmost clais quilk wes of reploch^r gray,
The vicar gart his clark cleik thame away.
When all was gane, I might mak na debeat,
But with my bairns passed for to beg my meat.
Now I have told you the black veritie,
How I am brought to this misery.
DILIGENCE: How did the parson? Was he not thy good friend?
PAUPER: The devil stick him, he cursed me for my teind:
And holds me yet under that same process,
That gart me want the Sacrament of Pasche.
In good faith, sir, though he cut my throat,
I have no geir except and English groat
Which I purpose to give a man of law.
DILIGENCE: Thou art the daftest fule that ever I saw;
Trows thou man, by the law remeid
Of men of kirk! Na, not till thou be deid.
PAUPER: Sir, by what law, tell me, wherefore, or why,
That a Vicar should take from me three kye?
DILIGENCE: They have no law, except consuetude^s
Whilk law, to them, is sufficient and good.
PAUPER: A consuetude against the common weal,
Should be no law, I think, by sweet St Geil.
Where will ye find that law, tell me gif ye can,
To tak three kye, fra a puir husband-man?
Ane for my father, and for my wife another,
And the third cow, he took fra Mald my mother.
DILIGENCE: It is their law, all that they have in use,
Though it be cow, sow, gander, gryse^t, or goose.

It is said that at the end of the performance James turned to the bishops present and told them in no uncertain terms that if they and their clergy did not mend their ways, he would send six of them to England to be dealt with by his uncle Henry VIII, whose reputation as a less than tolerant justice would have been well known to them. However, it seems that they continued much as before and were perhaps allowed to because James had more pressing problems.

Following the death of James, the battle between Catholicism and Protestantism took on a stronger hue. Mary of Guise, the Queen Dowager and effective ruler of Scotland, was an ardent Catholic. Her family, the Guises, were the predominant Catholic influence in France, where the battle between Catholicism, as represented by the Crown, and Protestantism, as represented by the Huguenots, was soon to reach a climax. Mary of Guise was determined that Scotland should remain firmly in the Catholic fold and in this she was supported by David Beaton, the Cardinal Archbishop of St Andrews. Beaton had been one of the personal favourites and close advisors of James V. There were, however, others with a different agenda.

In March 1543, Parliament sanctioned the reading of a version of the Bible in Scots and in 1545 a theologian called George Wishart returned to Scotland, having been forced earlier to leave the country on account of his preaching of Lutheran doctrine. Wishart was made of stern stuff and was well aware of the personal danger he ran in continuing to expound doctrines which the Holy Church regarded as extreme heresy. He had studied at Cambridge and in Germany and, under the title 'The Confession of the Fayth of the Sweserlands',[8] had translated 'The First Helvetic Confession' into Scots. This placed a major emphasis on preaching and faith and held that Christ is the only Head of the Church and that the ministers were its officers. Baptism and Holy Communion were to be the only Sacraments. It went on to assert that the Civil Authority had a duty to defend true religion and exercise government with justice. Towards the end of 1545, on his return to Scotland, Wishart embarked upon a preaching campaign. He was well aware that the doctrines he preached were regarded as heretical by the Holy Church and it seems that when he preached in public places, he always had with him a friend carrying a two-handed sword, presumably to defend him against arrest by the authorities. He preached mainly in the Dundee area and in Ayrshire, but he also visited Haddington in East Lothian. On that occasion his personal bodyguard and sword carrier was one John Knox. A few days after preaching in Haddington, while staying at the house of a friend nearby, he was apprehended in the middle of the night by the forces of the Queen Dowager and Cardinal Beaton, and taken captive to St Andrews, where he was condemned for heresy. A month later he was burned in front of the palace of the Cardinal, who himself observed the scene, something he would come to regret. Beaton had many enemies and in May the following year a group of them managed to gain entry to the palace in the early hours of the morning, while it was still dark, and found their way to his private apartments where they summarily despatched him. To add insult, the next morning his bloodied body was to be seen hanging from the outer wall of the palace for all to see.

Naturally the Regent, Arran and the Queen Dowager sought to apprehend and destroy those who had perpetrated this outrage. The perpetrators managed, however, to find sanctuary in St Andrews Castle, which they were able to defend with some strength. They were joined shortly after by John Knox, who had now taken over the mantle of Wishart. A siege ensued, led by Arran, but with little effect. Arran and Mary of Guise relied increasingly on their French allies, and in due course a French fleet arrived off St Andrews with a battery of guns, which, within a month, did such damage to the Castle that the defenders were left with no alternative but to surrender. All, including Knox, were taken prisoner. Those who were deemed to be gentlemen were imprisoned, while those who were not were forced to become French galley slaves. Among their number was Knox.

In due time Knox was given his freedom, largely due to English influence. He was clearly already recognised by the English authorities as being someone who could aid their cause in seeking to dominate Scotland because of his obvious resistance to the Catholic and French-dominated Scottish authorities. Perhaps in gratitude he moved to England, where he soon made his mark to the extent that he was appointed as one of six personal chaplains to the young King Edward VI. However, the succession of Edward's sister, Mary, to the throne after his early death, caused Knox to return to France and Germany and ultimately Switzerland. By 1555 the situation in Scotland was such that he was able to return there in safety, but after only ten months he was called back to Geneva to be minister to the English congregation based there. It was in Geneva that he became recognised as one of the great figures of the Reformation, along with Calvin, Beze and Farel, something which is acknowledged by the great memorial which stands in the Parc de la Reformation in Geneva. It was during his time in Geneva that Knox wrote his famous 'First Blast of the Trumpet against the Monstrous Regiment of Woman'. This was not directed at Mary, Queen of Scots, as is often thought, although she was frequently to experience the 'blast' of Knox in later years. Rather, it was directed against Mary of Guise and Mary Tudor, and possibly also Catherine de Medici, the Queen Dowager and effective ruler of France. It was a strange quirk of history that the rulers of three of the prominent nations of Europe were women at this time. The 'Blast' has also been seen as directed at Elizabeth I, something that she did not appreciate.

Knox finally returned to Scotland in 1559, where the stage was set for the climax of the confrontation between the Church of Rome and the reformed order. In a rear guard action, the Privy Council had tried to stem the inflow of Reformist literature and also to suppress the printing of works produced in Scotland itself, such as 'The Complaynt of Scotland' and 'The Gude and Godlie Ballatis'.

In 1557 a group of nobles and others supporting the Protestant cause, who called themselves 'The Lords of the Congregation', banded together and signed a document, which has become known as 'The First Covenant'. There were to be four further such documents in the subsequent years and together they had a major part in framing the history of the Church of Scotland and for which, in later years, men and women suffered, fought and died.

The final act was precipitated by the preaching of Knox. In a sermon given at Perth he portrayed the worship of the Church of Rome as idolatrous and deserving of destruction, but before the church had emptied, a priest somewhat injudiciously took it upon himself to assert the established order by saying a Mass. A riot ensued during which the pictures and images in the church were destroyed. The mob then made for two nearby monasteries and the Abbey Church, which they destroyed leaving only the walls standing. Knox disapproved, but he had set alight a flame which would not be extinguished, and similar action followed in towns across Scotland.

On 1 August 1560 the Scottish Estates or Parliament, now effectively in the hands of the Protestants, met in Edinburgh and within three weeks had passed an Act endorsing a Confession of Faith, largely drawn up by Knox. In addition, Acts were passed removing the authority of the Pope in Scotland. Any act of worship not conforming to the Confession of Faith was to be illegal. The celebration of the Mass was made an offence, with a succession of punitive measures culminating in death for the third offence. The Sacraments were reduced to two, Holy Communion and Holy Baptism.

Although a commissioner from Peebles, whose name is unknown, Lord Yester and Lord Borthwick, who owned property in the Northgait of the town, were in attendance at the Parliament, it seems that the burgesses of the town were divided as to whether to accept the new order or adhere to the old. There had already been signs of dissention in the spring of the previous year, when the town was occupied by Protestant soldiers anxious to add a degree of coercion to the argument. The Town Council had other ideas and on 5 May 1559 decreed that 'sojarries and allegit men of weir'[9] should leave the town immediately. Sometime later, in March 1560, two of the bailies declared their intention to remain in the faith 'and obedience to thair Prince bearand authorite for the time'. They complained about the new vogue for common prayers and preaching in place of their old liturgy. However, it seems that their protests were somewhat tempered by a declaration that they were made 'in na contemptioun of the lordis of the congregatioun'. It is perhaps understandable that there should be some confusion of mind on the part of the people. Peebles had long been a place of pilgrimage and retreat for the faithful to 'Haly Kirk', since the establishment of the Cross Kirk in 1261 and for nigh on 100 years. Since its inception in 1474, as the Conventual Monastery of the Trinity Friars, the convent and monastery of the Holy Cross of Peebles had been a dominating influence in the town and its surrounding country. Although the numbers of its occupants had dwindled, in spite of all their faults — and there were many — the master or minister and the brothers would have been a source of some good.

Shortly before the end of March 1560, the Master of Maxwell, with a detachment of troops, entered the town and took possession of the Cross Kirk. On 30 March Brother Gilbert Broune, who was the minister of the monastery, appeared before a Notary Public, Sir John Allan. Brother Gilbert is described as 'a venerable and worthy man'. He was clearly also a pragmatist. He explained to Sir John that when Maxwell and his men, acting on behalf of the Lords of the Congregation, had taken possession of the church and monastery, he had feared for his life and also the safety of the buildings themselves. He had, therefore, hastily changed his white friar's habit for a 'gray keltour goune"' and a 'howe black bonet"', but only out of fear. He asked the notary (who would be a priest and therefore sympathetic) to give a written statement confirming his adherence to the old religion. Brother Broune was the last Roman Catholic minister of the Cross Kirk, but he would not be the last clergyman in Scotland to 'turn his coat'.

In the ensuing years there would be many who changed allegiance to one or other form of the reformed religion, if not to the Church of Rome. Nonetheless, it does seem that, for the moment at least, Peebles still inclined towards the Church of Rome, but the tide was beginning to flow strongly in favour of the reformed order. In May, an officer acting on behalf of Lord Borthwick visited the minister and warned him to remove himself, his goods and his family from the lands and property belonging to Lord Borthwick adjacent to the monastery. Venerable and worthy the good Brother Gilbert may have been, but the reference to 'his family' might suggest that even he might have fallen from grace as far as the opposite sex was concerned, unless of course 'his family' is to be construed as referring to the brotherhood of friars. Brother Gilbert protested that the actions of Lord Borthwick were illegal, because he had paid all rents due on time and had not had sufficient notice as required by law. However, all this seems to have been to no avail. Whatever the detail, it is clear that pressure was mounting against the old order.

The meeting of the Estates in August 1560 finally brought that order to an end. In the context of Peebles, and having regard to the actions of Lord Borthwick in seeking the removal of Brother Gilbert from his property, it is curious that his lordship was among a total of five commissioners who were alone in objecting to the Acts effectively abolishing the authority of the Church of Rome, and protesting that they would 'believe as our fathers believed'. Perhaps like many, his was a confusion of mind in what must have seemed an apocalyptic situation, or perhaps in his dealings with Brother Gilbert he was merely being opportunistic.

The news of the events that took place in Edinburgh during August travelled fast, and on the day after the Confession of Faith was adopted, the somewhat bizarrely named Dionysius Elphinston of Henderstoun,[10] standing in the porch of what remained of the Church of St Andrew, took it upon himself to announce to all who would hear him that 'no ministration of the Common Prayers to the parishioners of Peebles was performed in the place where it ought to be done' by the rector or anyone else in his name, in accordance with the now established custom and practice. He seemed to have established himself as the leading advocate of the Reformed cause in Peebles, in contrast to his fellow landowner, Lord Borthwick, who still hankered after the old order. Elphinston went on to announce that until such time as the rector, or someone acting on his behalf, preached the Gospel to the parishioners in accordance with what was now the new order, he would no longer feel obliged to make any payments of teinds to the rector or his factors. In practical terms, public worship in the centuries-old Parish Church had ceased and the parishioners were without a place of worship. In order to protect themselves from the risk of confiscation of their properties, many of the clergy took steps to dispose of them. For example, the Dean of Peebles, who enjoyed the revenues of the Deanspark,[11] sold off the property in exchange for an increased feu-duty payable in perpetuity.

Peebles was now without a minister or the Ordinances of the Church, and on 20 November 1560 it was decided that the town's bailies should go to Edinburgh with the request that the Lords of the Congregation provide them with a preacher and minister. They seem to have met with instant success, for only a week later, on 28 November, the magistrates met in the Tolbooth to appoint John Dickson to the Kirk of Peebles. John Dickson was thus the first Reformed minister of Peebles and the sole representative of Church authority. In theory at least, the authority of the Pope in Peebles, as elsewhere, no longer held sway. Non-conforming clergy, together with Mass books and altars, were all removed. As Dr Gunn records:[12]

> The work which had for centuries carried on in the Parish Church, with its eleven Altars by dean, rector, curate and twelve chaplains, and choir of men and boys and at St Mary's Chapel was now abandoned. The minister alone was to discharge the sacred office, and carry on the whole religious duty of the parish. To enable this to be done a service of a very much simpler form was necessary; or rather, because the new Order was of so simple and severe a nature, one clergyman was considered sufficient to perform its offices.

The congregation essentially remained the same, the Common Weal of Peebles. They were, however, without a proper place of worship. The Parish Church, the Church of St Andrew, was a ruin, as it had been since it suffered from the ministrations of English invaders in 1549, and in December 1560 the Town Council presented a petition to the Lords of the Congregation on behalf of the burgesses and townsfolk asking that the Cross Kirk be granted to them as the Parish Church. The petition explained that the Church of St Andrew could not be rebuilt at reasonable cost or in reasonable time. They were in urgent need of a church where they could hear the Word of God preached and have the Sacraments administered. They further pointed out that the Cross Kirk, the Church of the Trinity Friars, was in good order, spacious and very suitable as a Parish Church. They would, however, need to refurbish it and remove all traces of idolatry. This petition was granted on 7 December and a few days later the bailies and Town Council went to the Cross Kirk to meet with Brother

Gilbert Broune, who, as yet, was still the Minister of the Trinity Friars. They read the petition to him and the letter confirming the grant. The compliant Brother Gilbert (he had little option!) seems to have accepted the situation with such grace as he could muster and agreed to give possession of the church to the bailies acting on behalf of the parishioners. He did so on the understanding that the current annual rents and profits, receivable by the monastery and convent, would continue to accrue to him as before. This was apparently agreed and confirmed in a document witnessed, among others, by Dionysius Elphinston, who, somewhat strangely, then put forward a petition on behalf of the landward parishioners, refusing to accept the Cross Kirk as their Parish Church, notwithstanding that it was to be acquired at no cost. Furthermore, these parishioners demanded the appointment of a minister or deputy to provide the service of Common Prayers and the Sacraments, in accordance with the custom and practice of the Church of Scotland, as now established. As he was unaware of the appointment of any suitably qualified minister by the Lords of the Congregation or the parishioners, Dionysius put himself forward for the role, although he appears to have been wholly unqualified. Quite what was behind this petition is difficult to understand. The Church of St Andrew was a ruin and likely to remain so, while the actual distance between the two churches was negligible, and the Cross Kirk would, in practice, be little further from the landward areas. It does, however, indicate that matters were far from settled, but the list of witnesses to the petition document, including the Dean and the Master of Yester, does indicate that the leaders of the old order had now accepted the Reformed order. There is also a suggestion that personal interest was involved as the Master of Yester was acting on behalf of his father, who claimed to have an option on the property of the Cross Kirk, which would be prejudiced by its transfer. The role of Dionysius Elphinston is even more obscure, although he may have been secretly persuaded to act in the interest of the Hay family. In any event, on the same day, the Master of Yester made a public protestation to the bailies, in the Tolbooth of Peebles, that the gift of the Cross Kirk, to become the Parish Church of Peebles, should not prejudice a prior agreement made with Brother Gilbert Broune. The outcome of these machinations is not recorded, but to this day the Hay family retain an interest in property adjacent to the Cross Kirk. Perhaps this is an early case of a difference of opinion between factions in a congregation and community, something not unknown in more recent times.

On the orders of the Lords of the Congregation the magistrates received the keys of the outer door of the Cross Kirk from Brother Gilbert Broune on 11 December, thus finally completing its transformation as the Reformed Parish Church. Although, at the end of 1560, there was no doubt a confusion of minds and conflict of allegiances on the part of many, the first part of the Reformation in Peebles, as in much of Scotland, was now complete.

Meanwhile in distant France, the now teenage Mary, Queen of Scots had married the Dauphin of France on 24 April 1558 in a splendid ceremony in Notre Dame, Paris. Francis, the companion of her childhood, was one year her junior and a sickly youth, but by all accounts they were a devoted couple in a childish way. In June 1559 her father-in-law, King Henri II of France, met an untimely and painful end as a result of a freak jousting accident. Mary was now Queen of France as well as Scotland, but her position at the pinnacle of the glittering French court was short-lived, for after a reign lasting only sixteen months, her husband, now Francis II of France, finally succumbed to the ill health which had attended him throughout his life, and he died on 5 December 1560. Mary was left alone. She had suffered another blow only a few months earlier, when Mary of Guise, the mother she had not seen for several years, but still revered, died on 10 June 1560. Her relationship with her formidable mother-in-law, Catherine de Medici, the Queen Dowager of France, had never been easy. As a now highly eligible widow herself, Mary had become a potential matrimonial target of those who were the political enemies of Catherine, and Mary's position at the court of France was no longer tenable. Furthermore, Scotland had been without the personal rule of its monarch for eighteen years and there was a strong feeling that she should return to the land of her birth.

So it was that in the summer of 1561 Mary set sail from Calais, with considerable regret and no doubt much apprehension. She arrived at Leith on 19 August 1561. The political and religious landscape of the Scotland to which she returned had changed beyond recognition from the Scotland she had left thirteen years previously.

Chapter Notes

a. discourse; **b**. at their ease; **c**. the rabble; **d** company; **e**. truly; **f**. grease; **g**. meat; **h**. idle lads; **i**. lazy wretches; **j**. deceivers; **k**. talk freely; **l**. prattling; **m**. trifling; **n**. fierce; **o**. clean; **p**. buying and selling of benefices; **q**. a payment extracted on the death of a tenant; **r**. coarse woollen cloth; **s**. custom; **t**. pig **u**. woollen garment; **v**. a hood.

5

The Queen Returns

The east coast of Scotland was shrouded in mist on 19 August 1561, when two ships of the French fleet arrived early in the morning at the Port of Leith, bearing the Scottish Queen and her Scottish and French retinue. Some regarded the inclement weather as an ill omen. In spite of the dismal morning, Mary was greeted by an enthusiastic crowd, anxious to view their long-absent monarch. The French courtiers who accompanied her were said to be somewhat shocked not only by the drab weather, but also by what they perceived as the equally drab appearance of her Scottish subjects and nobility, whom they regarded with no little disdain. Whatever the inward thoughts of the eighteen-year-old Queen, she gave every appearance of being delighted by her reception. That night, and for several nights thereafter, she and the court now established at Holyrood were serenaded by a large group of musicians and singers who, it was claimed by the French visitors, demonstrated all the worst features of enthusiastic amateurism by discordant playing and tuneless singing. The French were appalled, but Mary, exhibiting the charm and tolerance that were so much a hallmark of her character, made it known that she personally had taken great pleasure from the experience. Even John Knox, ever ready to carp and criticise, had to concede that her reception had been genuinely joyful.

From the outset of her return to Scotland, and fully aware of the cataclysmic religious change that had come about in her absence, Mary made it clear that she had no intention of interfering with the new order, provided that she could continue to worship privately in the Catholic tradition. However much it might have pleased her personally to see the Reformist order reversed, she was well aware that the pragmatic approach must be to preserve the status quo. Indeed it should be said that at no time during her personal rule of Scotland did Mary seek to re-impose Catholicism. Her links to, and covert promotion of, the Catholic cause are correctly associated with her later years as a captive in England, when willingly, knowingly or unwittingly, she became associated with the manoeuvring and plotting of the Catholic faction in England, who saw her as their figurehead and the rightful monarch of that country. It was this, rather than any of her actions in Scotland, which was to prove her ultimate downfall. In spite of her clearly stated religious tolerance upon her Scottish return, there were those to whom her personal adherence to Catholicism was anathema. Within one week of her return John Knox used a sermon in St Giles to give an outspoken condemnation of the Mass. This was clearly directed at the young Queen and it says something of the egotism and arrogance of Knox that he felt he could make such an outburst with impunity. It did not, however, pass unnoticed, and Mary summoned him to Holyrood. There followed the well-known series of interviews, which in the context of the times were remarkable. For here was a subject, and a mere commoner at that, presuming to debate and admonish his anointed sovereign on matters national and very personal. However much Mary may have lacked judgement on many matters, as time would show she was no feeble woman, and it seems that, using her considerable intelligence and learning, she was the equal of Knox in debate. It should be further remembered that she was still only eighteen years old. They agreed to disagree (or at least Mary did). At a different time, and in different circumstances, Knox would have been lucky to avoid imprisonment or worse. However, Mary was, at that time, very much influenced by her half-brother, Lord James Moray, and William Maitland of Lethington, who were both firmly in the Protestant camp. For a time at least she listened to and accepted their good counsel and adopted a pragmatic attitude to Knox, who had the tide of popular opinion behind him, as Moray and Maitland were well aware. Sadly, pragmatism and political and personal good judgement were in time to desert her.

In the meantime the effects of reformation were beginning to bite throughout Scotland. In Peebles the final act of the destruction of Papal authority and the establishment of the Protestant Church of Scotland had been concluded by Brother Gilbert Broune, handing the keys of the outer door of the monastery of the Cross Kirk to the magistrates of the burgh on 12 December 1560. The very next day the new minister, John Dickson, took possession of corn lying in the yard in the Old Town belonging to the Catholic archdeacon and the former Rector of Peebles, as it was the most accessible of their goods, out of the proceeds of which he could be paid a stipend as Reformed minister. However, Dickson seems to have acted a little precipitately, as two of the towns' burgesses, no doubt still sympathetic to the old order, came forward to act as surety for the value of the corn, which was returned to the former owners.

The appointment of John Dickson as minister seems to have been short-lived. Whether as a result of dissatisfaction with his performance or whether it had transpired that he was insufficiently qualified, within a matter of days the bailies were instructed to approach the Lords of the Congregation to appoint a new minister 'to shew the true word of God'.[1] This took some time to resolve, but on 5 February 1561, what was effectively the first Kirk Session of the Parish of Peebles was appointed when the magistrates and community elected ten elders and eight deacons. The Kirk Session, in turn, then elected John Allan[2] as minister, his admission being confirmed by John Willock, Superintendent of Glasgow.[3] It is noteworthy that they also sought the endorsement of this appointment by John Knox, Superintendent of Edinburgh. Just a year later, John Dickson, having been effectively demoted, was admitted as 'Reader and Exhorter'[4] by John Willock.

February 1561 does seem to have been a time of great activity. Destruction of the symbols of the old order was much in hand. Perhaps it was at this time that the font, now in the Old Parish Church, and supposed to date from medieval times, was cast into the Tweed.[a] The town treasurer was instructed by the bailies and Council to have the two bells of the Church of St Andrew removed, with one to be re-hung in the Cross Kirk, while the other was to be laid up in the Tolbooth. This bell was subsequently sold by the Council in 1564. In March the same year, it was decided that all the remaining vestments should be sold by auction, with the proceeds to be distributed among the poor of the town. One James Tweedy, together with seven others, was instructed to draw up a list of those most in need and to arrange distribution of the money at their discretion. The linen cloths, which had been used in the former Catholic services, had been taken to the steeple and, on 16 October 1562, the Council ordered James Wilson and John Dickson to give these to poor people for whatever use they deemed expedient. A short time later, on 10 December 1563, the Council decided that one of the chalices, which had been placed for safety in the Tolbooth, should be melted down and sold and that the proceeds should be used in whatever way the bailies might decide best.

Brother Gilbert Broune does not appear to have retired gracefully. Together with those of the Trinity Friars remaining, he was summoned on 13 February 1562 to appear before the newly established Kirk Session by John Dickson, now Reader and Exhorter. The exact details of the reason for the summons are not recorded, but there does seem to have been an ongoing dispute between the two clerics. Dickson's complaint seems to relate to a less than cordial conversation between him and Brother Gilbert, who refused to appear before the Session on the grounds that they had no jurisdiction over him. Brother Gilbert, in turn, claimed that John Dickson had 'back bited' him, to which Dickson responded that Brother Gilbert should show proof of this, failing which he should be punished for his error. Brother Gilbert did not have his troubles to seek. He was probably still living in part of the cloisters of the Cross Kirk, and on 28 May 1565 he accused John Wille of cutting down some of the ash trees which grew in the grounds, with a saw borrowed from William Kelle who was a weaver. The charges were strongly denied by both, but Brother Gilbert had somehow obtained a copy of a written statement from one of the bailies which purported to confirm that the bailie had found evidence of ash tree wood in the house of

John Wille. Brother Gilbert alleged that this was the same that had been removed from the Cross Kirk grounds. Once again there is no record of the outcome, but perhaps this is an indication that no action was taken, possibly because of a lack of sympathy towards the former minister. The disputes between John Dickson and Brother Gilbert seem to have festered on for some time, for on 8 July 1566 Dickson again presented a petition to the bailies, probably relating to a continuing lack of co-operation from the former minister and the other remaining friars. Brother Gilbert and the friars refused to comply and declined to appear before the bailies as instructed. The bailies, in turn, warned them that continuing failure to do so would result in their absence being taken as an admission of guilt. However, no more is heard of the outcome of these episodes, but they clearly show that tensions remained within the community between the old and the new orders.

Elsewhere in Scotland, Mary, Queen of Scots had spent much of the first two years since her return in trying to restore the authority of the Crown, particularly in the north of the country, where the Earl of Huntly, ironically a Catholic, was in rebellion. Mary personally took part in the campaign against him, which demonstrated that whatever else she may have lacked, it was not spirit or courage. It was not until the summer of 1563 that she turned her attention to the Borders, when she undertook a progress throughout the south of Scotland. Mary was less frequently in or about Peebles than any of the Stewart monarchs up to that time, something which her son did much to redress. Her first recorded visit to the town is on 27 August 1563 when she stayed overnight, probably at Neidpath Castle. The next day she followed the practice of her predecessors since James II by granting letters of protection to the burgesses, and these were reportedly written in her own hand.

A more frequent royal visitor to the town was her husband: Henry Stuart, Lord Darnley, who was the son of the Earl of Lennox. Initially Mary seems to have been much infatuated by him. He was several years her junior, but his youth and handsome appearance belied a weak and self-indulgent character. It was against all good sense, although perhaps all too characteristic of her, that Mary entered into marriage with him, something which she later regretted. Much as he aspired to it, Mary, for once applying some sense, never granted him the Crown Matrimonial. Nonetheless, in the Scottish court he was referred to as the 'King' and accorded the due deference that the title implied, little though he deserved it.

For Darnley, Peebles became a frequent bolt hole to escape the ire of his increasingly disenchanted wife and what he perceived as the tedium and restriction of court life. In and about Peebles, a day's ride from the capital, he could indulge in his almost continuous pastimes of hawking, hunting, drinking and wenching with his dubious band of cohorts. Towards the end of 1565 Mary was pregnant, something that would not necessarily fill Darnley with joy, as the birth of an heir would inevitably give the child precedence over him. He met with the Queen at Linlithgow at the beginning of December. In view of Darnley's blighted aspirations this was not a happy meeting, and shortly after he left for Peebles on yet another hunting and carousing sojourn. George Buchanan, as usual antagonistic to Mary, inferred that she had deliberately sent her husband to Peebles in the depth of winter with only a small retinue, and that he nearly died of starvation. Buchanan, in due course the boyhood tutor and tormentor of their son, James VI, seems to have been no supporter of the royal household of Mary and Lord Darnley. Certainly he was one of the greatest critics of the Queen and his account seems to be less than objective, rarely missing an opportunity of casting her and those about her in a poor light. The thought of Darnley's discomfort in Peebles doubtless gave him cause for rejoicing. Captain Armstrong recalls an extract from Buchanan in his history of Scotland:

Lord Darnly [sic] with his attendants, retired to Peebles, to avoid the fury of the Queen's jealousy, and courtiers envy; but throws an illiberal reflection on the country, which, Buchanan says, was so infested with thieves that King Henry was obliged to remove. Peebles, with its environs, has been particularly adapted for a hunting seat

In an apparent apology for the state of Peebles, the Notes to Pennecuik's Works[5] have this to say:

The real, unbiased, state of these facts seems to be, that King Henry, being fond of hunting and hawking, went to his Royal Hunting Forrest at Peebles, near which, as we have seen, the hawk used in falconry breeds, in Glendean's-banks, as a place much resorted to for sport, to enjoy his favourite amusements; to which he was, even according to Buchanan, so much addicted as to neglect public affairs on their account; taking with him but few attendants, that he might be at ease with himself, and less burdensome on the town. It being a very severe winter; the town being altogether unprepared for his visit, even with the small retinue he had; a quantity of snow happening to fall on his arrival, so as, probably, in a great measure to cut off, in so highland a district, convenient access to their flocks, herds, and other supplies, and leave them exposed to the swarms of Moss-troopers, Gipsies, and Thieves, with which Peebles, of course, in common with all Scotland, was infested, and whose depredations would appear more numerous and heinous than usual from the apparent indigence of the inhabitants, and the want of fuel, and provisions amidst beggars, gipsies, free-booters, and mountains of snow; its pastoral people, thus embarrassed as to their own means of subsistence, it is likely enough, would be unable to entertain others. The King himself, 'bred up at court, and used to a liberal diet', would, consequently, as in any other highland town in those days, have been very ill off, had it not been for the accidental arrival of the Bishop of Orkney, who, like a prudent and provident prelate, had taken care to provide against the poverty of the place, by carrying along with him, of the good things of this life.

While noting that the story as given by Buchanan is uncorroborated, Alison Weir[6], referring to the occasion of this visit, says that Darnley travelled from Linlithgow to Peebles on a hunting trip and, not having returned, that Lennox, his father, set out in search of him. However, Dr Gunn[7] mentions the occasion of one of Darnley's visits in 1565, which may well be the visit in question, and quotes the following from an earlier source:

Darnley was in great hazard of wanting necessities, unless the bishop of the Orcades had casually come hither; for he knowing the scarcity of the place, brought some wine and provisions for his use.

Adam Bothwell was the son of an Edinburgh burgess. While adhering to the Church of Rome he was, for a time, parson of Ashkirk and one of the canons of Glasgow Cathedral, before becoming Bishop of Orkney in 1558. He owned property in Peebles, and thus would have been well acquainted with the state of the town. The material privation suggested, together with Buchanan's report of the lawlessness of the place, hardly paint a flattering picture of Peebles at that time.

Dr Gunn also offers, in the same extract, a more likely reason for Darnley's visit:

About Christmas time the Queen's husband was residing in Peebles. The weather is stated to have been exceptionally severe, and much snow fell. The object of the journey appears to have been for the purpose of effecting a meeting between Darnley and his father, the Earl of Lennox, who was out of favour with the Queen at the time. Here is a letter arranging the interview:-
'Sir, - I have received by my servant Nisbet your natural and kind letter, for which I humbly thank Your Majesty; and as to the contents thereof, I will not trouble you therin, but defer the same till I await upon Your Majesty at Peebles, which shall be so soon as I may hear of the certainty of your going thither. And for that the extremity of the stormy weather causes me to doubt of your setting forward so soon on your journey, therefore I stay till I hear further from Your Majesty, which I humbly beseech you I may, and I shall not fail to wait upon you accordingly. Thus committing Your Majesty to the government and blessing of Almighty God, who preserve you in health, long life, and happy reign, - from Glasgow, this 26th Day of December, - Your Majesty's humble subject and father, MATTHEW LENNOX.'

This suggests that the true purpose of the visit was a meeting with his father, and as the quoted letter implies this was something which had been envisaged for some time.

At the time of the birth of her son James on 15 June 1566, there seems to have been unrest in the Borders. Mary was already heavily involved with the infamous James Hepburn, Earl of Bothwell and had appointed him to exercise royal authority in the Borders. Following her confinement, on his advice, she decided to hold a series of royal assizes in the area in order to dispense justice and due punishment to the many troublemakers who were the cause of the unrest. Among the assizes one was held at Peebles on 13 August, when her lieges were summoned to attend her in the Royal Burgh. August 1566 finds the royal couple apparently reconciled, for a brief period, in the area, hunting at Megget on the 14th of the month and again on the 16th at Rodono and Cramalt. A large number of the nobility were in attendance and no doubt Peebles and its neighbouring villages felt the effect of their presence. Sadly the sport was poor, so much so that, owing to the scarcity of deer, the Queen decreed that they were not to be shot, the penalties for non-observance being severe. They then moved on to Traquair on 19 August before returning to Edinburgh by the 21st.

At about 4 a.m. on the morning of 10 February 1567, the citizens of Edinburgh were awoken by a loud, rumbling explosion, which came from the far side of the Flodden Wall, on the eastern boundary of the town. The house known as Kirk O'Field had been completely destroyed, and nearby lay the body of Lord Darnley, who had been staying there overnight. However, he had not died from the effects of the explosion, but by strangulation. By whose hand has never been completely established, although James Hepburn, Earl of Bothwell, was then and still is the prime suspect. Although it is known that Mary had indicated a wish to be parted from her useless husband, whether or not she was implicated or even knew of the plot to do away with him has never been conclusively proved or disproved. Modern opinion seems, on balance, to exonerate her, although she is unlikely to have greatly grieved the loss of one whom she had come to despise. Whatever loyalty or love the people of Peebles may have held towards the royal couple, the murder of Darnley seems to have passed without comment. With their considerable experience of the debauched and wayward King, perhaps the good folk of the town heaved a collective sigh of relief.

But what of their attitude to Mary, Queen of Scots? Loyalty to the monarch of the day has been a hallmark of Peebles throughout its history and no doubt the town remained loyal to her, at least for a time. The provost, Lord Yester, was certainly a loyal follower of the Queen as his presence at Dunbar, when she rode there to be with Bothwell, and subsequently at the Battle of Langside, surely demonstrates. At Langside he fought alongside her together with his retainers, who presumably numbered among their company some who came from Peebles.

The career of Mary, Queen of Scots was all downhill after the murder of Darnley. In May 1567 she was married to Bothwell, willingly or unwillingly, but probably the former. Of all her many personal misjudgements, this last was arguably the greatest. It was the cause of a major rift among the great magnates who perceived it as a cynical attempt by Bothwell to gain ultimate power and authority in the kingdom, something particularly those who supported the Protestant cause could not accept. Bothwell retreated to his castle at Dunbar where Mary followed him, and shortly after he led his depleted forces to a confrontation at Carberry Hill, near Musselburgh, where the force led personally by himself and Mary was ignominiously defeated by the Protestant Lords. While Bothwell fled the scene, and ultimately Scotland, Mary was captured by the Lords and taken to Edinburgh. The cries of the Edinburgh mob, 'burn the whore', which rang in her ears as she was led through the streets, is ample evidence that she had lost the respect and trust of the very people who, not so long before, had acclaimed her on her return to Scotland. A few days later, she was moved to the Castle of Loch Leven and effectively held captive in that island fortress and there, on 24 July, she was forced to sign a Deed of Abdication and to confirm the appointment of her half-brother, the Earl of Moray, as Regent. On 29 July her infant son was crowned as James VI, King of Scots, at the Church of the Holy Rude in Stirling.

On 2 May 1568 Mary made her famous escape from Loch Leven Castle and headed for Hamilton, where forces loyal to her had been gathered together by her Hamilton cousins, who planned to link up with other forces loyal to her in the west of Scotland. But at Langside, near Glasgow, these forces, again led personally by Mary, were soundly defeated. Her courage for once deserting her, Mary fled the field and made for the south-west, stopping briefly overnight at Dundrennan Abbey, near Kirkcudbright, before setting sail across the Solway Firth the next day, from the place still known as Port Mary, for England, captivity and eventual execution. The final departure of Mary from Scotland brought to an end the first part of the great religious transition in Scotland from Catholicism to Reformed Presbyterianism. The reign of her son, James VI, would see the start of the second part of the battle for the minds and souls of the people, which was to become a battle between Episcopacy and Presbyterianism.

Chapter Note

a. It was found and retrieved many centuries later when the foundations of the Tweedside Mill adjacent to the Old Parish Church were being excavated. Today it may be seen beneath the baptismal table of which it forms a part.

6

God's Sillie Vassal

James, the son of Mary, Queen of Scots and Henry, Lord Darnley was little more than one year old when he was crowned King of Scots at Stirling on 29 July 1567. Indeed the crown itself, fashioned for his grandfather, James V, could only be held above his head as it was far too big to fit him.[1]

James VI of Scotland and I of England was described by Andrew Melville, the arrogant, vocal and self-opinionated Scottish divine, as 'God's sillie[a] vassal', and by the Duc de Sully, the principal advisor to King Henri IV of France, as the 'wisest fool in Christendom'. William Chambers, the Peeblesshire historian of the nineteenth century,[2] went so far as to describe him as an imbecile. In this he was no doubt influenced by his near contemporary and fellow Borderer, Sir Walter Scott. As with so many facets of Scottish history, distorted by Scott, it was he, possibly taking his lead from an English courtier, Sir Anthony Weldon,[3] who created the picture of the clumsy, ungainly, slavering and shambling King in his novel *The Fortunes of Nigel*, and who dubbed him as 'deeply learned without possessing useful knowledge; sagacious, without having real wisdom'. In his later years, when James was established in London, no doubt this view suited many of the English court, who despised this seemingly uncouth Scottish intruder and his rag tag band of followers. This is certainly the impression that has come down through history, yet it was those same English courtiers who were so frequently outwitted by him. Modern historians have, however, taken a different view of him. Silly, a fool, imbecile? James Stuart was none of these, despite appearances, which might have tended to that impression. On the contrary, he was highly educated, intelligent, shrewd (particularly in his dealings with his fellow men) and, yes, devious. He used all his talents and also his infirmities to his personal advantage. It is even thought by some that he deliberately played upon and accentuated his apparent deficiencies and thus trapped many of his adversaries into underestimating him. He was, in fact, arguably one of the most able and successful of monarchs; forget his later years, when he fell victim to some self-indulgence. Considering his strange and lonely upbringing, the trials and tribulations of his earlier years, and his long years of struggle (he could not remember a time when he had not been King) to control an unruly Scottish nobility and a self-seeking English court, this self-indulgence is something for which he might be forgiven. Deprived of any sort of normality, even by the standards of a royal household of the day, he was under threat from his earliest childhood, yet he learned the art of manipulation. Although often surrounded by less than suitable companions in his court, he survived, and not only survived, but brought peace and a measure of stability to Scotland, particularly in the Borders, and ultimately, through perseverance and subtlety, gained a second crown. Having gained that crown he departed to his new capital of London to find that the State coffers had been left virtually empty by his illustrious predecessor, Elizabeth I. Through his shrewdness and a cynical understanding of the workings of the English court, he once again survived and ultimately held that fractious court in thrall. By the avoidance of conflict and deft negotiation he brought to an end the state of war with Spain. He gained the respect of much of Europe and was able to link his family to the House of Bohemia by marriage, while, shortly after his death, his son, Charles, married the daughter of the King of France. Although money remained an ever-present problem, he managed to live throughout his reign with the minimum of recourse to Parliament for funds.

It was in 1578, at the tender age of twelve, that James commenced his active reign, although it was another five years before he took real control of the affairs of the realm. In the interim various factions sought to exercise influence and control over him. Foremost among them was his distant cousin, Esme Stuart, Seigneur d'Aubigny, who had been brought up at the French court and managed to establish himself as James's closest companion and advisor. In 1581 he was made a Privy Counsellor and given the dukedom of Lennox, vacant since the death of James's grandfather. By his French upbringing he was, of course, a Catholic and his presence and influence at the Scottish court was greatly resented. The Protestant Lords, with both the moral and financial support of Elizabeth of England, were able to persuade James to confirm the renunciation of Catholicism in a document counter-signed by his principal court favourites, including d'Aubigny. This was known as the 'King's Covenant' or 'The Negative Confession' and effectively renounced all Popery.

By the time James was sixteen years old there had been nine attempts to kidnap him and this no doubt accounts for his lifelong fear of assassination, which in time caused him to adopt padded clothing as a protection against the knife of an assassin. This can be seen in portraits of him, showing bulbous clothing, particularly about the midriff, which set a fashion for the court dress of others. What was effectively a 'kidnap' did occur in 1582. While out hunting in Perthshire, the Earl of Gowrie and a group of nobles, knowing where he was, surrounded his party and persuaded or coerced him to go with them to Ruthven Castle.[4] There he was held a prisoner, to all intents and purposes, while Gowrie and his cohorts, firmly Protestant and sympathetic to England, were thus able to exercise great influence over the government of Scotland. James escaped from Ruthven in 1583 and from then on was able to establish his personal rule.

James's passion was hunting. In spite of his physical deficiencies he was an able horseman and it is likely that he was a frequent visitor to Peebles to sample the delights of hunting in Ettrick Forest at Meggetland and Cramalt, as his grandfather, father and mother had done. However, it is not until 1585 that a specific visit to the town is recorded.

The reign of James VI & I did have a significant effect upon the development of ecclesiastical affairs in Scotland, and although James was inclined towards Episcopacy, particularly after he established himself at the English court, he was enough of a pragmatist not to allow this to altogether antagonise the rising tide of Presbyterianism. Bishops or no bishops? That was the question, and it has remained a question debated even in modern times in the search for an accommodation between the churches of Scotland and England. The political significance was that the appointment of bishops was the prerogative of the Crown. Appoint the bishops and the Crown controls the Church. Throughout his reign, in both England and Scotland, James sought to establish the authority of the Crown, so that Church and State were one. The King derived his authority from God and should therefore have authority over all the Estates of the two kingdoms, the Lords Spiritual, Temporal and the Common Weal. This was the Divine Right of Kings, a theory of government expounded by James and set down in his treatise 'Basilikon Doron', written primarily as a guide to kingship for his elder son, Prince Henry, who was sadly to die as a youth. It, however, sowed the seeds of destruction for the younger son, Charles, who succeeded him, with disastrous consequences for himself and many of his subjects.

The year 1560 had seen the demise of the Church of Rome as the ecclesiastical power in Scotland. In the years before James commenced his personal rule there had been developments that marked the first stage of the ensuing conflict between the forces of Presbyterianism and Episcopacy. Late in 1560 the first meeting of the General Assembly had taken place. This was a relatively small affair. For a time it met twice a year and in 1562 this body set up Synods or Provincial Assemblies, but the governance of the Church remained a contentious issue. In September 1571, without any discussion with the Kirk, archbishops were appointed to St Andrews and Glasgow by the Council, and the next year what is known as the 'Concordance of Leith' was endorsed against much opposition, by a meeting of the General Assembly. This effectively introduced Episcopacy and restored the position of bishops, although their powers were similar to the superintendents created by the 1560 arrangements. While in theory the appointment of bishops was to lie with local 'Chapters', in practice they were nominated by the Crown. They were known as 'Tulchan' bishops.[5]

On to the stage now stepped Andrew Melville, he who would later dub James 'God's sillie vassal'. Melville, like Knox before him, had spent some time on the European continent, part of it in Geneva, from where he returned to Scotland in 1574 to take up the appointment of Principal of Glasgow University. He became the focus of the Kirk's opposition to Tulchan Episcopacy. He asserted that the Kirk had its authority direct from God and not the King and State, and that the Bible as 'the Word of God' was the foundation of all religious authority and practice. Under that authority there was no precedent for the appointment of bishops. Pastors and ministers had equal authority. They were all the first among equals, although taking precedence over doctors (teachers), elders and deacons. Under Melville's leadership, opposition to the estate of bishops was confirmed by the General Assembly, which outlawed the office of bishop and required all bishops to give up their posts. In addition, bishops were not to administer the Sacraments or preach until re-admitted by the General Assembly. There was to be complete equality amongst all ministers and even the office of superintendent was abolished. Thus the Kirk was restored to its position in 1560 – for the time being at least. A 'Second Book of Discipline' was produced by Melville in 1581 and was approved by the General Assembly of that year.

However, James did not let matters rest there. The Scottish Parliament met on 22 May 1584 and passed a series of Acts which were to initiate a dispute between Crown and Kirk which was not ultimately resolved until the Revolution Settlement of 1690. These Acts, which came to be known as 'the Black Acts', introduced the principle that the King was the Head of the Church and that Assemblies could only take place with his assent. In addition, the appointment of bishops was to be the prerogative of the Crown and ministers should not preach against the Crown or State. Although the Black Acts re-established a form of Episcopacy, the church that emerged was something of a mixture. It remained Calvinist, but had a system of government that included bishops and had the Crown at its head. Andrew Melville and the leading Presbyterians were, of course, implacably opposed and in this they had wide support in the country, something which the pragmatic James recognised, and in 1592 a further Act of Parliament officially endorsed the 'Second Book of Discipline' and also the meeting annually of the General Assembly, but gave the King or his Commissioner the right to decide the time and place of the next meeting. Thus it was formally recognised that, in theory at least, Scotland was Presbyterian. James continued to seek the enhancement of monarchical power over all matters of State and religious practice. The vocal and fanatical utterances of Andrew Melville were becoming an increasing thorn in the flesh and in response James progressively took control of the General Assembly.

Meanwhile, what of Peebles? Throughout its long history, certainly since the days of Alexander III, the good people of Peebles and their leaders had been loyal servants of the Crown, but now to which crowned head should that loyalty be given? To the deposed Mary or to her infant son, James? Not only that, but in the years 1567 to 1578 a succession of Regents ruled over Scotland. In the wider sphere, matters were far from settled, and there continued to be a struggle for power between those who still supported the deposed Queen and those who supported the Regent and the young King. There was clearly some confusion in the minds of the townsfolk and this cannot have been helped by the fact that so recently, radical change had taken place in relation to religious belief and practice. It was without doubt a time of uncertainty which bred, not only confusion in the minds of the people, but also lawlessness and near anarchy. There is ample evidence of this in the burgh records. On 10 October 1567, a proclamation was issued that all should meet with the Regent, the Earl of Moray, bastard son of James V and half-brother of Mary, at Peebles on 8 November of that year. The purpose was to deal with thieves in Annandale and Eskdale, and in 1568 and again before Michaelmas in 1569, Moray wrote to the provost and bailies, urging them to use all their available financial resources in the building of a wall round the town to 'resist the invasioun of thevis'.[6] The building of the wall was indeed undertaken shortly after. Moray visited Peebles in person on 20 December 1569, when he gathered a force from the southern shires to combat those of the Earls of Northumberland and Westmoreland, who were in revolt against the English Crown and had sought refuge north of the border. Moray had had a great deal of support from Elizabeth and no doubt acted in some repayment of the debt he owed to her.

Moray was murdered, however, on 23 June 1570, when he was shot by a member of the Hamilton faction in the street in Linlithgow, the Hamiltons still being supporters of the deposed Queen. He was succeeded as Regent by the Earl of Lennox, grandfather of the young King, who continued to encourage the building of the town wall. There is a suggestion that certain of the burgesses had acquired some of the possessions of the former Catholic Church, including some of the contents of the church itself, by means that were less than transparent. This 'Kirk Graith[b]', as it was called, should, the Regent said in a letter to the Council of 11 September 1570, be used to pay for the building of the wall. 'Intromitters' (those admitting) were called upon to restore their ill-gotten gains to the Council for the common good. The Council did take steps to implement this instruction and it was noted that two of the town's bailies, at least, had benefited from what was little more than pilfering of former Church property. One of them, John Horsbruk, admitted that he had in his possession part of a chalice and he offered to make a payment equivalent to its value in restitution. There seems to have been other offenders as well and finally on 24 May 1571 the Council ordered all such to give back what they had illicitly acquired.

Lennox, in turn, was murdered at Stirling by supporters of Mary in September 1571 and was succeeded as Regent by the Earl of Mar.

Early in 1571 the town had been ordered to raise men to provide reinforcements for the army, which the Regent wished to raise in defence of the King's party. This was to assemble at Glasgow on 14 February. However, showing lingering support for the deposed Queen and her cause, the bailies and townsfolk showed little enthusiasm and decided instead to apply to be relieved of this duty and be allowed to 'byde at hame'. Whether or not this wish was granted is not known, but as with the transition from Catholicism to Presbyterianism in the religious sphere, it shows less than universal agreement with the government of the day and at least a degree of public ambiguity. Whatever wavering of loyalties to King James there might have been up to this point, the situation seems to have been clarified in September 1572, when a deputation consisting of two of the bailies and three of the town's burgesses travelled to Leith, where they appeared before the Regent Mar and the Lords of the Secret Council and at least acknowledged 'the King's majestie for thair onlie Soverone'.[7] Furthermore, they avowed that they would have nothing to do with 'traitouris and notorious rebellis'.[8] However, the provost was not a member of the deputation, which perhaps illustrates that loyalties in the town remained divided to a degree. Nonetheless, it seems that the majority of the townsfolk approved of the purpose of the deputation and its actions on their behalf, and on its return the relevant document was endorsed by the Council as confirmation of the town's obedience to the King 'as dewtifull subjects'.[9]

By 1572, perhaps still uncertain as to which of the parties presented the greater threat, steps were taken to improve the security of the town. On 19 May of that year all able-bodied men in the town were called upon to appear, complete with armour and weapons in a great 'wappinschaw'. Every man was to be in possession of a spear and those who were too poor to own one were to be supplied at the town's expense. It was further ordained that at the start and finish of each night and morning watch, 'the drum was to be struck by Robert Thomson, tavernour'.[10] At any other time when the drum or 'common bell' sounded, every male who could bear arms was to assemble at any place in the town which the bailies might decide upon, and they were to do so in their 'best and most honest substantious manner'.[11] These were anxious times, and on 28 May as Dr Gunn records:

orders were made regarding the fortifications of the town. One man was appointed who was to shoot the artillery from the east Wark, and another to superintend the gunpowder. Another man was appointed to walk nightly upon the bartizan of the East Wark, and keep watch from thence. The east port to be closed from nine at night until five in the morning ... A new gate was to [be] built in the new wall out of the readiest of the Kirk timber, beginning on the morrow. All through the summer these precautions were continued, and in the autumn they were increased. The watches, both by night and day, were augmented, and men appointed to walk outside the north gate, at which the expected trouble might come ... The clock was to be made to strike nightly, and to ring curfew, twelve and six respectively. All the gates and their wickets were to be closed in daylight, and opened also at daylight in the morning; and the key of each to be in the keeping of a different man. All who leaped the wall were to be put in irons for twenty-four hours for the first fault; banished for the second; executed for the third. All barn doors were either to be reinforced or else condemned under penalties. One man out of every house ordered to convene at seven in the following morning, and assist in heightening the wall.

These precautions do not seem to have been wholly successful. Dr Gunn adds:

Nothing certain is known now, but on January 6, 1572, they (the Council) inhibited Harry Thomson for all time coming from being found within the liberties of the town of Peebles; because it was notoriously known that he was at the plunder of the town of Peebles on the 27th day of March last.

Following the death of Mar in 1572, he was succeeded by James Douglas, 4th Earl of Morton, one of the less pleasant characters in Scottish history. Morton was a 'strong man', ruthless and competent, but also personally avaricious. He was recognised as leader of the Protestant faction and through force of character, unpleasant as it may have been, he was able to reimpose a measure of order in Scotland. That this required not only strength on the part of Morton, but also the backing of a strong army, is evidenced by an order issued by him as Regent on 16 July 1574, that all lieges between sixteen and sixty years old from within the sheriffdoms of Lanark, Peebles and Selkirk, were to assemble at Peebles on 26 July. They were to appear with food and provisions for four days and thereafter to accompany him 'and attend upoun service, under pane of tynsall[d] of lyfe, landis and gudies'. He was clearly serious about the matter. But strong as he may have seemed, Morton lost the Regency, not due to an untimely death as his predecessors had done, but by the pressure exerted by a coalition of his peers. He was forced to resign in 1578, and although he briefly regained a measure of power in 1579, his influence was effectively at an end and his life itself was ended in 1581. James had commenced his personal rule in 1578 and, under the influence of his cousin Esme Stuart and James Stewart, son of Lord Ochiltree, Morton was condemned to death and executed for his alleged part in the murder of the King's father, Lord Darnley.

Although Morton had brought about a measure of peace and stability, the almost endemic lawlessness of the Borders was never very far beneath the surface, and in 1583 four of the notorious Border clans, the Johnstones, Grahams, Elliots and Armstrongs, combined to carry out a raid on Peebles. Much damage must have resulted, because a complaint was lodged by the town with the Convention of Royal Burghs, who in turn appointed commissioners to take the complaint to the King, which had been put before them 'be the toune of Peiblis anent the greit injuris done to theme' by the four named clans and sought 'quhat redres may be ressonabliest obtanit thairof'.[12]

The first positive reference to James's presence in Peebles is in April 1585, when all the inhabitants aged between sixteen and sixty were ordered to meet the King or his deputy at Peebles on 2 May. If all responded it must have been a sizeable gathering. It is indeed described in Buchan as 'formidable'. It was called because of the continuing feuds between the Border families and crimes committed on the Borders, especially by Robert Maxwell, natural brother of John, Earl of Morton and others. It seems that Peebles had become a regular place of meeting, when the King sought to impose his authority on the Borders, and James was again in the town in 1592 and 1593 planning the pursuit, apprehension and punishment of those who flouted royal authority.

Mary, Queen of Scots had of course suffered death under the axe-man's blade at Fotheringay Castle in February 1587, and there was now no cause for uncertainty about where the town's loyalty should lie. James reigned supreme over most of Scotland, not least the Borders, and the age-old loyalty to the Crown of the Royal Burgh was no longer in doubt. It was a loyalty that James would recognise and reward in later years.

The practice of calling together his subjects from the Border shires at Peebles continued during the remaining years before James departed to his new kingdom of England in 1603. The last such gathering recorded took place on 15 October 1602, when he was present at a justice ayre held in the town on that date. This was appointed by the King 'for trying and punishing, the many enormities and insolences which have been committed during several years bygone'.[13] His Majesty and a number of his Council intended to be present in person as it was necessary 'that His Majestie be weel and substantiallie accompaneit by a force of his guid subjectis'.[14] James therefore directed that all his lieges and subjects aged between sixteen and sixty living in the shires of Peebles and Selkirk should meet him at Peebles on 15 October 'ilk ane of them weel bodin in feir of war[e]', and be prepared to attend on His Majesty for a period of fifteen days.[15] Again this must have represented a sizeable gathering and would have strained the resources of the town to its limits. Where such a gathering took place is not recorded. In practice, while the King's proclamation required all lieges aged between sixteen and sixty to attend, in reality perhaps this related more to the men of influence and representatives of the people, rather than the whole population.

In religious affairs the burgh had elected a body of elders and deacons in 1561, which in due time would constitute what was to become the Kirk Session. The General Assembly of 1580 had created Presbyteries for the first time, but as late as 1582 none had been established in Tweeddale, which, as the Assembly of that year noted, was due to the lack of qualified ministers within the shire; but in

1583 a new 'Synod' was created joining together Dunbar, Chirnside, Melrose and Peebles.

James was present at a meeting of the General Assembly on 4 August 1590. He was no stranger to voicing his opinions in public and was reported to have 'fell forth praising God that he was born in such a time as the time of the light of the gospel; to such a place as to be King in such a Kirk – the sincerest Kirk in the world'. And he went on: 'The Kirk of Geneva keepeth Pasche and Yule: what have they for them? – they have no institution. As for our neighbour Kirk in England, it is an evil said Mass in English, wanting nothing but the liftings[f]. I charge you, my good people – ministers, doctors, elders, nobles, gentlemen and barons – to stand to your purity, and to exhort the people to do the same; and I, forsooth, so long as I brook my life and crown, shall maintain the same against all deadly.' This certainly seemed to be a forthright endorsement of Presbyterianism by the King, although later years would modify this perspective.

A few years later there seems to have been a serious problem in relation to the use of the Cross Kirk as the Parish Church of Peebles. It will be remembered that when it became the Parish Church in place of the Church of St Andrew in 1560, Lord Yester had attempted to prevent this, claiming that he had an agreement with Brother Gilbert Broune that the property of the Cross Kirk should become his. At that time Yester failed in this endeavour, but it seems that sometime thereafter he had obtained possession, by means fair or foul. The congregation were, as a consequence, now worshipping in the Chapel of St Mary in the High Gait, which had stood there since 1362. However, the Presbytery, which had finally been established on 28 April 1597, instructed the minister of Peebles to stop conducting services in the Chapel and to return to the Parish Church (Cross Kirk) the following Sunday. This instruction was to be intimated to the Kirk Session. The reaction of Lord Yester is not recorded, but as the Cross Kirk appears to have been used as the place of worship thereafter, it must be assumed that he acquiesced or was thwarted. In any event, the matter was settled by the King, who instructed the granting of a Charter in the same year under the Royal Seal, granting the Cross Kirk to the town as the Parish Church.

Our sovereign lord ordains a charter to be made under the great seal, in due form, making mention that His Highness, after his perfect age, and all his vocation and the zeal His Majesty bears to the glory and service of God, and to the entertainment of policy and keeping of good order among His Highness' subjects, specially within His Highness' burgh of Peebles, where the Parish Kirk of the said burgh was burnt of long time bypast, in time of war betwixt His Highness' realm and that of England; with advice and consent of his lords of His Highness' secret council and exchequer, has given, granted and perpetually confirmed, and by the tenor hereof gives, grants, and perpetually confirms to the provost, bailies, burgesses, community and inhabitants of His Highness's said

burgh of Peebles, and their successors, heritable, all and whole the Kirk called
the Cross Kirk of Peebles, with the yards, place, and enclosure adjacent thereto,
and all their pertinents lying within the sheriffdom and parish of Peebles, to
the effect that the said provost, council, burgesses, community, and inhabitants
of the said burgh, and their successors, may sustain, build, and repair, and use
the same for the Parish Kirk of the said burgh of Peebles in all time coming.
Which Kirk, called sometime the Cross Kirk of Peebles, sometime pertained to
the friars of the said Kirk, called the Trinity Friars of Peebles, and their predecessors, and now pertain to our said Sovereign Lord, fallen and come into
His Highness's hands, and at His Highness' gift and disposition, by the acts of
Parliament and laws of this realm through the abolishing of the superstitions of
the said friars.[16]

On 24 March 1603, following the death of Queen Elizabeth, James Stuart VI,
King of Scots, was proclaimed King James I, King of England and Ireland, and
later that year he took himself off to his new capital of London, together with a
selected group of Scottish courtiers. He never again visited Peebles and, in spite
of a promise to return to Scotland every three years, he did not do so until 1617.
At the end of that visit he returned to London, never to set foot in Scotland again.

The year following the departure of James to his southern capital, Peebles
suffered the devastation of a major fire on 4 July. Nothing is known about its
cause, nor is there any detailed account of its consequences, but it must have
been an event of some note. The diary of Robert Birrel, an Edinburgh burgess,
who recorded events in Scotland between 1532 and 1605, notes under that date
'ane grate fyir in Peblis toun'.[17] Fires were not uncommon at that time, given the
nature of the materials used for building, much of it timber and thatch. However,
the reference to a 'grate fyir' suggests that this was something out of the ordinary,
and a major conflagration damaging or destroying many of the town's houses
and buildings. It was apparently sufficiently catastrophic for the Council to ask
the Convention of Royal Burghs 'for thair helpe to the re-edefying of the toun
… brunt with sudden fyre'. It is noteworthy that the town records for the period
1573 to 1604 are absent or have been lost. Very possibly they may have been
destroyed in that fire.

In spite of his absence from Scotland, James continued to exercise effective
power and authority over the country, mainly due to his careful selection of a
Privy Council, whose members were wholly loyal to him and his aims. As James
was to remark, he ruled Scotland with his pen. It was during the early years in
England that James brought his long-running battle with the Kirk to a head.
Although the Act of 1592 had established the right of the Kirk to hold a General
Assembly on an annual basis, albeit to be called by the Crown, James failed to
convene a meeting in 1603 or 1604, and in 1605, when the Kirk itself called a
meeting, the Privy Council made it known beforehand that anyone attending

would be outlawed. Nonetheless, some of the ministers constituted themselves as an Assembly and set a date and place for the next meeting. Thirteen of the leaders were prosecuted and found guilty, and of these, on the insistence of James, six were found guilty of treason and exiled, never to return to Scotland. The most prominent member of the 'dissident' ministers was Andrew Melville. He showed no respect for the King and continued to decry the practices of the English Church. By 1606 James had had enough of him and together with seven other Scottish divines he was summoned to London for a meeting and discussion with the King. Six of the eight were allowed to return to Scotland thereafter, but James Melville, his nephew, was required to live in the north of England, while Andrew himself was confined to the Tower for three years. Following his release in 1611 he became a professor at the University of Sedan and never returned to Scotland. James had drawn a great thorn from his side.

Meeting at Perth in 1606, the Parliament, which included the two Scottish archbishops, passed an Act that effectively restored the former position of bishops, with all their trappings of ancient revenues and privileges. Later in the year the King commanded that a 'convention' be held at Linlithgow in December. This meeting, which was not a General Assembly, decided that each Presbytery should have a permanent moderator or chairman. The bishops were to fulfil this role. To the astonishment of the ordinary clergy, it was learned that the convention was to be regarded as a General Assembly and that it had agreed to permanent moderators, not only for Presbyteries, but for Provincial Synods as well. The clergy were now subject to the authority of the bishops. Courts of High Commission were established under the jurisdiction of each bishop in 1610, and the General Assembly of that year meekly confirmed all the changes; these were further endorsed by the Scottish Parliament in 1612.

Peebles was in the diocese of Glasgow and an application was made to the Archbishop to have a Commissary Court set up in the town. One Henry Balfour, Advocate, was appointed to hold the office of Commissar for Teviotdale, Liddisdale and Tweeddale, 'with full power to the said Mr Henrie to sit within the burgh of Peiblis, sua that the said commissariat in all tyme heirefter salbe callit the commissariat of Peiblis'.[18] To the Council the Archbishop wrote, 'I dout not as ye haif bene ernest to haif your toun the seat of that judicatorie, so ye will haif care to se the judges and thair memberis of courte well usit'.[19] The necessary arrangements were put in hand to make the Tolbooth available to the Commissar on those occasions when the court sat, and all this seems to have met with the general approval of the townsfolk. At about the same time, the first commoner to hold the position was appointed provost. Until that time the provostship had been held successively by the Lord Yester of the time, but an Act of Parliament of 24 June 1609 required that in future the holder of the offices of provost and magistrates in a burgh could only be those who lived and worked in the burgh, and 'noblemen and gentlemen' were disqualified. An election was to be held annually and the first such election, in October 1609, elected John Dickisoun to the office of provost. The influence of the Hays was not entirely at an end, for the eighth Lord Yester, who became the Earl of Tweeddale, sat as a member of the Council for many years.

In the wider sphere of Church government and practice, James continued to turn the screw. His return to Scotland in 1617 was primarily to ensure that his views on these subjects would be fully implemented. Among his visiting party was William Laud, later to become primate of England. His presence was seen as an affront to many of the Scottish clergy and for once James's pragmatism seemed to have deserted him and he failed to persuade the Scottish Kirk to give the bishops more power. However, he recognised that the presence of Laud and the form of liturgy he represented was unacceptable to the Scots.

In 1618 a meeting of the General Assembly was held in Perth on 25 August. This meeting was called by the King and packed by him with his supporters. He sent a letter to the Assembly setting out what became known as the Five Articles of Perth. These dealt with the administration of the Sacraments of Communion and Baptism and the observance of Holy Days. Communion was to be received kneeling and could be administered to the sick in private. Baptism could be administered at home when it was not practical to bring the child to church. When they reached the age of eight, all children were to be brought before the bishop to be questioned by him on their religious knowledge and to receive his blessing. Christ's birth, passion, resurrection and ascension, as well as the coming of the Holy Spirit (Pentecost), were to be observed as Holy Days. The practice of kneeling to receive communion, in particular, was anathema to strict Presbyterians. The teaching of the Church of Rome was that the bread and wine were changed into the body and blood of Christ, and those receiving the elements of bread and wine should do so on their knees. To Presbyterians this constituted worship of the bread and wine, which was considered by them to be idolatrous. At an earlier time, before his departure to London, James himself had described the English liturgy as 'an evil said mass'. Nonetheless, he had now dictated what he considered to be acceptable practice. Congregations essentially remained Presbyterian, but there was far from uniformity, with many churches and ministers adhering to previous practice and a mixture of old and new.

Throughout his life James maintained an interest in witchcraft, even to the extent of involving himself personally, on occasions, in the trials of alleged witches, and most famously in the trial of Agnes Samson and the North Berwick witches, where he took part in their interrogations. They were inevitably condemned to death by burning. He was convinced that what he learned from their interrogation confirmed his notion of the Demonic Pact, and in 1597 he produced a book on the subject entitled *Demonologie*. To modern minds the whole idea of witches and demonic pacts seems to be nonsense, but in the sixteenth and seventeenth century it was very much an issue. The notion that witches existed and could wield an evil influence was widespread, and even as late as 1628–29 there is a record of three witches being strangled and then burned at Peebles.

James Stuart died on 27 March 1625. His legacy to his two kingdoms was to leave them in a state of relative peace, and at peace with the rest of Europe. His legacy to posterity was his commissioning of the King James Bible, which was first published in 1611 and is dedicated to him. It is one of the finest written examples of the English language ever produced and he is said to have personally supervised it, approving drafts from the team of writers involved in its production. Even if his personal involvement was more limited, he deserves credit for its inspiration. To Peebles he left a Charter. This document gathers together all that the earlier Charters bestowed upon the town, and confirms its special place in royal favour. It is a very lengthy document, as it set out in detail all the grants of land and privileges that the town would then enjoy, and to a degree continues to enjoy today. It remains the final and definitive grant to the burgh by the Crown. The preamble runs thus:

JAMES, by the grace of God, King of Great Britain, France and Ireland, Defender of the Faith, to all good men on earth, both clergy and Laity, Greeting:- Be it known that we, after attaining our lawful, full and perfect age, and considering all our revocations, as well as special as general, and the assiduous care and singular diligence which we and our noble ancestors of worthy memory have taken in the erection of royal burghs within our kingdom of Scotland, in the increase of which, the policy, advantage, and glory of our said kingdom consists, and itself daily augmented and renowned, and we calling to remembrance the ancient erection of our Burgh of Peebles, the great benefits, memorable and agreeable services performed by the Provost, Bailies, Burgesses and community of our said Burgh of Peebles, without any suspicion, fault, or guilt in every past occasion, performed and manifested, as well in peace as in war, not only by defending the country against foreign enemies, but also by exposing their persons and estates to open and evident oppression, as well by struggling on the borders of England as of Scotland, and likewise the great prejudice and loss sustained by them from thence, both in punishing transgressors and other disturbers within the bounds of our kingdom, the city being often spoiled, burnt, laid waste and desolated, lying contiguous to the said borders; likewise calling to our remembrance that our said Burgh of Peebles has always been a very convenient place where the administration of justice for the time might have a safe and secure residence and defence, for the punishing malefactors at the particular Courts of Justiciary, and has been always protected, preserved, and supported from open invasion, by the said Burgh and inhabitants thereof – and we being willing to defend the rights and privileges anciently granted to our said Burgh of Peebles and to the Burgesses and Inhabitants of the same, that henceforth a better opportunity might be given them of continuing in their faithful offices and services:

This is surely a confirmation of the special relationship between the Scottish Crown and the people of Peebles. It is James's reward for the steadfastness and loyalty of the burgh throughout the centuries. It was a steadfastness and loyalty that was to be stretched to its limits and beyond during the reign of his son, Charles I.

Chapter Notes

a. Scots usage – feeble; **b**. furnishings; **c**. show of weapons; **d**. loss; **e**. well-equipped in war gear; **f**. raising the host.

———❦———

7

Royal Supremacy

Charles Stuart was the very antithesis of his able and wily father. Where James VI & I had been sociable, Charles was reserved and aloof, characteristics that were exacerbated by a speech impediment, which made him ever fearful of public humiliation. He was not unintelligent or untutored. Indeed he was widely read, although not a scholar as his father had been. He had had a good broad education at the hands of his tutor, Thomas Murray, who was a Scot. He spoke several European languages and had a sound background of Renaissance culture. Where his father had been slovenly and often coarse, Charles was fastidious to the point of being effete. He knew nothing of Scotland.

Charles was born in Dunfermline in 1600, the second son of James and Anne of Denmark. He was a sickly child, so much so that when his father and other members of the family departed for England early in 1603, he remained in Scotland until the next year, before joining the royal family in London. Although he is said to have held on to traces of his Scottish accent, he could have retained little memory of his earliest years in the northern kingdom, and it was another twenty-nine years before he returned to the land of his birth. Charles had a further misfortune: he was the second son, and his elder brother Henry, the Heir Apparent, was treated and schooled as such, whereas Charles received little education in the affairs of State and none in politics. His brother, in any case, appears to have been a charismatic young man with all the intellectual attributes of his father, but added to that, great charm and a dashing extrovert nature, probably inherited from his mother. It is perhaps one of the tragedies of history, and certainly of the Stuart dynasty, that he died from an infection of some sort, possibly typhus, at the tender age of sixteen. James had taken some trouble to ensure that his firstborn received schooling in kingship. Indeed his tract *Basilikon Doron* was written primarily for the instruction of his son in this art. Perhaps the long years of struggle in Scotland, the stress of establishing his position in England and grief at the death of his son had left him devoid of the incentive to transfer his tutelage to Charles. In any case, even when Charles became Heir Apparent he was in no way prepared for the role and seems to have had little further preparation for kingship during the remaining years of his father's life.

Not all about Charles is negative. He had a fine appreciation of the arts, particularly the visual arts, and during his reign he assembled one of the greatest collections of works of art to be brought together in Europe. Although much of it was dispersed after his demise, this remains the core of the Royal Collection today and is responsible for the presence of many of the great works in the National Gallery and other national British collections.

Charles was fastidious and self-disciplined and sought order and conformity, not only in his personal life, but also in the world of politics and especially religion. It was his desire to impose uniformity of religious practice, both in England and his northern kingdom, that was to prove his undoing. The liturgy of the Church of England appealed to him. He felt comfortable with a form of service and worship that was prescribed and set down. The degree of pomp and ceremony appealed to his sense of the artistic and theatrical, and not least he felt it appropriate that he, as God's anointed, and not the Pope of Rome, was the earthly Head of the Church. Thus the supreme power in Church and State was brought together in his person. On the other hand, he distrusted the very idea of a Scottish Kirk, with its supreme authority, the General Assembly, independent and separate from, and in some ways superior to, the State. Like many ex-patriot Scots both before and after him, he harboured romantic notions about the country and nation of his birth, but knew nothing of the reality, and, like the later diaspora, Charles no doubt preferred to retain this idealistic view of Scotland and his forbearers in his mind, rather than witness the truth first hand.

Nonetheless, it seems that the people of Scotland may have harboured equally romantic notions of their sovereign lord, who after all had merely gone for a time to his southern kingdom and would return to take the personal rule of the land of his fathers. Whatever the consequences of the reigns of their earlier monarchs, the Scots still retained at least a sneaking admiration and even affection for the Stuart dynasty. In the case of Charles, that affection from afar was enhanced by his marriage in 1625 to Henrietta Maria, the fifteen-year-old daughter of Henri IV of France, once again uniting the partners of the 'Auld Alliance'. It was, however, not until 1633, eight years after his accession, that Charles finally made his first visit to Scotland. The ostensible reason for that visit was for his long delayed coronation as King of Scots, but in Charles's mind the perhaps more pressing reason was to ensure the imposition of greater personal authority over the Kirk. Although his alienation of the English nobility and Parliament was already an established fact, it was his alienation of the three Estates of Scotland which was to sow the ultimate seeds of his downfall. The process had started soon after his accession.

In 1626 the Archbishop of Glasgow (and later of St Andrews), John Spottiswoode, was appointed as President of the Exchequer and a member of the Privy Council, together with four other bishops, while every one of the Lords of Session was excluded from that elite body. Thus, not only did the bishops rule the Kirk, but increasingly their power and influence extended to temporal government as well; all this at the expense of the great lords and nobility. The weakening of the landowning classes had been further underlined when the already clerically dominated Privy Council passed an Act of Revocation at the behest of the King in 1625. This recalled all royal grants of land and property and their attendant revenues, which were once again vested in the Crown. Such Acts had been common in the past when a monarch reached the age of personal rule, having reigned as a minor, and by and large the revocation of grants would not be enforced against individuals. The particular significance of Charles's Act of Revocation was first, that he had not reigned as a minor, and more significantly it affected grants of former Church property and benefices, which had been made by the Crown since the Reformation. The property of some thirty-five religious houses had been transferred into the hands of the nobility, and many of the former Church revenues had been acquired by local lairds and often by those who had little or no interest in the parishes from which these benefices arose. No doubt Charles took this action in an attempt to ensure that the revenues from the properties that were their source should be used to provide for the proper support of the local clergy. Those who had benefited from these acquisitions were, however, horrified at the prospect of loss and, furthermore, as most of the great landed families had derived their lands and property as a direct grant from the Crown, this was an action that was perceived as a direct threat to their power and influence, and even their actual livelihood. While Charles might have thought his actions to be fair and reasonable, he made no effort to reconcile himself to those who now felt attacked unjustly. This certainly did not endear him to the Scottish nobility and was a major cause of the ultimate withdrawal of their traditional support for the Stuart monarchy.

Accompanying the King on his coronation visit of 1633 was William Laud, recently appointed Archbishop of Canterbury and a man upon whom Charles, unfortunately, greatly relied, although his wily and perceptive father had harboured a healthy suspicion of this ambitious cleric. With Laud's enthusiastic support, the King ordered that services in the Royal Chapel and the High Kirk of St Giles should be in accordance with the Episcopal liturgy. Edinburgh was created an Episcopal see. The coronation service itself was conducted in accordance with the Episcopal order, with all the pomp and ceremony that implied. This included the singing of choirs, bishops in grand vestments, while the spoken word was in English accents, which might as well have been in Latin as far as uncomprehending native Scots were concerned. It was an affront to Scottish

Calvinistic Presbyterianism. Charles, aloof and wrapped up in what he perceived as a glorious and totally appropriate celebration of his divine Kingship, was unaware, if he cared at all, of the outrage he provoked. Charles returned to his English capital determined to continue the pursuit of his policy of Anglicanisation, and of imposing uniformity of religious practice and observance in his two realms. A new Court of High Commission with extended powers was created by him in 1634, and the following year Archbishop Spottiswoode was appointed Chancellor. That same year, without seeking the approval of the Scottish Parliament or the General Assembly (which had not met since Perth in 1618), and using what he supposed to be the Royal Prerogative, he ordered the introduction of a Book of Canons. This named him as Head of the Church and required the use of a new form of liturgy to be derived from the English Prayer Book. This has come to be known as 'Laud's Liturgy', but although based on the English Prayer Book, it was largely the work of the Scottish bishops. If anything, it was more Papist than its English precursor.

On 23 July 1637 a service was held in St Giles, the High Kirk of Edinburgh, attended by Archbishop Spottiswoode, the Lords of Session, many of the bishops, members of the Privy Council, the Edinburgh magistrates and a large number of the ordinary citizens. At this service the new liturgy was to be used for the first time. The story is well known. It caused a riot. Stools were hurled at the officiating clergy, one allegedly propelled towards the unfortunate Dean by one Jenny Geddes, with the words, 'Traitor, dost thou say Mass in my lug'. This latter part of the story is perhaps apocryphal, but what is certain is that the service broke up in disorder and confusion. It is said that in a matter of days the news of the riot provoked a wave of protest, which rapidly spread through southern Scotland. No record remains of the reaction of the people of Peebles. Perhaps with its long history of loyalty to the Crown and its somewhat ambivalent endorsement of the Reformation not long before, the town retained some neutrality. However, events in Edinburgh are unlikely to have passed unnoticed. Even in those days, lacking modern communication, news travelled fast and subsequent events would suggest that leading members of the community, at least, would not have welcomed the new liturgy and probably supported its rejection.

In the intervening years since the accession of Charles, Peebles continued to be concerned with its own parochial affairs. One matter, which seems to have greatly exercised the populace and the local religious and civic powers, was witchcraft. It was the firmly held belief that warlocks and witches did indeed exist and could exercise their malign influence over their fellow men. Who were these warlocks and witches? In all probability they were the unfortunate few found in every age and in every community who were mentally afflicted or were nothing more than social misfits. Such people have always attracted a degree of fear and aversion from their compatriots. Those unfortunate enough to be accused of witchcraft were unlikely to receive a fair trial, and so-called 'confessions' were extracted rather than volunteered. The punishment varied from the mild to the extreme. Thus, on 4 January 1627, a Peebles widow by the name of Margaret Dalgleish was accused of witchcraft and charming, which she denied. The only thing that could be proved against her was that she had threatened someone with whom she had quarrelled. To this she confessed and asked for pardon, at the same time repeating that she did not practise witchcraft. It was a crime often associated with personal quarrels, and no doubt, in the heat of the moment, words were used and curses cursed, which were later regretted. Margaret was lucky, escaping with an admonition. Less fortunate were the three women who perished for their alleged crime of witchcraft during 1628 and 1629. They were strangled and then burned at a place called the Calf Knowe, which lay to the east of the town.[1] Who they were or how they came to be condemned is not recorded. It seems inconceivable that such a thing could happen in a place like Peebles, where every inhabitant would be known, although it is likely that the three wretches in question were less than popular in the community and were the subject of severe dislike. Possibly they were the victims of the sort of personal hatred that can still emerge in communities today, where unpopular individuals can find themselves blamed for the misfortune of others. Such was the interest that the records list in detail the associated costs of their execution, down to the smallest item. For making the gibbet, £4. For the hire of the lockman[a], £3 and for the amount drunk at his feeing[b], 26s 8d. To John Robene, for five loads of peat, with a quart of ale he gave to the peatmen, bought to burn the witches, 32s. Three loads of coals, 36s. A load of heather, 9s. Three fathoms of small cord to bind the witches' hands, 30d. Four fathoms of thick rope to hang them all up with, 6s 8d. Bread and drink fetched forth to the assytherees[c], 30s. Hangman's wages, £10. To his son for being doomster, 12s. The following verses relating to this affair are attributed to Dr Gunn:

Outwith the burgh stands a grassy mound,
Oft kissed by smiling sunbeams of the morn,
And bathed by evening dews, but hallowed ground
To us, though to our sires a place of scorn,
To which were led old dames of friend forlorn,
To yield in lambent flame and pungent smoke
Their lives in martyrdom oft bravely borne
In name of justice, but too oft a cloak
For spite and jealousy of neighbour folk.
A redder glow than sunbeams fired it then,
The dew was human tears from spirits broke,
Hearts torn and robbed of hope by cruel men.
This mound thus takes to-day the form of passing eyes
Of one vast altar raised for human sacrifice.[2]

On the ecclesiastical front, Peebles seemed, for the time being at least, to have been reconciled to Episcopacy, and in May 1636 Patrick Lindsay, Archbishop of Glasgow, in whose diocese Peebles was situated, made an official visit to the town. Such was the importance of this visit that a delegation of the townsfolk went out to meet the Archbishop and his entourage at Lyne Bridge, some 4 miles west of the town. The cost of the reception (24s) was borne by the town and later there was a formal meeting with the provost and Council, when the diocesan party were entertained with 'confections, ale and shortbread'.[3] Further endorsing the link between matters spiritual and temporal, a new pew for the town's magistrates in the Cross Kirk had been completed in 1637, and in November of that year, the Council ordered that all its members should sit every Sunday in the town's stall in the Kirk. On the day of the inauguration of the magistrates' pew, every member of the Council was to wear a new hat 'to enhance the dignity of the council'. Failure to do so would result in a fine of 40s.

Meanwhile, in the wider world of Scottish affairs, the ripples and recriminations stemming from the failed attempt by the King and the Episcopal hierarchy to introduce the new Prayer Book were developing rapidly. In December 1637, representatives of all the main interests in Scotland, the towns, the nobility, lairds and the Kirk, came together in Parliament House in Edinburgh, where they formed four committees, each one sitting at a separate table. One table was for members of the nobility who had joined the common cause. The second had a gentleman representative from each county. The third had a minister from each Presbytery, and the fourth, a burgher from every town. In common with all Scottish burghs, Peebles was invited to send representatives to this crucial event. Who they were is not recorded, but in view of later events, it seems almost certain that the former, and soon to be again, provost, James Williamson, would have been among the delegation. This was the start of the rebellion and the rebel-steering committee became known as 'the Tables'. It was also the start of a nationalist movement led by John Leslie, Earl of Rothes and James Graham, Earl of Montrose.

At the same time as the Tables was being established, a document was being drafted by a prominent minister, Alexander Henderson, and a lawyer, Archibald Johnston, which was to become the keystone of the rebellion and one of the great iconic statements of Scottish nationhood. This became known as the National Covenant. It incorporated in full the 'Negative Confession' accepted by James VI in 1581. Thus it confirmed Reformed Presbyterianism as the religion of Scotland. It repudiated all recent Acts of Parliament and royal decrees which were incompatible with it. It included a reaffirmation of loyalty to the Crown, 'in defence and preservation of the aforesaid true religion, liberties, and laws of the Kingdom', and also set out the importance of Parliament and the rights and liberties of the people. On 8 February 1638, before a great gathering in the Kirk and Kirkyard of Greyfriars in Edinburgh, the Covenant was signed by the nobles and gentry. Ironically the first to sign was Montrose, he who would later desert the cause of the Covenant and turn in support of the beleaguered King. Also among the early signatories was Lord Yester. The next day the signatures of the ministers and the representatives of the burghs were added, to be followed by members of the general populace. Duly signing on behalf of Peebles was Provost James Williamson. In the following days copies were distributed for all the people throughout the country to sign. Provost Williamson returned with one copy to the Royal Burgh, and on the bright, late spring morning of 5 March 1638 (the probable date) the magistrates, Council and people of Peebles gathered at the Tolbooth of the town to add their names to this epoch-making document. Standing with his father among that great crowd, perhaps bemused, but sensing the excitement of the occasion, was a small boy of a mere five years. His name – James Nicol.

Chapter Notes

a. executioner; **b.** hire; **c.** assessors.

PART II

—◦◦◦—

8

Joshua Made a Covenant

So Joshua made a Covenant with the people that day.

The Book of Joshua 24:25

It is 5 March 1638. A tolling bell rings out across the burgh of Peebles, through the haze of wood and peat reek, rising from many houses into the still air on a cold but crisp late winter's day. The bell rings out from the fortified town steeple, standing close by the West Port and forming part of the town walls at the west end of the High Gait. Facing it on the high ground to the west are a few isolated dwellings and what remains of the foundations of the King's Castle, long since fallen into decay and ruin.

The population of the town is 1,000 to 1,100 souls, of whom perhaps 100 or more are burgess householders, owning their own property. Most of the houses are one storey, built of whinstone and thatched with heather or straw. The larger houses have an upper storey, faced with wood. The access to the upper floor is by way of an external wooden stairway to a projecting balcony, again built of wood and lacking any protecting hand rail. The construction of all these dwellings makes them very susceptible to destruction by fire, and some of the older citizens can recall the great fire of their childhood years in 1604, when huge destruction of property resulted from a major conflagration in the High Gait, its cause still unknown. Some of the houses have a bastel door, which can be barred and bolted against unwelcome intruders, in days which still see unruly and felonious behaviour, while beneath the projecting stairs and balconies of the larger houses, the affairs and gossip of the day are discussed by townsfolk in huddled groups.

The High Gait is a wide open space and scattered about it are the market stalls of merchants and the purveyors of the bodily needs of the population. These vary in number and position as from time to time the Town Council seek, perhaps ineffectually, to keep them under some semblance of control, a matter often on the agenda of their meetings. The alignment of houses is haphazard, with no attempt to adhere to a common building line, the only defining feature along the High Gait frontage being the open drainage channels running down either side. These are frequently blocked by steadily growing middens, especially at the mouths of the many wynds and vennels that run north and south from the High Gait itself. These middens are a further source of concern to the Council, whose regular attempts to remove or reduce them are thwarted by the need for house-holders to be rid of their own and their animals' ordure.

On the north side, not far from the West Port, stands the Chapel of St Mary, which has occupied its position for nigh on 300 years. Close by and also on the north side is the Tolbooth, the centre of the town's administration, meeting place of the magistrates and Town Council and place of incarceration for felons and those committed there by the Council for various misdemeanours, of which there are many. Few buildings stand outside the walls that encircle the town. Most are situated in the Auld Toun, the original settlement of Peebles, which lies across the Peebles Brig and stretches westwards on both sides of the road leading to the Kirklands and the gait to Neidpath beyond. The walls themselves run northwards from the West Port, until meeting the Peebles Water, which they then follow in an easterly direction passing by a gate giving access to St Michael's Wynd, and further on to a second entrance to the Briggait opposite the Trie Brig.[1] That bridge gives access to the Cross Kirk, some distance to the north, and to the Auld Mill further along the Peebles Water, standing close by the riverbank. From there it turns east along the length of Usher's Wynd to the Auld North Port at the end of the North Gait, and continues east before turning south along the edge of the Foul Myre to the East Wark, crossing the road to Traquair and Selkirk and on southwards along the margin of Skinnersheuch, before turning west again along Tueid Grene to rejoin the West Port. In this last section there is a further access to the High Gait by way of a gate and vennel which issues more or less opposite the Tolbooth. These walls have been originally constructed in their present form in 1569, in accordance with an agreement drawn up between the magistrates of the day and the town clerk, Sir John Allan and Thomas Lauder, a mason. This agreement had specified a continu-ous wall (ports and gates excepted) four and a half ells in height and three feet broad at its top. The work was to be completed within four years. Substantial and effective as this wall has been, the passage of time and lack of adequate maintenance has caused its decay, while the relative calm of recent decades has provided little incen-tive for its restoration. Parts of it are in poor order and little deterrent to any hostile force, and the East Wark in particular is in a near-ruinous state.

Just beyond the East Wark, a road branches northwards from the route to Traquair and beyond, and leads to the town's common pasturage at Venlaw and the place of execution of witches. The main route east passes by the Quhyt[a] Stane. It is the custom for travellers to Traquair and more distant Selkirk and the eastern Borders to stop there and drink a stirrup cup to set them on their way. Lord

Borthwick's property lies outside the walls beyond the Auld North Port, while the Grene Yairds, which are the property of the Council, lie opposite, behind which the few dwellings of Biggiesknowe line the road to the Trie Brig.

The steeple has several bells, each for a different purpose. Thus there is a bell to signify the start and end of the working day and to summon those who attend school. Today it is the Great Bell that is tolling. Usually that bell is rung to alert the townsfolk of the approach of hostile forces, mercifully a rare occurrence these days. It has a sonorous quality, as does any large bell, but this is combined with a sharper, livelier timbre, which lends it a sense of urgency. Today it is tolled as rapidly as the town Bell Ringer and Crier, John Frank, is able. It is rung to summon the townsfolk, and there is not unnaturally a buzz of expectation and excitement as young and old make their way towards the High Gait and the Tolbooth, stepping over a midden at a vennel mouth here and avoiding a marauding pig there, while in the rush scattering squawking poultry in every direction. Uncontrolled livestock are a further source of regular irritation to the magistrates and Council, and their control equally ineffective as is their control of markets and middens. Among those making their way to the Tolbooth is a small boy, not yet six years old, holding tight to his father, Walter, and mother, Jennet. His name is James Nicol, and although at such a tender age he cannot fully comprehend what all the fuss and excitement is about, he is aware that it is an occasion of some importance.

A few days earlier the provost of the burgh, James Williamson, together with a modest retinue, had set out for Edinburgh. He had been summoned there, as had the civic leaders of all Scotland's burghs and shires, by the Lords of the Council. His route to Edinburgh was by way of the Auld North Port and out past the Grene Yairds and the Dean's Park, pausing, as was the custom, to partake of a stirrup cup to set him and his companions on their way to the capital, a day's ride distant. The purpose of the visit was to join in the signing of the National Covenant, which had been drawn up after much debate by Alexander Henderson, the minister of Leuchars, and Archibald Johnston of Warriston, an eminent Edinburgh lawyer. Its purpose was to set down in a written document a statement by Scottish people of their commitment to the Reformed religion and the principle of a non-established church not controlled by the Crown, yet still remaining loyal to the monarch as Head of State. It was a reaction to the clumsy and foolhardy attempts by Charles I to control the Kirk and to impose Laud's, and thus Episcopalian or near Popish, liturgy on the people of Scotland. The resentment of the people was universal and rarely had there been a time when the main body of the Scottish people were more united. The National Covenant was in every sense the culmination of a national rise of feeling. The signing itself had taken place in the Kirkyard of Greyfriars on 28 February 1638. Thousands attended and the principal copy of the document had been signed, firstly by the great lords, who included such as Argyll and Montrose, but also by huge numbers of the Common Weal. More copies were signed in the following days by the representatives of the burghs and shires present,

Provost Williamson and his entourage signing on behalf of Peebles. Further copies had been prepared to be distributed throughout Scotland to be signed by the mass of the people. The provost, having no doubt enjoyed the fellowship and hospitality of his peers and thereafter duly refreshed and rested, had returned to Peebles on the previous day, bearing the copy to be signed by the people of Peebles and the surrounding community. This morning he would present it to the crowd now gathered about the Tolbooth so that as many as were able and willing (as all were expected to be) could add their name or mark.

Having completed the tolling of the Great Bell, John Frank now hurried to the Tolbooth to carry out his further duties as Town Crier and, after a brief pause, mounted the steps at its front to call the crowd to order and pray silence for the provost. The provost himself was hardly to be counted among the least affluent of the town's citizens. He owned property a few miles outwith the bounds of the burgh, as his family had done for generations, and also a sizeable townhouse in the Northgait.[2] Yet he was a man of the people and his popularity among his peers, as well perhaps as his powers of persuasion, caused him to be elected provost on many occasions in the years before and after.

In front of the Tolbooth a large table has been set up. It is an ancient table of which there are two in the possession of the Town Council, both having formerly been part of the furnishings of the Monastery of the Red Friars at the Cross Kirk. Upon it lay a copy of the great document itself. Copies such as this were being displayed through the length and breadth of Scotland at this very moment. After a brief speech, the provost informs the assembled crowd that he will read the whole document from beginning to end so that all may know its contents, whether able to read or not, although most will be able to do so. In a clear voice he begins to read.

We all and every one of us under-written, protest, That, after long and due examination of our own consciences in matters of true and false religion, we are now thoroughly resolved in the truth by the word and Spirit of God: and therefore we believe with our hearts, confess with our mouths, subscribe with our hands, and constantly affirm, before God and the whole world, that this only is the true Christian faith and religion, pleasing God, and bringing salvation to man, which now is, by the mercy of God, revealed to the world by the preaching of the blessed evangel; and is received, believed, and defended by many and sundry notable kirks and realms, but chiefly by the kirk of Scotland, the King's Majesty, and three estates of this realm, as God's eternal truth, and only ground of our salvation; as more particularly is expressed in the Confession of our Faith, established and publickly confirmed by sundry acts of Parliaments, and now of a long time hath been openly professed by the King's Majesty, and whole body of this realm both in burgh and land. To the which Confession and Form of Religion we willingly agree in our conscience in all points, as unto God's undoubted truth and verity, grounded only upon his written word. And therefore we abhor and detest all contrary religion and doctrine; but chiefly all kind of Papistry in general and particular heads, even as they are now damned and confuted by the word of God and Kirk of Scotland. But, in special, we detest and refuse the usurped authority of that Roman Antichrist upon the scriptures of God, upon the kirk, the civil magistrate, and consciences of men ... [at this there is an audible murmur of agreement].

There then follows a long list of the iniquities of the Pope.

And finally, we detest all his vain allegories, rites, signs, and traditions brought in the kirk, without or against the word of God ...
[a louder murmur of agreement].

But this was not the end. There was much more to come:

And because we perceive, that the quietness and stability of our religion and kirk doth depend upon the safety and good behaviour of the King's Majesty, as upon a comfortable instrument of God's mercy granted to this country, for the maintaining of his kirk, and ministration of justice amongst us; we protest and promise with our hearts, under the same oath, hand-writ, and pains, that we shall defend his person and authority with our goods, bodies, and lives, in the defence of Christ, his evangel, liberties of our country, ministration of justice, and punishment of iniquity, against all enemies within this realm or without, as we desire our God to be a strong and merciful defender to us in the day of our death, and coming of our Lord Jesus Christ; to whom, with the Father, and the Holy Spirit, be all honour and glory eternally. Amen.

Again, a murmur of agreement, but still not the end. Far from it. The next part sets out at length all the preceding Acts and Statutes, which in the minds of the Covenanters establish the rights of their position. There were a great many of them, going back as far as the reign of James I and including those during the reign of the present King, Charles I. Having dealt with the establishment of the Kirk as God's true Church, the document addresses the obligation of the King to maintain and defend that true Kirk, and the peoples' obligation to be loyal to the King. The provost reads on:

Likeas, all lieges are bound to maintain the King's Majesty's royal person and authority, the authority of Parliaments ... And therefore, for the preservation of the said true religion, laws, and liberties of this kingdom, it is statute ... 'That all Kings and Princes at their coronation, and reception of their princely authority, shall make their faithful promise by their solemn oath, in the presence of the eternal God, that, enduring the whole time of their lives, they shall serve the same eternal God, to the uttermost of their power, according as he hath required in his most holy word, contained in the Old and New Testament; and according to the same word, shall maintain the true religion of Christ Jesus, the preaching of his holy word, the due and right ministration of the sacraments now received and preached within this realm ... and shall abolish and gainstand all false religion contrary to the same; and shall rule the people committed to their charge, according to the will and command of God revealed in his foresaid word, and according to the laudable laws and constitutions received in this realm, nowise repugnant to the said will of the eternal God; and shall procure, to the uttermost of their power, to the kirk of God, and whole Christian people, true and perfect peace in all time coming: and that they shall be careful to root out of their empire all hereticks and enemies to the true worship of God, who shall be convicted by the true kirk of God of the foresaid crimes.' Which was also observed by his Majesty, at his coronation in Edinburgh 1633, as may be seen in the order of the coronation.

Then the final oration:

We Noblemen, Barons, Gentlemen, Burgesses, Ministers, and Commons undersubscribing, considering divers times before, and especially at this time, the danger of the true reformed religion, of the King's honour, and of the publick peace of the kingdom ... do hereby profess, and before God, his angels, and the world, solemnly declare, That with our whole heart we agree, and resolve all the days of our life constantly to adhere unto and to defend the foresaid true religion [cheer] ... And in like manner, with the same heart, we declare before God and men, That we have no intention nor desire to attempt anything that may turn to the dishonour of God, or to the diminution of the King's greatness and authority; but, on the contrary, we promise and swear, That we shall, to the uttermost of our power, with our means and lives, stand to the defence of our dread sovereign the King's Majesty, his person and authority, in the defence and preservation of the foresaid true religion, liberties, and laws of the kingdom [more cheers] ... seeing what we do is so well warranted, and ariseth from an unfeigned desire to maintain the true worship of God, the majesty of our King, and the peace of the kingdom, for the common happiness of ourselves and our posterity ... most humbly beseeching the LORD to strengthen us by his HOLY SPIRIT for this end, and to bless our desires and proceedings with a happy success; that religion and righteousness may flourish in the land, to the glory of GOD, the honour of our King, and peace and comfort of us all. In witness whereof, we have subscribed with our hands all the premises.

The end at last! There is a moment of silence. And then a great cheer and many press forward, eager to add their name by signature or mark to this momentous document. As always, precedence, or imagined precedence, takes hold. The first to sign are the magistrates and members of the Town Council, but in the following hours a steady stream makes its way towards the table, though the enthusiasm is not entirely universal.

In November 1638, the General Assembly convened in Glasgow Cathedral. The Provost of Peebles, James Williamson, represented the Royal Burgh. In the meantime, the King had done all he could to thwart the Covenanters who were now demanding an Assembly and a Parliament free of the King's absolute control. It was clear to all that if their wishes were not granted, they would set up a government of their own in place of the present regime, although they were at pains to make it clear that such a government would, nominally at least, remain under the King's authority. Charles was well aware that any such arrangement would leave him effectively powerless and this would be the case as long as the Covenant remained in being. As so often in the past, Charles misjudged the unity, strength and resolve of those opposed to him. He attempted to avoid a conclusion and played for time. In September he had instructed the Lord High Commissioner, the Marquis of Hamilton, to offer a free Parliament and Assembly. At the same time he sought support for his own King's Covenant, which echoed the Covenant of James VI & I of 1581, but also repudiated the National Covenant and denied the right of lay elders to take part in the Assembly. All this was in vain, and when the Assembly met in November it continued to sit despite being officially dissolved by the Commissioner, and it once more abolished Episcopacy and its liturgy as set out in the 'Five Articles of Perth'. In addition it confirmed the right of lay members to attend and removed from office all bishops and clergy who would not support the National Covenant.

The attempts by the King to gain support for the King's Covenant certainly did not impress the townsfolk of Peebles, and the Town Council confirmed this when it decided that 'protestatioun sal be maid quhensoever the samynsalbe proclamit'. On the other hand, although it seems that every effort was made by the Town Council to ensure that the National Covenant was signed by the maximum number of townsfolk, they were by no means universally successful, in spite of the clear messages sent out from the Assembly. A number of orders were issued early in 1639 requiring all those who had not done so to sign forthwith. Clearly the number of signatures up until then was not considered sufficient. Once again public ambiguity in the minds of the people of Peebles was evident. The Town Council were, however, adamant and on 30 April 1639 it threatened defaulters that 'they sall incur the panes contenit in the instructions sent … be the nobleman, barones, and ministrie thairout'. As Buchan comments, liberty of conscience was not a matter of personal choice at that time, but Peebles and its people would not have been alone in this confusion, and doubtless similar situations occurred throughout Scotland.

Chapter Note

a. white.

9

———

Bishops' Wars

Sir John Stuart, laird of Traquair, had been a man of ambition from his earliest youth. Unlike his near neighbour, James Williamson, who had been content to lead and represent the people of Peebles as their provost, John Stuart had loftier aspirations. His was from a noble family of ancient lineage, claiming kinship with the Royal House of Stuart. Indeed, perhaps to emphasise that connection, the French spelling of the family name had been adopted, as it had by the Royal House since the days of Mary, Queen of Scots.

The origins of the Stuarts of Traquair stretched back to the reign of James III, when the King granted the lands of Traquair to his half-uncle James, Earl of Buchan, who in turn granted them to his son, James Stewart, who died at Flodden, following which they passed to his son William. Traquair lay a few miles to the east of Peebles on the banks of the River Tweed, and for centuries had been a royal castle, and at the time of its separation from Crown ownership was a place of defence and fortification rather than the lordly country house it would become. It had been the first Stewart laird, James, who had begun the transformation, only completed some 150 years later by Sir John and his son.

The first ancestor to receive royal preferment was another John Stewart who was Captain of the Guard at Holyrood, and had received a knighthood at the hand of Mary, Queen of Scots. She had further demonstrated her favour by staying at Traquair with her dissolute husband, Lord Darnley, in August 1566.[1] John Stuart had been born in 1600 and had been largely educated by the Bishop of Galloway, Thomas Sydserf. His public life started quite early, when he was elected Commissioner for Tweeddale in 1621. It was not long before he had caught the eye of the King, who within a short space of time granted him a knighthood, and in 1628 further advanced him by making him Lord Stuart of Traquair. In 1630 he had risen further in the Royal esteem, becoming Treasurer-depute. At last, ambition had begun to reap material reward, and wealth and power had become his to enjoy. When, in 1633, King Charles I made his first visit to Scotland after his accession, the loyal John Stuart had been granted the earldom of Traquair on 23 June, and with it came the lordships of Linton and Caberston and the right of his male heirs to bear those titles. He gained yet further advancement in 1636, when he was appointed Lord High Treasurer of Scotland, one of the great offices of State. He clearly aspired to even higher things and must have made his frustration known. In response to his irritations, on 20 November 1637, the King wrote:

> Traquaire I have taken this occasion to aseure you that I have not delayed your upcoming out of anie displeasure against you or the least distrust of your Councels; but to show you the contraire, I have commanded Roxburgh not onlie to show you the verie secrets of my thoughts, but also, to have your judgement, as well as your industrie, concur in my service: So referring you to Roxburgh I rest
>
> > Your asseured frend
> > Charles R[2]

In spite of these signs of royal favour, his appointment as Lord High Treasurer was to prove the apogee of his ambitions, and although appointed Lord High Commissioner (and thus the King's representative) to the General Assembly of 1639, the conflict between the King and the Covenanters proved to be his downfall. In fairness, he had tried to reconcile the opposing factions, but this only led to him being distrusted by both sides.

In the spring of 1639 the King attempted to lead an attack on the Scottish forces opposed to him and had gathered a sizeable army at Berwick, but it was badly trained and its members less than enthusiastic to lay down their lives in the royal cause. Charles soon became aware that the Covenanters had been able to muster a formidable army under the able and experienced Alexander Leslie. The Scots army was encamped at Duns Law and there the two forces faced each other. The Covenanters were still loyal to the Scottish Crown and, if it could be avoided, they had no wish to take arms against their anointed King, but Charles realised the weakness of his position and agreed to concede virtually all of the Covenanters' demands. There was to be a free General Assembly and a free Parliament and, provided the Tables were disbanded, the army stood down and the occupied castles handed back, the King's forces would be withdrawn. A formal document incorporating this agreement and known as the Pacification of Berwick was signed by the parties on 18 June 1639. Sadly, sincerity was absent from both sides. Having failed to influence the outcome by his personal presence, Charles departed southwards and did not attend either the General Assembly or Parliament, and when the Assembly met late in 1639, it endorsed all the proceedings of the 1638 Assembly and, in addition, instructed the Privy Council that acceptance of the Covenant should be a matter of obligation. The Privy

Council had given its consent and John Stuart, now Earl of Traquair, as Lord High Commissioner, ratified all the Acts passed by the Assembly. However, he was well aware that the King would not give way and also that the Covenanters' attitude, which demanded freedom of worship for themselves while seeking to deny the same to others, severely weakened their case. The Marquis of Hamilton (later created the Duke of Hamilton) had written to him on 16 August 1639,[3] informing him that the King thought it would be to his prejudice to agree to the establishment of an annual General Assembly. Traquair was to do all he could to avoid a dispute and was to take special care how he proceeded in the matter of the 1580 Covenant, which Charles wished to see implemented as it had been in the reign of his father, James VI & I. Hamilton wrote again on 2 September[4] to tell Traquair that he was commanded by the King to say, as Parliament was likely to have met before this letter reached him, he was to be sure that at its conclusion he should 'make a protestation in those termes as may give his Majesty groundes legally to readres whatt hath now beine donne to the prejudice of his service and lykwyes that you be myndfull to make a right distinction (in those particulares) betwixt giving way and permitting the assemblie and parl[iament] to proceed and concenting to their actes'. In terminating the Parliament, the quicker the better, provided that 'nothing be omitted that may prouve advantageous' to his Majesty.

The meetings of the Estates between August and November caused further problems. As there were now no bishops, Lord Traquair had taken it upon himself to nominate those of the nobility who should sit on the Committee of the Articles, yet when the Articles approved all the Acts of the Assembly and recommended permanent exclusion of the clergy from their Council, as well as other changes of a constitutional nature, John Stuart declined to give the Royal Assent and, without consent of Parliament, prorogued that body until June 1640. All these somewhat contradictory actions inevitably caused John Stuart to be regarded as a vacillator and one who tried to trim his sails and be all things to all men. The result was total distrust of him by both sides. When a quantity of ammunition, ostensibly under his control, was seized by the Covenanters at Dalkeith, the King held him to be responsible. On the other hand, his ambiguous actions as Lord High Commissioner made him the enemy of the King's opponents. He appealed to his royal master. The King, now overlooking the lapse at Dalkeith, was sympathetic, and on 1 July wrote:

Traquair/ Since by your owen desire, & my permission ye are retired from my Court, to satisfie the needless suspitions of your Countrimen; I have thoughts, fitt by thease lynes, to asseure you, that I am so far, from having chased you away as a delingquent, that I esteem you to be as faithfull a Servant as anie I have, believing that the greatest cause of malice, that ye are vext with, is, for having served me as ye ought: Therefor I desire you to be confident, that I shall bothe fynde a fitt tyme, for you to wype away all these slanders, that are now against you; & lykewais, to recompense your past sufferings for my service: So, you shall trewly see, that I am

Your asseured frend

Charles R[5]

In spite of, or perhaps because of, the King's support, he did not survive long thereafter in the office of Treasurer and, in addition, after this fall from grace, he was accused of a number of crimes against the Church and suffered the indignity of a fine of 40,000 merks, which made a sizeable hole in the resources he had so carefully gathered to himself. He was ordered to confine himself within the sheriffdoms of Roxburgh, Tweeddale and Peebles.

The personal misfortunes of the Laird of Traquair were doubtless of little concern to the people of Tweeddale. What was of concern was the clear possibility that the argument between the King and the supporters of the Covenant would inevitably lead to war. On 1 May 1639, the burgh of Peebles and the local lairds received a letter from Lord Yester, written the previous day, telling them that twenty-eight warships of the King's navy had sailed up the Forth to Leith. To defend against what was effectively an invading force, every fourth man in the Scottish kingdom would be required to take up arms. There had been a formal proclamation to that effect. So, one quarter of the men of the Royal Burgh was to set out for Leith that very day, fully armed and ready to join with his Lordship and his colours. Acting on this instruction, the magistrates and Council decided that the first quarter of the men named on the burgh roll and one of the magistrates should be sent to Leith for a period of ten days and nights, and at the end of that time, the men of the next quarter and another magistrate would replace them, and that those of the third and fourth quarters would replace them in turn at the end of each ten-day period, during the time of the emergency. The arms to be carried were to be muskets and picks. Later in the year the cost of this armoury was to be raised from the inhabitants by the provost and bailies.

Further preparation for conflict was made in the following year. A colour with the arms of the Royal Burgh on it was purchased. It was decided that every fourth man going on service to the army should take his own arms and armour with him. However, if any man was unable to provide the full compliment, he was to be supplied by the other three members of his group of four. In August of that year, manpower was supplemented by two horses fully equipped at the town's expense with saddles and creels[a]. Not only did the town provide manpower for the anti-Royalist force, but soldiers from elsewhere were for a time billeted in the town, the provost and magistrates undertaking to pay for every soldier who was not paid for by the Commissary General.

Early in August, General Leslie led a sizeable army from Edinburgh towards the Borders. As they had done previously, they camped first at Duns Law and no doubt they were augmented by the Peebles contingent. There is certainly evidence for this, as an entry in the town records notes that upon their return the bailies were instructed to 'tak tryell of the airmour cum hame fra the camp'. It was later noted that this comprised forty-one 'musquettes' and forty-one 'pickes'.[6] Leslie's army broke camp on 21 August and marched south, across the Tweed, into England. At Newburn, just outside Newcastle, they met and defeated a force led by Lord Conway, sent against them by the King, and by the 30th they had taken Newcastle itself. Before long the whole of Northumberland was occupied and with it came control of the coal trade. Charles was powerless to resist and was forced to summon a Parliament in England and then to meet with the Scottish Commissioners at Ripon, where it was agreed that the Scottish army should be paid a subsistence allowance of £850 per day, provided they halted their advance. The Parliament that met in November remained in session and refused to be dissolved without its own consent.[7] In 1641 it endorsed the terms of the agreement reached at Ripon and a well-satisfied Scottish army marched back home, £200,000 richer.

In an attempt to regain control of affairs and to seek support from his Scottish subjects, now that his activities in England were under threat from a Parliament that refused to bow to his wishes or to agree to dissolution, Charles made his way north to Scotland once again. He reached Holyrood Palace on 14 August and, in the week that followed, he personally opened the Scottish Parliament, which nonetheless decreed that no one could sit in it unless they had signed the Covenant. This included the nobility. Many noble egos were bruised.

Charles was no doubt aware that all was not united. There had been a significant de facto transfer of power to lairds and ministers from the Crown and the nobility. Constitutional changes had been effected, which seemed to go beyond the spirit of the National Covenant, if not its legal boundaries. In particular, the two great marquises, Montrose and Argyll, were at loggerheads. Charles hoped to bolster his position by signifying his agreement to the Acts, which had abolished Episcopacy in 1639, but this failed to satisfy the Covenanters, who demanded that all major State appointments should only be made by the King with the advice of Parliament. He was not helped by the exposure of plots by some of his supporters to kidnap Argyll and Hamilton. Failing to make any real progress, in spite of these divisions, Charles returned to London, where he was greeted with the news of a massacre of Ulster Protestants. Perhaps he thought this disaster would cause the people of England and Scotland to support him in avenging this atrocity and those who had perpetrated it. As so often before, however, Charles misjudged the mood of the people. Since the reign of James VI & I there had been a sizeable settlement of Lowland Scots in Ulster. These were Protestants. For centuries before, Ulster and Scotland had had strong links, first as part of the Kingdom of Dalriada, which joined the north of Ireland with the west and south-west of Scotland. Later the Macdonald Lords of the Isles had dominated much of the same area, largely in defiance of the Scottish Crown, and in the latter part of the sixteenth century it was the Highland and staunchly Catholic Macdonalds who conquered

Antrim and settled there. The resentment of the Catholic settlers against their later Protestant rivals created a volatile mix, which finally exploded. Charles needed to raise an army to deal with the situation, but the English Parliament, now dominated by the Puritans, refused to grant the King the necessary funds, unless it and not the King had ultimate control of the army. This was something Charles could not accept. The Commons were immoveable and, in January 1642, Charles personally entered Parliament to arrest five leading members of the Commons. He failed and shortly thereafter he headed north to York. After more abortive negotiations, on 22 August 1642 he raised his standard at Nottingham. The Civil War had begun.

The first battle at Edgehill was indecisive. The Scots now found themselves in the enviable position of being courted by both sides. The Covenanters saw their vision of a Scotland, England and Wales united under a single Presbyterian order within their grasp. Negotiations between the General Assembly and the English Parliament were begun and in August the Assembly agreed to accept the terms of a treaty, which became the Solemn League and Covenant. Scottish loyalty to their King was sold in exchange for a promise to preserve the reformed religion throughout England, Wales and Ireland, and to eliminate all remnants of Popery and bishops. The great blessing of Presbyterianism would descend upon the length and breadth of England. Hardly was the ink dry on the treaty document than steps were taken to enlarge and enhance the Scottish army. The Estates had ratified the Solemn League and Covenant on 17 August 1643 and a proclamation was issued a few days later, which required all males aged between sixteen and sixty to arm themselves, have provisions for forty days and be ready to mobilise on forty-eight hours notice. Committees of War were formed throughout the country and in Tweeddale this included most of the local lairds, with Lord Yester as their colonel. A contribution towards the costs of fitting out every fourth man for the war was required from every householder in Peebles and from every manservant aged between sixteen and sixty, and each man fitted out was to receive five dollars as pay and allowance for equipment. The town's walls were to be repaired and the ports locked each night.[8]

The General Assembly of 1643 added its approval of the Solemn League and Covenant to that of the Estates. The prospect of the Scots taking the lead in converting the English Church to the Scottish form of Presbyterianism was a considerable inducement. In England the two Houses of Parliament had set up the Westminster Assembly in July 1642 with the avowed intention of creating a united reformed Church. A deputation from the English Parliament had been sent to the General Assembly and, in response, the Assembly sent commissioners to London where they met with members of both Houses of Parliament and the members of the Westminster Assembly of Divines in St Margaret's Church, Westminster, on 22 September. The text of the document[9] having been approved, it was then signed by all parties.

At the head of a Scots army of some 18,000 infantry and 3,000 mounted troops, Alexander Leslie, now Earl of Leven, crossed the border in January 1644. This was a well-trained force, subject to rigid discipline under Leven, who issued 'Articles of War', which decreed that every soldier was to swear allegiance to the principles of the Solemn League and Covenant and to observe strict morality, as well as giving their best in the performance of military duty. The Scots had little difficulty in overcoming such Royalist opposition as there was before reaching York, and joining with the English Parliamentary army, now led by Oliver Cromwell, which was besieging it. The King's nephew, Prince Rupert, headed north to raise the siege, but was defeated by the combined forces of the Scots and Parliamentarians at Marston Moor. The first signs of division now appeared. Cromwell, beginning the personal campaign which was ultimately to lead to his domination of England, Scotland and Ireland, claimed credit for the victory, although the Scots had played a significant part. In something of a fit of pique, Leven took his forces back northwards and, after occupying Newcastle in October, he remained there over the following winter, in spite of the entreaties of the Parliamentarians to return south. Leven was aware that the Scots were less than welcome to the broad mass of English people, and considered as little more than interlopers. He was also concerned by what he heard of the activities of Montrose, who had now come out against the Covenant and the Scottish government and was gathering such Royalist opposition as there was under his command.

The Scots did make a foray as far as Hereford, but this was short-lived. On their return north, they besieged Newark, but were then surprised by the arrival at their camp of the King himself. His arrival immediately caused the Parliamentarians to doubt the sincerity of their Scottish allies. Charles certainly knew when and how to create divisions among his enemies. In any event, although having accepted the Covenant, the English hardly found favour with it. In addition, there was growing division in the English Parliament itself. The Presbyterian faction, which did support the Covenant, remained largely loyal to the Crown, but was increasingly at odds with the Puritan Independents, whose clear aim was the defeat and overthrow of the King. The situation at Newark was confused. Charles clearly tried to exploit the emerging divisions and, although he still refused to sign the Covenant, some sort of agreement was reached. He was able to obtain the surrender of Newark and thereafter he joined the Scots on a return march to Newcastle. It is little wonder that the English Parliamentarians were nonplussed by these events. Such was their displeasure that in May the Commons voted to have the Scottish army removed from the territory of England. The Scots demanded a payment of £2 million to pay off its forces. In return the Commons offered £400,000 on condition that the King was surrendered to them before the Scots departed. They reluctantly accepted. They had little choice. They were unwelcome in England, but to return to Scotland with the person of the obdurate King among them was unacceptable. They attempted to ensure the safety of the King before their departure, but had hardly gone far before Charles was arrested in Northamptonshire by the Parliamentary army. The Solemn League and Covenant, short-lived as it was, had failed.

The supporters of the Covenant still held sway in Scotland and exercised their power and authority with severity. Those who failed to acknowledge the Covenant were grievously punished. There was a fresh outbreak of destruction against any vestige of Papist idolatry in churches. Intolerance and cruelty prevailed. There was a renewed purge of witches. The General Assembly of 1643 gave specific instructions as to how they should be dealt with. In Peebles the Calf Knowe was once again the focus of gruesome attention and the records note that on 8 January 1644, 'Alexander Lauder is ordained to go to Edinburgh or Musselburgh to fetch an executioner to the impanneled witches upon Thursday next January 11th; and if he refuses, the provost and bailies to cause another, on Alexander's expenses.'[10] Perhaps Alexander had expressed some sympathy for the poor and probably witless but harmless women who stood condemned to a frightful end?

Across the length and breadth of Lowland Scotland there were emerging men and women utterly opposed to Popery and Prelacy, intolerant, narrow-minded, but with an unshakeable belief in the Word of God revealed, as they believed, in the Holy Bible. These were the true Covenanters and in the years to come many of them would cling to their beliefs in the face of torture and even death.

Chapter Note

a. baskets.

10

---ᴓᴓ---

Montrose Rebuffed

It is 13 September 1645. Towards evening the Great Bell rings out from the steeple over the Royal Burgh of Peebles. This bell is usually rung to warn the citizens of the approach of a hostile force. It is many years since it has been rung in earnest and at its ringing, those charged with the defence of the town move swiftly to their pre-ordained positions and tasks. Messengers have ridden fast from further down the valley of Tweed to report the approach of a group of mounted soldiery, coming from the direction of Selkirk, some 25 miles to the east. The East Port is closed, as are all the other ports of the fortified town, and all about the East Wark and the West Port, the steeple and the defensive walls, the townsfolk that are trained or able to carry arms gather in nervous anticipation. They are certainly not untrained. On 6 May of the previous year the Council had decreed that a muster and Wappinschaw should be held on the following Saturday; everyone in possession of a musket was to provide himself with a pound of powder and a pound of balls. The town would graciously provide matches. Peebles has been at peace for many years, although it has to be said that the town itself is hardly peaceable and lawlessness is prevalent. As the men await the approach, memories are stirred by stories of days long gone when the town was laid waste by 'our auld enemies of England', but this is something different.

The supporters of the National Covenant have become a well-ordered and disciplined army under the able leadership of General Alexander Leslie, Earl of Leven. The Covenanting army seeks the preservation of a pure form of Presbyterianism in Scotland, while remaining loyal to the Crown. Opposed to it is the army of King Charles I, now led with some success by the charismatic James Graham, Marquis of Montrose. This is the same Montrose who, but a few years earlier, played a leading part in the preparation of the National Covenant, and who had been the first to sign that great document in Greyfriars Kirkyard. While that document had proclaimed loyalty to the King, it proclaimed Presbyterianism as the true religion of Scotland and the freedom of the people of Scotland to worship according to that form, without interference from King or State. With the passage of time Montrose had decided, whatever the consequences, that his loyalty to the King and the House of Stuart had the greater call upon him. Thus, while initially he had supported the actions of the Covenanting army under Leslie during the time immediately following the signing of the Covenant, and had led the campaign to enforce the Covenant in the north-east, by 1644 he had become disenchanted with the turn of events and in particular the alliance between the Covenanters and the English Parliamentarians; an alliance whose principal purpose was the defeat of the King. Early in 1644 he travelled to Oxford and there pledged his allegiance to King Charles. Although this was accepted with some scepticism in view of his recent activities, the King recognised that here was a personality of some substance who might well be able to revive his fortunes north of the border. So it was that not long after Montrose was appointed Viceroy and Captain General in Scotland, he turned his skills to the defence of his King.

Initially his forces consisted of his own Graham clansmen, who for a time were unwilling to follow his lead, but then a force of 1,000 or more wild Irishmen and Islemen landed on the west coast. Their leader was the legendary Alasdair MacDonald, known as Colkitto; a giant of a man, experienced as a guerrilla fighter in Ireland where he had gained a reputation for ruthless slaughter in the Ulster massacres. Backed by these near savages led by MacDonald, Montrose was able to embark on a campaign, which to begin with met with consider-able success. He took control of Perth after destroying a Covenanting force at Tippermuir in September and two weeks later sacked Aberdeen. In December, in spite of a severe winter and taking a route over high mountain passes, thought to be impassable in such conditions, he took his army into the west and created havoc in the heartland of the Campbells. Then, before retreating from the area in February 1645, he destroyed the Covenanting forces led by the Marquis of Argyll at Inverlochy. Thereafter he gained control of Dundee and in May defeated a Covenanting army at Auldearn, near Nairn. He followed this by a further victory at Alford in July. Encouraged by these successes, and his almost total domination of the north and east, he headed into the Lowlands with a large force and again gained a significant victory at Kilsyth, near Stirling, where the carnage inflicted by the Irishmen and the Highland caterans in battle and in its aftermath was merciless, bloody and brutal. Among the defeated force was a small contingent from Peebles. Totally confident now of his ability to defeat the 'rebels' he decided to head south across the border with his considerable army, with the intention of coming to the aid of the remnants of the royal forces, which had been badly beaten at Naseby in June. But then things started to go wrong. He found little new sup-port in the Lowlands, and many of the Highlanders who had formed a large part of his army started to drift away back to their homelands in the north and west, and while the Irishmen remained, the Covenanting army had now regrouped. Nonetheless, Montrose would not be deflected from his chosen course, and he and what remained of his force made their way south towards the Borders.

News had reached Peebles that the Covenanting army, now led by David Leslie, nephew of the Earl of Leven, had marched north from a raid into England and was camped near Selkirk. The town had been alerted to the possible approach from the north of Montrose at the end of August, some two weeks earlier, and made suitable preparation. The word from Selkirk, on this 15th day of September, is that the Covenanters will try to ambush the forces of Montrose nearby and draw them into battle, but the outcome is as yet unknown and Peebles, which is now firmly for the Covenant, must be at risk of attack from Montrose and his Highland caterans and wild Irishmen. This is not a happy prospect and many are the stories of the ferocity and bloodlust of those northern and Irish savages, as those of the small Peebles contingent in the defeated army at Kilsyth can testify. If an attack was to come, it would be resisted with all the strength that the town could muster.

As evening approaches, those posted at the West Port watch a cloud of dust rising a few hundred yards away from the direction of the Kings Meadows and moving fast along the south bank of the Tweed. Soon it becomes clear that this is a detachment of horsemen and, after some minutes of watching, guardians can see that there are perhaps thirty to fifty of them making for the Tweed Bridge and the town itself. The West Port gate is firmly closed and minutes later the fast-moving group clatters over the old bridge and up the Port Brae, drawing to a rapid halt in front of the gate itself. Their leader is a tall, handsome man, clearly of noble stock, although now covered in the grime of physical effort and fast travel. He announces himself as the Viceroy and Captain General of Scotland, and demands, in the name of King Charles, that the gate be opened up and that he and his men be given entry. It is Montrose himself and the men with him are the rag tag remnant of his army, which have suffered an ignominious defeat at the hands of Leslie at Philiphaugh earlier in the day, although this remains unknown to the Peebleans.

Consternation and no little anxiety follow. The reputation of Montrose and his men is all too well known. What is to be done? After a hurried conference the leader of the guard, John Robene, sends a messenger to the provost and magistrates gathered in the Tolbooth further up the High Gait. Montrose is not welcome. The traditional loyalty of the good people of Peebles has been strained to breaking point by their foolish and arrogant King. There must be resistance. The provost himself will go to the West Port. Nervous crowds have now joined the guards, and, as he makes his way through them to the steeple, which rises above the town wall and gives a view over the Port Brae and the route to the Auld Toun, James Williamson musters his courage and such dignity as he is able. As he mounts the steps to the upper gallery he hears the voice of Montrose once again demanding entry in the name of the King. The provost is clear. There will be no entry given this day to the lackeys of Charles Stuart. Peebles is well enough equipped with men and weapons to ensure that this is so. This is now evident from the large numbers of armed townsfolk who have assembled along the walls around the West Port. Montrose would be well to be on his way. The options for Montrose are few. Perhaps he and his highly trained and battle-hardened men could overcome these anxious folk, more used to hiding behind the walls than mounting their defence, but this would take time and doubtless the forces of Leslie, whom they had been able to outrun in their hasty retreat from Philphaugh, would not be far behind them. Pragmatism prevails and, after further attempts at persuasion and threat, Montrose accepts the inevitable, and, wearily turning towards the north-west, sets off at speed across the Peebles Brig and up the Auld Toun, disappearing from view in a cloud of dust. In denying Montrose access to the town, Peebles had perhaps precipitated the remarkable campaign of flight and pursuit that carried Montrose far and wide across Scotland to inevitable defeat, capture, trial and execution in Edinburgh.

On that September day the twelve-year-old James Nicol followed the events from a safe vantage point on the walls. The town had the right of it. This was one more slap in the face to an arrogant and ignorant King and one more victory for the true religion. In the years since the great day of the signing of the National Covenant, some seven years earlier, James had come to learn something of the importance it now held in the religious life of Scotland. Although only twelve years old, and not understanding the beliefs of Presbyterians, there stirred in him some comprehension that it was something worthy of preservation, even if it meant that loyalty to the King of Scots took second place. He had heard that the King of Scots, Charles Stuart, held himself to be divinely ordained as Head of the Kirk as well as Head of State, but James had been taught that no man is divine, and he had read and heard it repeated that only Christ was the Church's Head, or so at least said the Holy Bible, which he had also been told was divinely inspired as being the Word of God himself.

A few miles to the east, as these events unfolded, John Stuart, Earl of Traquair pondered upon the past glories and misfortunes of his life. His rise to the heights of Lord High Treasurer of Scotland and the King's Commissioner had been spectacular, as had been his rapid fall from grace, caught in the maelstrom that was the conflict between King and Covenant. He had tried to be loyal to the King and yet had also tried to accommodate the forces ranged against the monarch. His reward had been impeachment and a virtual destruction of the wealth he had so assiduously garnered from the rewards of high office. In his heart John Stuart considered it still to be his duty to be loyal to the King. Indeed, there still remained the possibility that the King would in the end overcome his foes and re-establish his authority. John Stuart would not be the first courtier to suffer a fall from grace and yet be able to reingratiate himself with the monarch and return to favour.

These thoughts were much in his mind this day of 13 September 1645. A few days previously, aware that the great Montrose was on his way south to the border with his Highland and Irish army, John Stuart had sent his son, Lord Linton, with a troop of horses to meet up with Montrose and join him in opposing the Covenanting army of Leslie. Like father, like son, Lord Linton prevaricated and then, assessing the strengths of the opposing armies, made a strategic retreat back to Traquair before the battle of Philiphaugh had begun. To the Royalist cause this was seen as treachery, although as Linton had not actually committed himself to either army, this could not be proved. In any event his return had caused consternation to his father. That consternation had been more than heightened later that day, when the defeated Montrose and his bedraggled troop, having made their way in haste over Minchmoor, knocked at the door of Traquair House and sought admittance. Here was a dilemma: loyalty to the King's cause, lost at least as far as Montrose was concerned, or fear of Covenanting reprisal, probably imminent? The earl was well aware that local feeling, so long supporting the Royal House of Stuart, had now turned against it and given its full-hearted backing to the Covenanters. He was also well aware that James Williamson, his near neighbour and Provost of Peebles, was fulsome in his support of the Covenant and that he had the town of Peebles with him. John Stuart had been all too conscious of the feelings of the Royal Burgh on his frequent passages through the town on his journeying to and from the capital. Pragmatism or fear prevailed. Both the earl and Lord Linton denied Montrose entry and he, in sad acceptance, had made his way to Peebles and the rebuff that followed.

—◦◦◦—

11

Divine Retribution

In the five years since the great Montrose was sent packing from the town follow-ing his defeat at Philiphaugh, the town of Peebles and its inhabitants had been able to go about their business in relative peace. True, the aftermath of Philiphaugh had descended into bloody slaughter, not only of those who had fought for Montrose, but also women and children who were their camp followers. Although this was doubt-less seen as retribution for the similar treatment meted out to defeated Covenanters by undisciplined and savage Highland and Irishmen after earlier battles, it did no credit to the Covenanting cause and was perhaps a precursor to the bloodletting which would be inflicted on Covenanters of later years.

In 1647 the Scottish army retraced its steps across the border following the final rift with the Parliamentary army and the failure of the Solemn League and Covenant. It had assisted in the defeat of the King, but had failed in its attempt to see Covenanted Presbyterianism established south of the border, in spite of English agreement. The purity of the form of worship and theology of Covenanted Presbyterianism had been diluted by the acceptance by the Scots of the Westminster Confession. The English Parliamentarians, to whom the Scots had given whole-hearted support, were now intent upon ignoring their side of the agreement.

King Charles was a prisoner of the Parliamentary army on the Isle of Wight, but he still harboured notions of recovering his position and plotted to that end. He thought that his best hope still lay with his native Scotland, and in secret he met with three Scottish Commissioners who pledged the support of the Scottish army provided that Charles would agree to re-establishing Presbyterianism for at least three years and also that he would suppress the more extreme elements of the Covenanters. These discussions became known as the 'Engagement'. Those in sup-port were known as 'Engagers' and they rapidly gained in influence, so that when the Estates met in 1648, it was they, led by the Duke of Hamilton, who were in the ascendant, and the General Assembly and the Covenanters no longer comprised the majority. Such fluidity of power suggests many transient and changing opinions. A letter was sent to the English Parliament demanding that the King be released, that the agreement to uphold the Covenant be observed and finally (and somewhat rashly) that the New Model Army should be disbanded. The Duke of Hamilton set off across the border with a Scottish army bent on enforcing the Scottish will. As now seemed to be common practice, the burghs and counties were expected to contribute to the manpower of the army and Peebles had duly raised a contingent of some forty-five men from the Royal Burgh to accept this honour. However, the Council had some difficulty in achieving this due to the unpopularity of the expedition. During the time of preparation soldiers from furth of the town were once again billeted in it, placing a considerable burden upon it and the people, adding to the unpopularity of the venture. In the event, the expedition was a disaster. The English army, led by Cromwell, crushed the Scots at Preston and again at Wigan, and finally destroyed the remnants at Warrington in August. Hamilton was taken prisoner at Uttoxeter and was beheaded a few months later outside Westminster Hall, the English Parliament (led by Cromwell's Independents) showing total disregard for legality. Hamilton was a Scot acting under instruction from a legally constituted and independent Scottish Parliament.

Back in Scotland the pendulum of power swung back, this time from the Engagers to the Covenanters ('The Protesters'). A force of some 6,000 from the Covenanting strongholds of Ayrshire, Renfrewshire and Lanarkshire marched to Edinburgh to add weight to the debate.[1] The Protesters, headed by Argyll, who had always opposed the Engagement, took control of affairs and immediately started to treat with the Puritan Cromwell, now firmly leader of the Independents, and those opposed to the imposition of the Covenant. Nonetheless, Cromwell recognised that both parties should unite to defeat the 'Malignants' as the Royalists were now labelled. When they met at the beginning of January 1649 the Estates set aside the Engagement and once again reinstated the Solemn League and Covenant. In addition, they passed the Act of Classes, which defined areas of conduct by the enemies of the Covenant that they regarded as 'sinful'. Those who would not publicly repent of these 'sins' were to be barred from holding any sort of office.

The governing elite of both countries regularly kept in touch and the Scottish Commissioners in London were given the unenviable task of treading the line between giving the English any grounds for going to war, while at the same time avoiding any suggestion that they concurred with any penalty that might be imposed on the King. Cromwell had what he wanted, an acquiescent Scotland. Secure in that knowledge, he now took the lead in the final act of destruction against the King. On 20 January of that same year, the trial of Charles I commenced in Westminster Hall, in spite of Scottish protestations. Whatever Charles may have been, he was not a coward. He conducted himself throughout with a dignity that he maintained all the way to the scaffold outside Westminster Hall, where, on the cold morning of 30 January, he was beheaded. In Scotland there was outrage. Charles may have been a foolish and arrogant despot, but he was the anointed King of Scots, and he and his forbearers had been monarchs of Scotland for centuries past. The Scots had not been consulted, let alone given their consent. As they had done with Wallace and Mary, Queen of Scots, the English had acted in complete disregard of Scotland, its laws and sovereignty as a nation state.

No sooner had the news reached Scotland than the Estates proclaimed the late King's eighteen-year-old son as Charles II, King of Scots and King of Great Britain, France and Ireland, these being the royal titles used since the reign of James VI & I. But Scotland's troubles were far from over. Commissioners were sent to the Hague in Holland where Charles was living. If he would accept the Covenants, Scotland would accept him as King. Charles prevaricated. A further attempt, more disastrous than the first, was made by Montrose to win back the Crown by force of arms. Montrose, who had also been in exile since the debacle of Philiphaugh, landed in the Orkney Islands and crossed to the mainland. He got no further than Carbisdale in Sutherland, where on 27 April 1650 he and his small force were annihilated. A few days later he was captured, taken to Edinburgh, and hanged and dismembered at the Mercat Cross on 21 May. The sad ending of Montrose finally brought Charles to the realisation that if he was to be King of Scots he could only become so by accepting the Covenants. Unlike his father, whose beliefs were so strong that he could not accept religious compromise, Charles cared little for religion and in the end was more than willing to accept the situation, at least in order to gain the Scottish Crown, much as he would have preferred not to be circumscribed by the principals of the Covenants. He gave his agreement at Breda on 1 May and signed both Covenants. Seven weeks later he set foot on his Scottish kingdom at Garmouth on the Moray coast.

The arrival of Charles in Scotland, and what was seen as the perfidy of the Scots, prompted the Commonwealth, as the English government was now known, to order their forces to march north under the leadership of Cromwell, who, on his appointment as commander, had taken the title of Lord-General (a title of his own devising). Nonetheless, it seems that Cromwell hoped to avoid engaging the Scots in armed conflict. He recognised that the Scottish supporters of the Covenant were essentially at one with the English Puritan Independents as far as religious observance was concerned, although they may have differed from them in their continuing support of the Crown. Cromwell appealed 'To all that are Saints, and Partakers of the Faith of God's elect, in Scotland' whom, as he said, 'we look upon as our brethren'. He pled that the killing of the King had been justified. He further suggested that although the Scots might be a God-fearing people, they were nonetheless mistaken in their support of the Crown, but both parties were of 'the Elect' and should thus seek to avoid conflict with one another. These pleas fell on deaf Scottish ears and, when this became apparent, Cromwell advanced into Scotland with all the ruthless vigour with which he had become associated. Once again the Borders would feel the effects of our 'Auld enemy of England'.

Rumour and fear march hand in hand. The news of Cromwell's advance into Scotland travelled fast and Peebles was gripped by fear and alarm. The revived Scottish army, again under the command of the able David Leslie, had succeeded in forestalling an attempt by Cromwell to take Leith, which would have provided him with a maritime supply route from the south. Unable to ensure supplies by that route, Cromwell withdrew to Dunbar where the two armies confronted each other. Wrongly assuming that the New Model Army of the Commonwealth was heading for a seaboard retreat, the Scots, who were also suffering from atrocious weather, abandoned their position on the high ground of Doune Hill. Too late to realise their mistake, the Scottish Covenanters found that they had no room to manoeuvre and suffered a severe defeat; 3,000 of their number were killed and around 10,000 were taken prisoner and treated appallingly. Of those who survived many were exiled to the Plantations. Edinburgh was occupied and thereafter Cromwell set out to subjugate the Lowlands and the Borders. The news of the rout at Dunbar was not long in reaching Peebles. In preparation for the town's defence, orders were issued that the town walls be 'repairit be all the heritouris effeirand to the parties[a]'. A watch was to be 'keipit ilk nicht[b]'. A further order was made on 7 October 'to keep nichlie a scout watche, sex at the North Port, and the remanent at the uther portes proportionallie, with armes, to adverteis the toun of the enemies approache'. As an additional precaution, two mounted scouts were despatched to report 'newes anent the motiown of the enemie'.[2]

James Nicol, now seventeen years of age, watched and listened to all the talk and preparation with mixed feelings. Some two years earlier he had experienced an event that was to profoundly affect his life until its end. As he himself would later say, this was when he began to 'pray and give praise to his Lord and Saviour Jesus Christ who converted me'. Whatever the circumstances of his conversion, James was now firmly anchored to Covenanted Presbyterianism. To him and many others the defeat at Dunbar was a signal that the Lord was not on their side. Indeed, the fact that the Scots had every advantage over their adversaries before the battle commenced and that they had, by their own fault, lost that advantage and that there was now division among Covenanters, had surely attracted divine retribution. One faction was opposed to supporting Charles as King because they doubted his sincere support of the Covenant. These were the 'Protesters'. The other faction, called 'the Resolutioners', believed that in spite of Charles's lukewarm support of the Covenant, he was unlikely to try to restore Episcopacy, given the unfortunate end brought upon his father. James was firmly in the former camp. To his life's end he would remain implacably opposed to all who did not give wholehearted support to the Covenant and, in particular, all, including the ruling monarch, who did not accept the will of the monarch to be subordinate to the will of the Almighty.

Chapter Notes

a. the parts which were their responsibility, to be repaired by the heritors; **b.** kept each night.

—◦◦◦—

12

Noble Neidpath

The noble Neidpath, Peebles overlooks,
With its fair bridge, and Tweed's meandering crooks:
Upon a rock it proud and stately stands,
And to the Fields about gives forth commands.

Alexander Pennecuik

It is the month of December 1650. The castle of Neidpath stands about a mile to the west of Peebles, as it has done for long years past. It is a solid edifice, with immensely thick walls, no less than thirteen feet at their base. It sits on a bluff overhanging the River Tweed at a place where the valley narrows into a pass at the lower end of a wide, semicircular bend in the river. Opposite, a wooded bank rises towards the surrounding hills. For about a mile in each direction the rising ground is covered in woodland of poplar, beech and fir. Between the house and the water a parterre and several terraces lend an air of domesticity to what is essentially a place of defensive fortification. The castle was once the family stronghold of the Fraser family, whose crest forms the keystone of the courtyard gate. In time it has come into the ownership of the Hay family and now it is garrisoned by the retainers of John, Lord Yester. The outlook to the south-west takes in the wooded sweep of the valley as it broadens out towards the meeting place of Tweed and Manor Water and the broader expanse of the lands of Barns beyond. To the east it looks loftily over the winding green parks to the town of Peebles itself, nestling in the basin of the rolling southern hills, which surround it on all sides. This winter day the usual haze of peat reek and wood smoke hangs, seemingly peacefully, above the town. Yet all is not peaceful.

On the hillside to the south there is great activity. Winter sunlight flashes from the near round helmets of a large body of soldiers toiling up the slope and driving on teams of horses, dragging up their cumbersome load. These are the soldiers of the New Model Army, commanded by Major-General Lambert. The loads the horses are straining to pull upward are cannon. On the hillside, at a point directly opposite the castle, axes are being laid to the bases of many trees. This is hard work. Many of the trees at this part are among the finest in the county, the beech growing especially tall and thick; but they must be felled to allow a clear line of fire to the castle.

Some weeks earlier, the Great Bell of Peebles sounded across the town as midday approached. Shortly before, William Patersone, one of the scouts who had been posted as an outlook far to the north of the Royal Burgh, at Gladhouse Mill on the route from Edinburgh, had ridden into the town in agitated haste to report a movement of mounted troops heading towards Peebles. It was difficult to say how many, but it was a sizeable number, and had sufficiently impressed the returning scout that in his agitation he had little difficulty in conveying a real sense of alarm. In fact, it was a force of some 3,000 led by Major-General Lambert and Colonel Francis Hacker. This Hacker, although unknown to any of the perturbed company now assembled, was the same Hacker who had assisted in supervising the execution of the late King, Charles I, and on the scaffold had read the warrant for his execution. Peebles was not unused to seeing the approach of mounted troops, but usually those rarely numbered more than one or two hundred at the most, a sight intimidating enough, but such a host as apparently witnessed by the scout was unknown in these days. Opposition would be pointless. The very presence of such numbers, were they to halt at Peebles, would be an impossible burden.

The day wears on and excitement mixed with apprehension rises with each passing minute. Following Patersone's initial warning, more scouts have been posted along the northern route to mark the progress of the approaching host. The head of the great cavalcade is now approaching Winkstoun. Those waiting there are amazed at the sight of the advancing column. Never in living memory has such a mighty force been seen in the vicinity of Peebles. The tales handed down from earlier generations of the great force assembled at Peebles by the Earl of Angus to repel English marauders a hundred years before, had spoken of 1,000 men-at-arms, large enough by any standards, but here was a column stretching into the distance, its tail probably yet to pass Athelston[1] a mile or more to the north. It had been said that the force that left Edinburgh had indeed numbered 3,000 mounted men, but to that would be added armourers, cooks, grooms, farriers and camp followers, which such a force brought in its wake. The total populace of Peebles numbered little more than 1,200 bodies, and the descent upon it of such numbers threatened not only the folk of the town itself, but also the folk of the ferm touns that dotted the surrounding countryside, which would be stripped of every source of food and sustenance, to the inevitable detriment of those who relied on those sources for their own survival. The arrival of General Lambert could not be looked upon in anything other than dismay.

In the event, their arrival in Peebles is relatively peaceable. Well informed in advance of their approach, the provost, bailies and Council have met and decided that co-operation, rather than opposition, should be the order of the day. The head of the column is now threading its way through the narrows of the Auld North Port and down the Northgait, eventually passing the Mercat Cross and spilling out into the wider expanse of the High Gait. The Council, fully robed, is drawn up before the Tolbooth. Provost Williamson steps forward to greet General Lambert and his senior officers. What they make of each other can only be guessed at. The provost, dignified and yet a man of the people, is now advanced in years, but presiding as he does over a town in which fun and festivity are far from unknown, that dignity conceals a personality not lacking in humour and conviviality. His newly arrived guest, by contrast, exhibits a somewhat different aspect. Puritan, constrained by military discipline and his elevated status, he does not seem a man of much humour. Nonetheless, he is aware that the town at least has the merit of firm support for the Covenant, although that implies a mistaken loyalty to the former King and tyrant, and possibly to his son, who contrary to the will of the English Parliament has sought to have himself proclaimed as Charles II, King of Scots. Without the courtesy of descent from his mount, General Lambert makes it clear who is now in charge. He will require food for the troops and lodging for the more senior members, who will be billeted upon the townsfolk. He is aware that the Lord Yester has perversely and foolishly garrisoned the Castle of Neidpath and indicated defiance towards what he perceives as impertinent English demands to surrender the castle. In this he shows either great fortitude or great stupidity, as Neidpath remains the only fortification in the south of Scotland yet to have conceded surrender. It is but a few weeks since the similar castle at nearby Borthwick had surrendered in similar circumstances – following some persuasion from cannon fire. Perhaps the provost could remind Lord Yester of this? In any event, the general makes it clear that the surrender of Neidpath is a minor matter for the present and one which can no doubt be dealt with satisfactorily in due course. It was the intention to remain in Peebles briefly before moving on into Lanarkshire to attend to a Scottish force led by Colonel Ker which had gathered there.

By now the High Gait is packed with a milling mass of mounted troopers and still the tail of the cavalcade has yet to pass the Auld North Port. The youthful James Nicol, and those of his friends brave enough to do so, wander among the horses and men with a mixture of excitement and awe. These Puritans, thought James, though they might not be overly friendly, were surely on the side of the true Kirk and that could not be bad. Their sojourn in Peebles would be a trial to the town. Not only would they take bread from the mouths of those that had it, but no doubt some might yet prove troublesome. Puritan or not some would likely find their way to the taverns of the town, and perhaps not all the woman folk would escape their attentions.

What do these Puritan English soldiery think of Peebles? They see a small proud and ancient town, now well walled around its principal parts. They would see houses, thatched in the main, but walled in whinstone and timber, some not insubstantial and of more than a single storey. Unlike the high, narrow, dark and fetid thoroughfares they had left behind in Edinburgh, the streets or gaits, especially the cobbled High Gait, are moderately wide and airy. From them run numerous narrow alleyways or wynds, usually descending steeply. All, however, are strewed with the signs and debris of a rural community, where town merged with country. Poultry, geese, pigs and dogs roam the streets at will and leave their mark, in spite of rules laid down by the Town Council to prevent such chaos. Even cattle are not unknown in the crowded streets in these winter days when the grazing of the town's common lands is not possible. The people on the whole are of a healthy appearance, well fed from good country fare and the harvest of river and stream. Those of the burgess class have the right to take salmon from that part of the Tweed within the town's bounds, although others, not so entitled, doubtless also benefit from the harvest of the river, in spite of the dire conse-quences of what is judged a felony. Many of the better sort are well dressed in good cloth and the poorer sort, reploch[a], the product of the many websters or weavers who work in the town's principal industry, using wool from the sheep of the neighbouring hills and such as was not sold on by the merchants of the town, among whom James Nicol was now numbered, following in the footsteps of his father. This trade, and the purchase and sale of other merchandise, give James the opportunity to travel furth of the burgh, as far as Lanark, Selkirk, Edinburgh and even Berwick and beyond the border; travels that bring him in contact with many sorts of men and many ideas.

In the days that followed the arrival of the English force, the town became used to their presence in sizeable numbers. For those not benefiting from the com-fort of billets in the houses of the town, the ruined Church of St Andrew, and such buildings as remained about it, became their base and provided some shelter against the winter cold for the many horses stabled there. The main body did not remain long and after a few days it moved off westwards to confront Colonel Ker and his Covenanters. A token force remained in the burgh as a mark of the town's submission. Brief though the sojourn of the larger force had been, it had not been without trouble or strife. The Council had found it necessary to make payments to numbers of soldiers injured in disturbances, while at a more serious level some deaths had occurred. The Council apparently felt obliged, or was required, in the circumstances to meet the cost of 'kists[b]' for the dead. Official papers stored in the steeple for safe keeping had been damaged by the English.

On 1 December, in Lanarkshire, Lambert had inflicted a severe defeat on the much larger Covenanting army of Colonel Ker, and with no further threat remaining he returned to Peebles. They would now deal with Neidpath. Lord

Yester was not intimidated by the huge English force that surrounded the castle and, with all English attempts to succeed by gentle persuasion having failed, sterner methods would now be employed. So it was that the lumbering column of horse-drawn cannon began to wend its way from the old Church of St Andrew, down through the Auld Toun and across the Peebles Brig, past the West Port and across the Tweed Brig, and on by way of the cowparks and the gait to Menner, across the Edderston Burn and up the gentle slope which led to the point across the River Tweed from Neidpath itself, where the tree-felling soldiery had now cleared an avenue, giving a clear sightline to the old fortalice. All along the route anxious folk had stood in expectant anxiety. James Nicol was impressed by the spectacle, much as he now resented these English who he heard had inflicted huge slaughter on honest and faithful Covenanters in Lanarkshire.

With two cannon now drawn up on the hillside, the crude preparations for their firing were made, a flare to the breech of first one and then the other initiated a huge explosion, followed by flame and smoke through which, at great speed, two heavy round balls raced across the valley to impact with a sizeable 'thud' at the base of the castle wall. Renewed preparation and adjustment of the elevation of the barrels preceded a further bombardment, this time the balls impacting the wall midway up its height with considerable force. Just as it had been at Borthwick a few weeks earlier, the effect was dramatic, and before a further salvo could be fired, a white flag appeared on the high gallery of the castle. The siege of Neidpath was at an end and the last stronghold in the south of Scotland had fallen to the New Model Army.

Chapter Notes

a. a type of worsted cloth; **b**. coffins.

13

~~~

The Protectorate

He that prays and preaches best will fight best.

Oliver Cromwell

The fall of Neidpath signalled the virtual subjugation of southern Scotland, and although elsewhere armed activity continued, a sort of peace now descended across the Lothians and Borders. The continuing presence of units of the New Model Army in Peebles, as elsewhere, remained an irritation and a source of friction, not least because of the burden that their presence placed upon the local population. Since his arrival in Scotland in June 1650, following his proclamation as King of Scots, Charles II had remained in the north of Scotland, protected by those magnates who remained loyal to the Royalist cause, chief among them the Marquis of Argyll.

In the Kirk quarrels and factional disputes continued unabated. Those who sought proof that Charles would abide by those agreements he had accepted at Breda, including the Covenant, issued a 'remonstrance' to the Committee of the Estates, requiring that Charles be rejected as King until he had shown proof of his sincerity. But in November 1650 the Committee rejected the remonstrance. Most of the clergy who had not already done so now moved into the camp of the Resolutioners. Charles moved south to Perth and at Scone, on 1 January 1651, it was Argyll who crowned him King of Scots, but not before he had to listen to a lengthy sermon by Rev. Robert Douglas, extolling the Covenants.

The confusion and discord in the Kirk had played well for Cromwell. The success of the 'Protesters' in imposing legislation, such as the Act of Classes, had resulted in the effective debarring from office and high military command of many men of quality and ability. It could be said that this had been a major contributory factor in the debacle of Dunbar, but at a meeting of the Estates in May, the now dominant Resolutioners were able to have the Act of Classes rescinded.

The Scottish army, under Leslie, was revived and was enough of a sufficient presence to cause Cromwell to halt an advance against Stirling. Thus thwarted, he sent a force commanded by Lambert into Fife, which overcame a Scottish contingent at Pitreavie. As the route north was opened to him, Cromwell entered and took control of Perth. With the invading English in close proximity, the Scots saw that there was a route southwards open to them and, with Charles in their midst, spotted an opportunity for a counter-offensive across the border, in the hope that they would be joined by supporters of the Royalist cause along the way. In this they failed miserably and, with Cromwell in hot pursuit, the two armies headed south and met in a final confrontation at Worcester, where Cromwell gained a crushing victory. Charles escaped into ignominious exile in France, in a trail of hide and seek with the aid of many disguises and bizarre hideouts, not least of which was the famous oak tree. Although in time he would regain the Scottish throne, he never again set foot in Scotland. For the moment Cromwell was totally triumphant.

Oliver Cromwell was a man in touch with the Almighty. Like so many who claim that advantage, he believed that through the power of prayer he could achieve all his ends. When he prayed for God's blessing on his endeavours and enterprises and then succeeded in them, he assumed that his success betokened God's favour. Although his beginnings as the son of a minor landowner in Huntingdon were relatively humble, his climb up the ladder of power was spectacular, first as Member of Parliament for Huntingdon and then Cambridge. This was followed by appointment as a colonel in the Eastern Association in 1643 and as lieutenant-general in 1644, and finally, in 1653, as Lord Protector (a title he again chose himself) of the Commonwealth of England, Scotland and Ireland, with a virtual grip on absolute power. The Divine Right of Stuart Kings had been swept aside to be replaced by the Divine Right of Oliver Cromwell.

For the soldiers of the New Model Army fighting was to be combined with prayer and preaching. With a body of troops still remaining encamped and billeted in Peebles, Cromwell wrote to their commanding officer, Colonel Francis Hacker, on 25 December 1650. The letter concerned a discussion about the choice of an officer to be appointed to a particular commission. In the course of this letter, 'For Col. Francis Hacker, at Peebles or elsewhere', Cromwell wrote the following:

Sir – I have the best consideration I can for the praesent in this businesse, and although I believe Capt Hubbert is a worthy man, and heere soe much, yett as the case stands, I cannott, with satisfaction to my selffe and some others, revoake the commission I had given to Capt. Empson, without offence to them, and reflection upon my owne judgment. I pray lett Capt. Hubbert knowe I shall not bee unmindful of him, and that noe disrespect is intended to him. But, indeed I was not satisfied with your last speech to mee about Empson, that he

was a better praecher than a fighter or a souldier, or words to that effect. Truly
I thinke Hee that prayes and praeches best will fight best. I know nothing will
give like courage and confidence as the knowledge of God in Christ will, and
I blesse God to see any in this armye able and willinge to impart knowledge
they have for the good of others. And I expect itt bee encouraged by all Chiefe
Officers in this Armye especially: and I hope you will doe soe. I pray receive
Capt. Empson lovinglye. I dare assure you hee is a good man and a good officer.
I would wee had noe worse. I rest your lovinge friend.

O. Cromwell

To the seventeen-year-old James Nicol, the notion of praying, preaching and
fighting seemed a noble one. These Englishmen might be a sore burden on the
town, but they would see to it that those of the Kirk adhered to the truth of the
Gospels and the proper practice of religion.

The Commonwealth of England and Wales, established by the English
Parliamentarians following the capture of Charles I and the final extinguishing
of the Royalist cause, was now effectively extended to include Scotland, which,
to all intents and purposes, became a mere province. The English Commons had
succeeded where, in the past, successive English monarchs had tried and failed to
extinguish Scottish nationhood. However, the new rulers, no doubt mindful of
their own notion of equality under the law, stemming as it did from their religious beliefs, sought to create a unified state, where all might enjoy equal rights.

At the beginning of 1652 a declaration of the English Parliament was brought
by their commissioners to a meeting of the Estates at Dalkeith. The declaration
stated that England and Scotland were to be one unified Commonwealth. The
Gospel was to be preached, but there was to be religious toleration. The same
rights and privileges as were now enjoyed by the English would be available
to the Scots. On the debit side, the costs of the English campaign north of the
border were to be met from the estates of such as the Duke of Hamilton, who
had taken part in the ill-fated incursion into England, which ended at Worcester.
The burghs and shires were to elect representatives to convene for the purpose of
acceding to the union.

Following the assumption of the office of Lord Protector by Cromwell, an
Ordinance of Union was produced by the Council of the Commonwealth in
1654. The united Parliament was to have 460 members, of which only 30 were
to represent Scotland. Of them, 20 were to come from the shires and 10 from
the burghs. Edinburgh was allocated 2 representatives, while the 56 other burghs
were to form groups to elect one for the group. Thus Peebles was to be joined
with Selkirk, Jedburgh, Lauder, North Berwick and Haddington. In practice, the
influence of the Scots at Westminster Parliament would count for little and in
reality the appointed representatives had little choice but to accede to what was
proposed.

Although the Puritan form of religion, as now practised in England, had many similarities to that of the Scottish Kirk, it did not extend to Presbyterianism, which in practice tolerated no other form. What was established was therefore a more tolerant system. This was made possible because it was evident to all that the Lord Protector himself was God fearing and a man of genuine religious conviction. His call to the Elect, who, as he said before Dunbar, 'we look upon as our brethren', had not gone unheeded, in spite of his success in that battle, which in any event the Scots came to regard as the result of divine intervention signifying the error of their cause. Besides, the continuing internal disputes in the Kirk between Remonstrants and Resolutioners ensured that no single Scottish voice dominated. Naturally the government leaned more towards the Protesters and Remonstrants rather than the Resolutioners, as the latter still supported the broad principle of monarchy. In reality Kirk Sessions, Presbyteries and Synods were left to their own devices so religious practice continued much as it had done. They were, however, no longer empowered to inflict civil penalties upon those who were subject to their discipline. The General Assembly was a problem and remained dominated by Resolutioners until July 1653, when it was forcibly closed down by a troop of soldiers under the command of Colonel Cotterell. The General Assembly did not thereafter meet during the life of the Protectorate. Effectively debarred from involvement in politics, ministers now had more time to devote to parochial affairs, particularly the morals and discipline of their flocks.

The Commonwealth was at first welcomed by the more extreme elements in the Kirk, who, taking the lead from their strict Puritan masters, embarked on an orgy of disciplinary enforcement. In spite of the loss of right to impose civil penalties, the least minor demeanour did not escape the attention of the Kirk authorities. As Dr Gunn records:[1]

> The records of this time teem with cases of discipline. Punishments are inflicted for gossiping in the churchyard, ricking[a] corn on a Sunday, flyting[b], drinking, keeping the mill going on Sunday, absenting from Church, hiring on Sunday, gathering nuts on Sunday, carrying meal on the same day, and for hounding a dog on sheep 'mair thoroughly than orinar'. These were indeed terrible days of Church discipline. Much attention was paid to evidence of a merely hearsay character; the result being that opportunity was afforded to the envious, to the malignant, to the slanderous and the revengeful, either to pay off old scores, or to destroy the reputation of a neighbour. To these causes also must be attributed the awful delusion of witchcraft ... which in this seventeenth century obsessed the Church like a hideous nightmare. Some of its victims were undoubtedly insane; others were the subjects of an aggravated hysteria which prompted them to confess to horrible practices out of a mere craving for notoriety; but very many suffered from false and vindictive accusations of their neighbours in order to afford the gratification of spite or revenge ... There was the fanatical

massacre of the prisoners of Philiphaugh ... There was the slavish worship of the Sabbath, with a literal attention to detail, rather than the God of the Sabbath ... There were the degrading humiliations of the cutty stool and of the jougs^c, which served merely to render the culprit callous and vindictive, rather than truly penitent.

The principal emphasis of the Kirk's philosophy towards the people was discipline and damnation rather than pastoral care, and in this respect the Kirk in Peebles was no better or worse than anywhere else in Scotland. For many of the clergy the rapidly changing religious order naturally presented serious problems. In 1638 they had to adjust to the transition from Episcopacy and now the pendulum had swung much further towards the extremes of Presbyterianism, very far removed from Episcopacy. This was a sore test of conscience to many, unless they were like the English Vicar of Bray, who at a later time had no difficulty in trimming his sails to the prevailing circumstances as a means of survival:

In good King Charles's golden days,
When loyalty no harm meant;
A furious High-Churchman I was,
And so I gain'd preferment.
Unto my flock I daily preach'd,
Kings are by God appointed.
And damned are those who dare resist,
Or touch the Lord's Anointed.
And this is law, I will maintain,
Unto my dying day, Sir,
That whatsoever King shall reign,
I will be the Vicar of Bray, Sir.

In most cases it was a question of survival. Conform to change or lose home and livelihood. An outward show of support for the changed order and a suppression of private feelings to the contrary was nothing other than pragmatic. It was a dilemma suffered by ministers throughout Scotland and Rev. John Hay, Minister of Peebles, was no exception.

John Hay, BD, was a Resolutioner of the stronger sort. Indeed, if pressed in the privacy of his own home and among company he could trust, he would even admit to Royalist leanings, like his father the venerable Dr Theodore Hay. However, to avoid the unpalatable label of 'Malignant' this was something which he assiduously sought to conceal from public scrutiny. Born in 1613, he had studied at the University of Edinburgh, there gaining the degree of Master of Arts in 1630, and later at Cambridge, where he held a Fellowship, and gained the degree of Bachelor of Divinity. His father had been appointed Minister of Peebles in

1. Medieval Scottish town market.
Reproduced by permission of Scottish
Borders Council, Museum and
Gallery Service. (*Photograph by Alastair
MacFarlane*)

2. The Cross Kirk of Peebles before the
Reformation of 1560. (*From a drawing by
Alex Blackwood*)

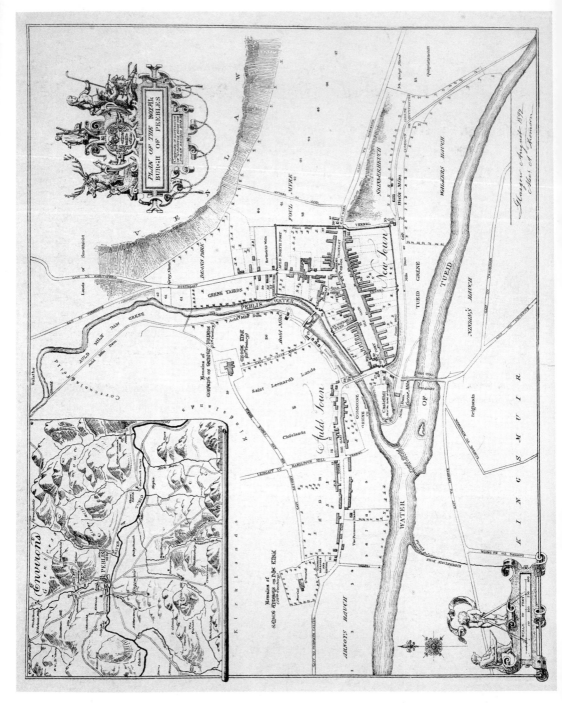

3. Plan of Peebles, *c.* 1609–52 as drawn by Alex A. Thomson, 1892, from Burgh Records. Reproduced by permission of Scottish Borders Council, Museum and Gallery Service. (*Photograph by Alastair MacFarlane*)

4. Siege of Neidpath. Reproduced by kind permission of Elizabeth Benson. (*Watercolour by Jack Roney. Photograph by Alastair MacFarlane*)

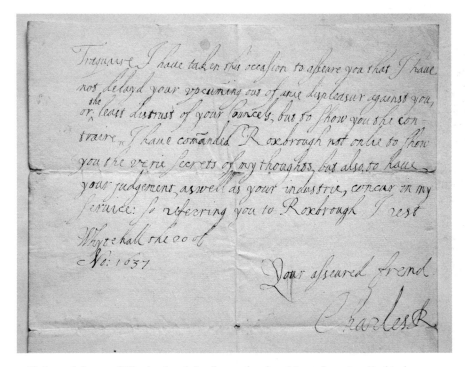

5. Holograph letter of Charles I to John Stuart dated 20 November 1637. By kind permission of the Traquair Charitable Trust. (*Photograph by Alastair MacFarlane*)

6. Four silver communion cups, dated 1684. By permission of the Kirk Session of Peebles Old Parish Church of Scotland. (*Photograph by Alastair MacFarlane*)

7. George Jamieson's *Portrait of John Stuart, 1st Earl of Traquair.* By kind permission of the Traquair Charitable Trust. (*Photograph by Alastair MacFarlane*)

8. Sir George Harvey's *The Covenanter's Baptism*. By permission of Aberdeen Art Gallery and Museums Collections.

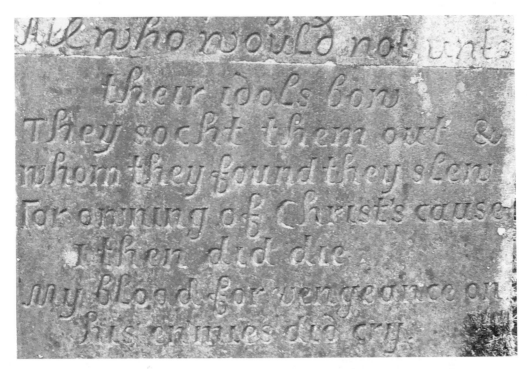

All who would not unto
their idols bow
They socht them out &
whom they found they slew
For owning of Christ's cause
I then did die
My blood for vengeance on
his crimes did cry

9. Detail of the inscription on the gravestone of John Hunter, Tweedsmuir churchyard. (*Photograph by the author*)

10. Talla Linn. (*Photograph by the author*)

11 & 12. The Martyrs Memorial, with detail below, Greyfriars Kirkyard, Edinburgh. (*Photograph by the author*)

From May 27th. 1661. that the moſt noble Marquis of Argyle was beheaded, to the 17th of Feb.ry 1688. that Mr. James Renwick ſuffered; were one way or other Murdered and Deſtroyed for the ſame Cauſe, about Eighteen thouſand, of whom were execute at *Edinburgh*, about an hundred, of Noblemen, Gentlemen, Miniſters and Others noble Martyrs for JESUS CHRIST. The moſt of them lie here,

For a particular account of the cauſe, and manner of their Sufferings, ſee the Cloud of Witneſſes, Crookſhank's and Defoe's Hiſtories.

13. The Martyrs Cross, Grassmarket, Edinburgh. (*Photograph by the author*)

14. Covenanters' Prison, Greyfriars Kirkyard, Edinburgh. (*Photograph by the author*)

1610. He was still in post in 1643, but was then already an old man and, concerned about his age and poor health, the bailies and the majority of the councillors of the town had sent a request to the Presbytery, asking that John Hay be appointed as his assistant. His exact status was, however, a matter of some controversy. The initial request had come from the Kirk Session and had been presented on its behalf by one Andrew Watson (of whom more later), asking that John Hay be appointed as colleague. The Council were of the view that the appointment should be limited to his assisting with preaching during the remainder of the lifetime of Dr Theodore. They went so far as to say that if the Presbytery went beyond what the Council intended, they would dissent and require that dissent be included in the Presbytery record. Perhaps thirty-three years of one Hay ministry up until then had been enough for them. Dr Theodore had eventually retired in 1648 and died in 1651. Now, in the midst of Cromwellian occupation, John Hay must once again adjust to changing circumstances. Dr Theodore had achieved the remarkable feat of presiding over the Church of Peebles for a period of thirty-eight years until his retirement, a time of change and change again. He had had the honour of meeting King James VI himself in 1610, shortly after he began his ministry in Peebles as an Episcopalian, in which order he continued until 1638, when Presbyterianism became re-established, albeit against the will of the reigning monarch, Charles I. In 1645 he had to further trim his coat to the discipline of the Westminster Confession. He had greatly disliked the resulting changes to the liturgy, which extreme elements had succeeded in imposing upon the Kirk, such as discontinuing the reciting of the Lord's Prayer and singing of 'Glory to the Father', and even the reading of scripture. The change to the drab blackness of Presbyterianism from the colour and magnificence of Episcopal vestments was a further cause of regret.

For his son, John, the passage of time had been equally painful. All his early scholarship and practice had been in the Episcopal tradition and no doubt this had been further enhanced by his time at Cambridge. Although he had welcomed and gladly accepted the opportunity to return to Peebles to assist his aged father in 1643, both men privately lamented the change to Presbyterianism, which had been imposed upon them and which was against all their liturgical and theological instincts. Now to add insult, he had to suffer the usurpation of these Puritan English, who would doubtless appeal to the worst elements of Covenanting bigotry. He was well aware that there was among his flock several of that persuasion, including some of the younger element, such as James Nicol. He could, of course, have demitted office, but to what end? There was no place in Commonwealth Scotland for Malignants (although John Hay would not have accepted that term as applying to himself). Those who had stood up for the older order had been cast out from the Kirk, their livings and their manses, to live without succour or sustenance. Material considerations prevailed. John Hay allowed himself the indignity of hearing the Word of the Lord proclaimed in his own

church with much praying and preaching by ranting and narrow-minded officers of Cromwell's occupying army. Even on the matter of discipline John Hay
had to accept the unacceptable in the face of a Kirk and Kirk Session committed
to rooting out what they saw in others as the work and ways of the Devil. The
arrival of Cromwellian forces and their sojourn in the town brought not only a
semblance of order to civil affairs, but also to the Kirk.

John Hay, although now established as minister and a less than enthusiastic
practitioner of Presbyterianism, no doubt secretly hankered after the Episcopal
order. The situation was not helped by the presence of his vicar, Andrew Watson;
a man seemingly more concerned with his own well-being and survival, rather
than the proper performance of the duties of a religious leader in the community.
His was a talent for survival, which had maintained him in prominent positions
in society for thirty years or more, first as schoolmaster and then as vicar. In both
of those roles he had periodically been taken to task for his idleness and lack
of attention to duty. The practice of medicine was one of his additional talents,
particularly in the repair of physical injuries often inflicted by sword or knife in
altercations and brawls in the town. Even in the exercise of those skills he had
often become involved in disputes concerning payment for his services. All in all,
his lack of popularity was evidenced by a number of incidents when his life and
property had been put in danger by some of those aggrieved by his behaviour. On
one occasion, while he was absent from the town, an angry parishioner climbed
on the roof of his house and removed part of the thatch so that the contents
inside were soaked by a following deluge of rain. On another occasion, again
during an absence from the town, a group of men invaded his house and removed
floorboards from an upper floor. On his return, it was said 'but for the providence
of God' he might have fallen down the stairway with fatal consequences. While
John Hay could not, in all conscience, approve of the officers of the New Model
Army demanding the right to occupy his pulpit, with lengthy praying and much
haranguing of his parishioners, at least they brought order and discipline to the
worship of the Kirk.

James Nicol, by contrast, was much impressed by these solemn and upright
men. Did they not favour the Protesters? Their worship was centred on prayer,
a great deal of prayer, and the exposition of the scriptures through extemporary
preaching was much to be preferred to formal and repetitive prayers, scripture
reading and the unholy sound of voices raised in song, with all their Episcopal
and even Papist formality. In October 1653, with some satisfaction, he could write
in his diary, 'There was no reading of the chapters nor singing of psalms on the
Sabbath day'. He generally approved of the rule of the Lord Protector, Cromwell,
and the civic powers of his Commonwealth, at least as far as religious observa-
tion was concerned. It favoured the Protesters rather than the Resolutioners and
James was very much in the camp of the former, with their strong devotion and
emphasis on much preaching. This, for the time being at least, also found general

favour with the common folk, though these same folk must have been sorely tried in the practice of their faith, especially on the Sacramental Fast Days or Holy Fairs that the Protesters had recently inaugurated.

The celebration of Communion was to take place once a month, but as the Protesters were much exercised by the original sin of mankind and its continuing failure to achieve perfection, it was generally ruled that at any celebration of the Sacrament, only one half of the communicants might receive it, the remaining half being judged as sinners, unworthy to attend the Lord's Table. Quite how this division was arrived at is unclear, but for such as James it was a system accepted as God's will. He had no difficulty in recalling whether or not he had been judged as worthy or unworthy at the last celebration, and thus whether or not it was his turn to be deemed sufficiently free of sin. Holy Fairs were held at intervals and were altogether more challenging for the faithful. Two or three sermons on the Saturday immediately preceding the Sabbath served to whet the appetite. The service on the Sabbath day itself was wont to last throughout the day, with a succession of sermons lasting eight to ten hours. Not content with such a plethora of preaching, those of the faithful who had survived the marathon of the preceding two days returned on Monday to submit themselves to the challenge of three or four sermons of thanksgiving, leaving them at peace for the remainder of the week to reflect on the wonders of the Almighty and the Damnation which would come to those who did not heed the Word – at least as it had been delivered and expounded to them at such length by his faithful clergy. This was indeed an endurance test to be marvelled at, but one which James felt only to be right and proper. The less arduous observance for weaker souls would follow, as usual, on the coming Sabbath.

With at least the tacit support of the occupying Puritans, the Protesters continued to hold increasing influence, and for the next few years they were the dominating force in Synod, Presbytery and Kirk Session in spite of the suppression of the General Assembly by the Commonwealth government. Although they did not entirely approve of them, as long as there was relative peace across the country the government saw no point in antagonising those forces in the Kirk that had a broadly similar view of the place of the Church in society and, furthermore, had the great merit of being anti-Royalist. These years did see disputes between the government authorities and those in their charge. They mainly concerned the cost of feeding and housing the troops billeted upon them. Their numbers in a town such as Peebles were not large, but sufficient enough to be a visible presence and to maintain public order. In time the occupiers and the occupied were able to reach some sort of reasonable understanding, but debate and negotiation about the costs of occupation were a continuing concern of the provost and Council. Not all was sweetness and light. Humble and prayerful as most of the occupying troops were, there were some who took advantage of their position. When Colonel Twistleton's troop was stationed in the town there was theft of local property. The thieves attempted to dispose of their ill-gotten gains to local folk and the Council issued a public order that no one should purchase goods from the 'enemy' or reset them, but, if opportunity arose, the goods should be returned to their rightful owners. The burden of losses in the town was particularly heavy in the autumn of 1651, when a large number of occupying troops remained there. Steps were taken to raise the matter with Major-General Lambert, now based in Edinburgh, and commissioners were appointed as a deputation to him. In August 1651 old Provost Williamson had died, much mourned for his resolute defence of the interests of Peebles over several decades. His place was taken for a brief period by John Lowes. Perhaps he had been less forceful than his worthy predecessor, for in any event, in December a further deputation was sent to General Lambert to speak to him about the losses the town had suffered due to the activities of the English soldiery.

Early in 1652 an event occurred that further emphasised to a defeated and dispirited populace that they had not yet fully atoned for their folly in lending support to the Royalist cause; indifferent and feeble though that support may have been. That event is described by Thomas Smyth, the town clerk of Peebles at the time:

Mirk Monday 29th March 1652. The sun eclipsed from eight houres to haif hour to ellevine or thereby befor noon, the sun eclipsed 11 digittes, the darknes continwit 8 minutes or therabout: the people begane all to pray to God; a little therafter ther was seene upon the south side of the firmament ane clear perfyte star. Some affirmed they saw two, but I saw one onlie.
Et Quonian Hoc Fuit Rarum Prodigiosum
Idcirco Registari Dignum Existimavi
[Since this was an unusual wonder
Therefore I thought it worth recording]

This seemingly sinister event did nothing to alleviate the mood of sullen forbearance that had descended on the town and much of Scotland. Throughout the next six years virtually the whole country remained occupied by Cromwell's forces under the control of their religiously imbued officers. Austerity prevailed, not only in the conduct of worship. Fun and laughter, such a feature of burgh life, were extinguished. The holding of fairs that fell on a Sabbath Day or on a Monday were considered to be profane and those that were allowed had now to be held on a Tuesday and were but a pale shadow of their former selves. Even fairs such as the St Andrews Fair, 'thes mony aiges bygane been kept',[2] held each year in November, were severely restricted. The Beltane horse race and its accompanying games were strictly forbidden. 'Peebles and the Play' became a distant memory.

The continuing presence of soldiers billeted on burgh households was a costly burden, not only to the burgh but also to burgesses saddled with the inconvenience of soldiers insinuated into their households and needing to be fed and watered. Monthly assessments had to be levied on the townsfolk to meet the expense. Attempts were made by the Council to recover the costs and once more deputations travelled to Edinburgh to the Commander-in-Chief to seek reimbursement. Typical was the deputation of two councillors who made their way to the capital on 25 August 1653, but their journey seems to have been in vain because the following appears in the records dated 21 September:

> in respect ther is added monethlie to the tounes assessments twentie four punds more than was before; therfor, and for preventing of quartering, the counsel ordeanes the inhabitants to pay the same proportiones they payed in the month of Julij last, and the thesaurer to pay twelve pundes, which, with what is already collected for the inhabitants, will compleit the monethes assessment of Julij and August last by past, being monthlie thrie scoir pundes.[3]

The monthly sum was considerable, but reasoned argument made way for the persuasion of corruption when a further attempt at recovery was made in November. A deputation was sent with the instruction to 'ryde in to Dalkeith upon Moonday nixt to present the tounes supplicatioun anent the assessment, and allowes him to *give the secretarie tuo rex-dolleres*' (author's italics).

Church affairs in Peebles had reached a state of calm equilibrium. Sabbath keeping was strictly enforced. The power of the Kirk Session was supreme. Perversely, this did not produce a peaceful or law-abiding community. Theft, riots and disregard of Council injunctions were commonplace and the enforcement of discipline was the paramount concern of both Kirk Session and Council. The conduct of worship throughout Scotland had descended into a state of barren and colourless uniformity, which only a major political and ecclesiastical upheaval could reverse. That upheaval was about to happen. On 3 September 1658 Oliver Cromwell died.

Chapter Notes

a. putting it into a heap; **b**. scolding; **c**. iron rings fixed to the wall of the kirk, used as a pillary.

14

Restoration

The death of Oliver Cromwell was not immediately marked by any great change in the condition of Scotland. It remained occupied by the soldiers of the New Model Army, controlled by General George Monk. Oliver Cromwell had ruled as a virtual dictator with all the power of an absolute, but uncrowned monarch. The Crown had been offered to him, but he had declined to accept it, although with what conflicts of ambition and conscience is difficult to say. Yet such was the perception of him as absolute ruler of the Commonwealth of England and Wales, Scotland and Ireland, that his family acquired dynastic status. On his death, his eldest son Richard was recognised as his successor. A man less like his father is difficult to imagine. Richard Cromwell was no soldier and less of a politician. His had been living the life of a country gentleman. Weak and ineffective, in the space of less than a year he who had been hailed as next in line of the Cromwell dynasty, born to carry forward the torch of his illustrious father, had been removed by the army, reviled and derided, first as 'Queen Dick' and finally as 'Tumble down Dick'.

The Protectorate, which the army had created itself, was dissolved by that same army. The Rump Parliament was revived on 7 May 1659 and immediately passed legislation declaring that all the Acts introduced by Cromwell since Parliament was dissolved six years previously were invalid. All the steps that had been taken to create a union between the kingdoms collapsed. An attempt was made to revive the process. A Union Bill was introduced and passed the initial stages, but Scottish Presbyterian demands that it should provide for freedom of conscience, at least for those of their persuasion, which excluded Episcopalians and Catholics, delayed the passage and the Bill finally collapsed when the army once more took charge of affairs. They dissolved the Rump Parliament in October and appointed a Committee of Public Safety to undertake the roll of government. Throughout England as well as Scotland there was a weariness of military rule, and although north of the border the well-trained and disciplined occupying army of General Monk continued to keep a firm hold on the country, Monk himself was preparing to play a crucial role in the future of both countries. General Monk, although authoritarian, commanded considerable respect both north and south of the border. He was a man of common sense, fair-minded and an able military commander. Such was the esteem in which he was held that he had gained the popular soubriquet of 'Honest George'. He was well aware of the failing popularity of the military government and, from his distant northerly viewpoint, he was concerned by the prospect of a government composed of a group of officers driven by Puritan fundamentalism, who showed every sign of being more careless of personal liberty than their great, lately deceased leader. News from the south spoke of English Presbyterians and Royalists joining together to demand a free Parliament to halt the advance of military tyranny. There was an ever-louder clamour for the return of a King.

Monk called a convention in Edinburgh, which elected the Earl of Glencairn as one of its presidents. Glencairn was a committed Royalist and so the tide was turned in favour of a royal restoration. On 1 January 1660, satisfied that the government of Scotland was in safe hands, Monk crossed the border at Coldstream at the head of his formidable army. As in the past, the descent of an army from Scotland into England, albeit this time an English one, was to change the course of British history. A parliament, of sorts, had met in London in December, but achieved little. The arrival of Monk concentrated minds. Lambert, the Puritan scourge of Scotland and leading military commander of the Puritan faction, found both his political and military power ebbing away. Sir Thomas Fairfax, the other great commander of Cromwellian days, backed Monk and by February he was firmly in control of the political agenda. In March a convention met at Westminster and in due course decided upon a return to the former constitutional arrangements. The Union was no more and Charles was recognised as the rightful King of England. There had already been contact with him and on 1 May 1660 his envoy came to London to present what was to become known as the Declaration of Breda. This promised a general amnesty and conclusion by Parliament of all questions arising from the confiscation of property and settlement of the arrears of pay for the army, which was much overdue. Of prime importance, however, was the question of liberty and toleration. Charles promised:

A liberty to tender consciences and that no man shall be disquieted or called upon for differences of opinion in the matter of religion which do not disturb the peace of the Kingdom, and that we are ready to consent to such an act of parliament as upon mature deliberation shall be offered to us for the full granting of that indulgence.

It was enough. On 8 May Charles was proclaimed King in London and a few days later, at the Mercat Cross in Edinburgh, he was proclaimed King of Scots once again. Although restored to the throne of his Stuart ancestors, Charles was never to travel to his northern capital to receive the crown and regalia of Scotland.

The restoration of the monarchy brought a collective sigh of relief to the Scottish kingdom. The English occupation had at best been an embarrassment to national pride and at worst a sore burden of heavy taxation and much else to support the occupying forces. There was wild celebration throughout the country. In douce Edinburgh there were fireworks and even a banquet in the High Street. Fountains flowed with claret and bells rang. Bells also rang in Peebles. The Royal Burgh, which for a time past had lost its loyalty to the Stuart dynasty, regained its fervour for the Scottish Crown. There was a bonfire and, on 19 June, a Thanksgiving Day for the King's restoration, both provided for at the town's expense. Fun and laughter returned and, after an absence of some years, the Beltane Fair and its horse race were revived in 1661. It was a happy and care-free event. Ale and wine flowed. Four gallons of ale were provided at the Town Cross for the townsfolk by command of the magistrates as a prelude to the race, some days in advance on 22 April. It must have been a jolly and boisterous affair, because the Town Treasurer carefully notes that three ale cups were broken at a cost to the town of 6s. However, this was but small beer compared with the Edinburgh celebration, when someone estimated that 'three hundred dozen of glasses' were broken in 'loyal toasts to the King'. There was further celebration on 1 May when the Beltane Cup, gaily decorated with red ribbons, was displayed at the Cross, while on the day of the race itself the Council expended the substantial sum of £27 12s for 'wyn and uther furnitor when the King was crownd, and at Beltan fair when the earl of Tuedell came to the toun'. There was an additional item of 16s for 'four stowps [of ale] to the mure wher the race hors did run'. Released from the shackles and restrictions of extreme Presbyterianism, which was never the town's ally, Peebles returned to 'the Play'.

Not all would welcome the new levity. There were those who still adhered to the bigotry of the Protesters and regarded any deviation from its narrow confines as Prelacy and Popery, and regarded as 'Ba'al's priests' those ministers who dared to suggest a return to Episcopacy. James Nicol was one such. Now twenty-seven years old, married and with a family, he had become increasingly attracted towards the extremes; the teaching and preaching of the remaining Protesters who were raising an ever-louder clamour in support of the fundamental principles of the Covenants. In his solitary journeyings across the great open spaces of southern Scotland in pursuit of his merchant trade, James had much time to reflect on these matters and, in that solitude, to lift up his eyes to the hills and contemplate the greatness and wonder of the Almighty who sustained him.

—◦◦◦—

15

The Merry Monarch

He [King Charles II] said once to myself, he was no atheist, but he could not think God would make a man miserable only for taking a little pleasure out of the way.

Bishop Robert Burnet

Charles II was the first member of the Stuart dynasty to be born out of Scotland. Indeed, the last Scottish monarch not to be born within the realm of Scotland was the ill-fated 'Maid of Norway' in the far-off thirteenth century. In spite of his dynastic heritage, Charles had little regard for the land of his forefathers. His early years at court in London had been happy enough. For all his political failings, his father, Charles I, was a loving and caring parent. Charles II had been sufficiently educated and had a sharp and incisive mind. He developed a real interest in science and, like his forbearers, James IV and James V, he took a keen interest in maritime matters. Unlike those ancestors, he had little interest in the arts or literature, preferring instead outdoor pursuits. Of Scotland he knew and was taught little. By the age of eight he had his own household and court at Richmond, but the Civil War was to shatter this youthful idyll. He and his brother James, Duke of York[1] were present at the Battle of Edgehill, but the war was at an end before he could personally play any part in it. On 4 March 1645 he saw his father for the last time and then began his years of exile, first in Paris where his mother, Queen Henrietta Maria, had removed from the dangers of England, and then to Calais and finally Holland, which was to be his base until his restoration in 1660 (apart from a brief and inglorious foray into Scotland in 1650 to claim the Scottish Crown).

The years in exile left an indelible mark on Charles. They were years of humiliation and anxiety, tinged with forlorn hope. He was Prince and King in name, but a royal pauper in reality. His experience in those years, where he was the

centre of intrigue and deception, left him cynical, unhappy and distrustful. Upon
his restoration he resolved never again to suffer the indignation of those years
and never again to 'go on his travels'. The events of that time had undoubtedly affected his attitude towards Scotland and its people, who had had no little
influence and part in the downfall of his father; a people riven by bigotry and
intolerance, which had been among the decisive effects in that downfall. In spite
of his apparent acceptance of the Covenants, which was a major influence in
his gaining the Scottish Crown in 1651, Charles determined that Covenanting
Protestantism should never again hold sway. He could not forget the indignity
visited upon him by the Covenanters, then in control of government, when he
arrived from Holland at Garmouth on the Spey in June 1650. They had insisted
that the price of his Scottish crown was not only the recognition of Covenanted
Protestantism as the religion of Scotland, but its imposition on England and Wales
as well. He had been prepared to accept the former, but resisted the extension of
the Covenants beyond the borders of Scotland. Twice he declined to accept the
Covenanters' advances and only on the third attempt, when a declaration had
been drawn up and ratified by the Committee of the Estates, did Charles give
in to the pressures upon him. In the face of an invasion of Scotland by 16,000
soldiers of the New Model Army, he finally signed, accepting the Covenants and
agreeing to their imposition on his greater kingdom. In return he received the
Crown of Scotland at Scone. Little good it did him. The previously well-trained
Scottish army had been purged of most of its best-trained men and officers by the
fanatical Covenanting ministers, who deemed any who did not subscribe to their
view of religion as unworthy to fight for the cause of Scotland. At Dunbar, even
the skills and leadership of Leslie could not prevent the disastrous defeat at the
hands of Cromwell, which was the inevitable result of religious fanaticism over
military pragmatism. Charles had to start the long journey into exile for a second
time by way of Worcester, clandestine escape and the indignity of refuge in an
oak tree. Scotland had delivered his father into the hands of his enemies and had
done little service to his son. Scotland could take care of itself, for what little he
now cared. Covenanting Protestantism would never again be allowed to hold the
power of the Crown and State in its hands if he could help it.

Charles was not a tyrant by nature. Rather he wished peace and stability in his
kingdoms. He was personally amiable, and although his rule was absolutist in style,
this arose as much from his wish to avoid the rise of warring factions, which too
much tolerance might encourage, rather than any desire to play the tyrant. After a
long and uncomfortable exile he wanted to avoid the tedium of fractious government so that he might indulge in the worldly pleasures so long denied, but which
now beckoned. In reality he did not care much about anything. Scotland hardly
concerned him, although he had in the past regarded his northern kingdom as a
potential source of danger; a danger which stemmed from its ecclesiastical heritage and those fanatical Covenanting ministers who seemed more concerned

with separating themselves from the temporal authority of the Crown than in the pastoral and spiritual care of the people. As Agnes Mure MacKenzie has succinctly commented, 'He was not cruel – far from it, both by nature and the fact that he cared so little for most things. But the men who governed Scotland shared his fear and he did nothing to relieve or check them, and more of them had the status of a king, or, as events were to prove, the power to be one.'[2] No doubt those who now governed in his name had good reason to be fearful and those fanatics who stood by the principles of the Covenants were their enemies. The inevitable result in the years to come was what came to be known as 'the Killing Times'. While blame cannot be laid directly at the door of Charles, his tacit support of the Scottish government in their subsequent policy of repression of the Covenanters leaves him ultimately with a heavy responsibility for the wave of violence which encompassed the aftermath of Rullion Green and later Bothwell Brig, which were to rank among the most ignominious events of Scottish history. The 'Merry Monarch' in the safety and decadence of seventeeth-century London he may have been, but his absent hands became covered in Scottish blood.

Scotland, by the time of the Restoration, was a country in considerable disarray. For seventeen years there had been periodic strife, including a civil war. Nine years of Cromwellian occupation had brought a measure of internal stability and peace, but it was a stability and peace bought at the expense of heavy financial burdens upon the populace. There had been increasing prosperity in the 1620s and '30s before the civil unrest began, but that was now all undone and Scotland was in a sorry and confused state. Much of that confusion arose from the continuing religious divide between the Resolutioners, who were now essentially Royalist while remaining loyal to Presbyterianism, and the Protesters, who remained vehemently committed to the narrow confines of the Covenants. A further, though less dominant element, were the remaining Roman Catholics, but these represented perhaps no more than one and a half per cent of the total population, then about 1 million.

The new King's first task was to assert his full authority and control over the government. Whether or not it was ever his intention to return personally to Scotland to assert that authority is unclear, although his view of both his and his father's treatment by their Scottish subjects would suggest that it was not. His choice of Officers of State was, therefore, of great significance, and the nature, qualities and personal affiliations of his appointees would give a clear indication of his intentions and how he meant to govern, as well as his attitude to the religious problems. The Scottish Parliament was not immediately recalled, but a Committee of Estates was set up to undertake the function of government. The chosen participants were those upon whom Charles felt he could rely and those who would maintain a strong association with their counterparts in England. Those selected as Officers of State were, in fact, a mixture of persuasions. Rothes, who was made President of the Council, nominally a Resolutioner, was an able man, although his most remarked characteristic seems to have been his fondness for alcohol. Crawford, again a Resolutioner, was appointed Treasurer. Glencairn, who was an Engager and an Episcopalian, was made Chancellor, while Middleton, also an Engager, became Commissioner. The new Secretary of State was the Earl of Lauderdale, who had spent nine years in prison following the Battle of Worcester. He was a Resolutioner, described by Agnes Mure MacKenzie as 'a gross lump of a man with a queer thick vitality ... a distinguished scholar, enthusiastic for theology to the point of learning Hebrew to study better'.[3] He would be the effective ruler of Scotland for most of the next twenty years.

Initially there were scores to settle and heads to roll – literally. In January 1662 Parliament met and its first business was to remove those deemed to be the enemies of Charles. The King had directed that everyone involved in the past troubles should be tried. In practice all but four of the leading Protesters were set free and the gallows were reserved for Argyll, Rev. James Guthrie and Lieutenant William Govan. Two years later, Archibald Johnston of Warriston, one of the architects of the National Covenant document, was captured in France and brought back to Scotland and the Edinburgh gallows.

The Parliament sat for six busy months passing no less than 393 Acts. Most significant among these was an Act that gave the King sole authority in the appointment of the Officers of State, Privy Councillors and Lords of Session. The Lords of the Articles were restored, while one Act required all holders of public office, local as well as national, to take an oath of allegiance to the King, acknowledging him as 'Supreme Governor of this Kingdom, over all persons and in all causes'. The King was to have the sole authority to call a Parliament. Absolute power of the Crown was effectively restored. The Solemn League and Covenant was to be binding no longer and a Rescissory Act effectively annulled every Act passed by the Estates since 1633. The principal result of this was to return statute law to what it had been in that year. This included the government of the Church of Scotland, although the powers of Kirk Sessions, Presbyteries and Synods were to be preserved. That government thus reverted to the Episcopal form established by James VI. Bishops were back. Not surprisingly, these arrangements were not universally welcomed. Scotland was seriously split as evidenced by the reactions of the Synods when they met to consider the new order. Those of the north heartily endorsed the change. Covenanted Protestantism had never found much favour north of the Tay. The Synod of Fife was against the change, but not strongly so and confirmed its loyalty to the King. Lothian was deeply divided as there were many Episcopalians in its bounds, but also a number of strong Presbyterian Resolutioners. Some Protester ministers were suspended and while, on balance, the new order was ultimately accepted, the Synod would not go so far as to allow the Lord's Prayer in public worship. Glasgow (which included Peebles) and Ayr supported the status quo of 1660. However, Resolutioners who had leanings towards Episcopacy carried the day, although a resolution was passed against 'preletical Episcopacy'. This was intended to placate the Protesters among them, but in practice it became a source of aggravation as it did not preclude Episcopacy as such. The Glasgow Protesters were further aggrieved that the Covenants had not been demanded. Dumfries and Galloway were unequivocally opposed to any change. They were almost universally Protester and continued to demand that the two Covenants should be sworn by all throughout the kingdom, and that any who supported Prelacy should be deposed. It was there that the seeds were sown for the escalating and bloody conflict of the next twenty-eight years. The flame of rebellion was firmly alight in the south-west of Scotland and, although remaining concentrated there, its flames would spread outwards north and east in the years to come.

In Peebles, the decision of the Synod of Glasgow was accepted quietly. Episcopacy was re-established, although the Kirk Session remained, as did the Presbytery of Tweeddale. The Rev. John Hay, Minister of Peebles, no doubt thankfully accepted the changed circumstances. He had always been an Episcopalian at heart and had initially been educated in that tradition. His enthusiasm for the Episcopal cause was quickly realised. In October 1661 he had even been proposed as Bishop of Caithness, an offer which he seemed to decline, but a year later he became perpetual moderator of the Presbytery, an appointment made by the Archbishop of Glasgow under the new order. On 14 October 1661 the Town Council met. The record for that day reads:

> This day Alexander Williamsone, lait proveist, reports that all the commissioners of burrows in the last session of parliament wer verballie ordeaned to present the oath of alleadgeance to the burghes from whence they wer commissionat, and this day desyred the said oath might be administered to the magistrates and counsel to be elected. The saids magistrates and counsel, all in ane voice, declaired they ar most willing to take the oath of alaedgeance, so soone as ther shal be public order issued furth from the King, his parliament or secreit cousell, for administrating thairof.

Thus were the leaders of kirk and town united in their professed allegiance to the 'Merry Monarch'. Others were perhaps not so far inclined.

The Protesters, those who continued to hold fast to the Covenants, had an essentially simplistic view of religious belief and practice. In the main they were simple folk. Their leaders may have been well educated, and those of their number who were, or had been, ministers were theologically trained, but it was the ordinary country folk that provided the main body of support. These were people who lived and toiled in the isolation of the uplands and southern glens rather than in gathered communities and towns. They were shepherds or the smaller sort of tenant farmers with time to contemplate life as they went about their daily affairs, and time to dwell upon the ways of the Lord and his servants. They did not have the advantage of the regular social intercourse found in towns and larger communities, which opens the mind to a broader vision of life. Their isolation bred narrowness of mind and intolerance of ideas other than their own, which all too easily descended into bigotry. It was not unduly difficult for the rising group of fanatical Protester preachers to underpin and elevate that intolerance and bigotry into a creed that saw no other way than its own, owing no allegiance on matters of religious belief and practice to King or State. What those Protester leaders wanted was not just the freedom to follow their own religious beliefs, but also to deny the whole of the rest of the populace (of which they themselves formed no more than a quarter) the freedom to follow theirs. As Agnes Mure MacKenzie notes, 'To accept toleration would have been to allow, by inference, freedom of thought to those who differed from them: and they quite honestly believed that this was the ultimate sin against the Holy Ghost'.[4] It was a dangerous creed which in time would ignite a campaign of disobedience to the civil authority to the point of armed conflict.

Protesters, with their blinkered vision, saw the changes that the new order had brought about as a renewed journey on the road to Rome. What else could the recreation of bishops signify? Covenanting Protestantism saw them and the clergy they ordained not just as near Papists, but as possessed of all the iniquities of the priests of Ba'al, with their worship of idols. In place of the Golden Calf was a decadent King who, in their eyes, had placed himself at the Head of the Church and thus usurped the position of the Almighty himself. In their narrow view, which stemmed from those days before the Reformation, now lost by time in myth and legend, they saw bishops as 'gluttonous, Epicurean, belly-god Prelates, who are riding in coaches in great pomp'.[5] The truth was somewhat otherwise.

In practice, little changed. Bishoprics conformed to the previous Synods, which continued to operate as before, but with the bishop as permanent moderator. The bishop did have sole authority to ordain clergy and admit to membership of the Kirk, but in reality they did so on the recommendation of local parties. In the main, those who now became bishops exercised their authority in a moderate manner, generally avoiding change from the previous order. The Prayer Book was not reintroduced, although some might have wished it. There was no change in worship or discipline. Doctrine was still essentially Calvinistic. Worship was conducted without ceremony. There was no liturgy. Divine Service did now include the Doxology and the Lord's Prayer (although even that was not universal). Elaborate vestments were not worn by the ordinary clergy, who retained the sombre black of the Geneva gown. The Creed was used in the Sacrament of Baptism. Communion was rarely celebrated. Synods, Presbyteries, Kirk Sessions and elders continued as before. At one end of the spectrum Episcopacy had its most extreme adherents in the north, which had retained the strongest associations with Catholicism since the Reformation; at the other end of the spectrum, the south-west had hardly wavered in its support of Covenanted Presbyterianism since 1638. In the years immediately following the restoration of Charles II and the return of an Episcopal Church of Scotland, it would be from the south-west that opposition would grow. It would grow from gatherings known as 'conventicles'. At first these were gatherings of the Covenanting faithful in houses and barns, but as time went on and as numbers grew, and the fame (and notoriety) of Protester preachers increased, these gatherings moved out most notably into the hills, where, in time, those preachers could command an audience of thousands.

It is perhaps strange that James Nicol, born and raised in the close-knit community of Peebles, should become a fanatical adherent and active supporter of the Covenanting cause. As a young merchant operating from the old Border town, with its associations with the wool and textile trade, the world of his trading would be towards the east, to Berwick, Edinburgh and Leith, but it would also take him into Lanarkshire and the high sheep lands of the upper Tweed, which were not far removed from the northern reaches of Dumfries and Galloway. In his journeying into those parts he could not have been immune from or blind to the Covenanting ethos so strident there. The Kirk Session records of Tweedsmuir certainly paint a picture of a parish and congregation firmly in support of the Covenants and its elders regularly attended conventicles. No doubt James had the opportunity to listen to harangues of preachers and to be carried along by the emotion that they generated in their assembled listeners. On the long ride back to Peebles he would have plenty of time for reflection. Although Peebles, in its central position at the crossroads from the south-west to the east coast and north to the capital, would have ample knowledge of the growing ferment in the south-west, it was clearly not now a Covenanting town, whatever its earlier adherence to the National Covenant might have been. It had accepted the return to Episcopacy with apparent equanimity and its Council had confirmed its allegiance to the King and accepted his absolute authority. So, perhaps not the only 'odd man out', James was certainly in the minority and a small minority at that. He was one of those not at ease with his fellow townsfolk. One of those who, for reasons best known to themselves, do not conform; a loner, perhaps regarded by his peers as anti-social, with strange, irrational opinions; the sort of person who cannot accept the majority view and cannot be dislodged from their own different view, however illogical that outlook may seem to the rest of society. Whatever the reason, James made no secret of his support for the Covenanting cause and was marked, in consequence, as someone different – a zealot; not an outcast, but certainly strange and unworldly.

—⦿—

16

The Making of a Martyr

It has been my desire these twenty-four years to die a martyr for my Lord.

The Testimony of James Nicol, August 1684

What makes a martyr? What makes someone, apparently blessed with a comfortable life, a loving family and the protection of a solid community, prepared to surrender to an unseen God that most precious thing, the gift of life?

It is the first week of June 1661. Charles II has had his kingdoms restored to him for more than a year, but the early promise and spontaneous outburst of joy at his restoration has begun to pall. The promises made by the King to preserve 'a liberty to tender consciences' and to protect those with 'differences of opinion in the matter of religion' have begun to lose their integrity. Tolerance of those who have steadfastly adhered to the principles of the Covenants is wearing thin and some of those who have dared to proclaim that Crown and State have no authority over the Church have suffered the severest penalty. As he makes his solitary way across the rising uplands on his way from Edinburgh to Peebles, James Nicol ponders these things. He is almost oblivious to the motion of his horse as it plods its way onward towards Kingside Edge and into the broad expanse of Athelston Water. In recent days good men have been put to death in Edinburgh. James has not witnessed these things, but in the immediate aftermath Auld Reekie has been abuzz with talk of those events and the hearing has much affected him. On 27 May the great Marquis of Argyll, stalwart supporter of the National Covenant and its first signatory, had been beheaded in the Grassmarket by 'The Maiden', a kind of guillotine. His severed head, as James was able to observe, has been mounted on a pike high above 'The Heart of Midlothian'. It was Argyll who had placed the Crown of Scotland on the head of Charles Stuart at Scone in January of 1651, Charles at that time having accepted the Covenants. His own adherence to those Covenants had led Argyll to lend support to the government of Cromwell and, when he had travelled to London to see Charles following the Restoration, he had been arrested in the audience chamber. After some nine months confined in the Tower he had been returned to Edinburgh, where he was condemned to death for his allegedly treasonable support of the Cromwellian government. He had, by all accounts, died with great courage and Christian dignity. A few days later, on 1 June, Rev. James Guthrie and Lieutenant William Govan, valiant upholders of the Covenant, were hanged at the Mercat Cross. All three, reflected James, had been men of honour and courage and true martyrs to the truth.

Reverend James Guthrie, the son of an Angus laird, had been born into the Episcopalian tradition. He studied at the University of St Andrews for the priest-hood in the Episcopal Church and, after serving for a time as assistant Professor of Moral Philosophy at St Andrews, he was licensed for the ministry and became parish minister at Lauder in 1638, where he remained until 1649. Although he had been strong in Episcopacy in his early years, and may even have harboured thoughts of a bishopric, by the time of his arrival at Lauder he had begun to turn against Prelacy and the idea of the supremacy of the Crown over the Church. So it was that he had travelled to Edinburgh as a representative of the Parish of Lauder and went to Greyfriars Kirkyard to add his signature to the great document, the National Covenant itself. From that day he had become a passionate advocate of the Covenant and all that it stood for.

Of course James Nicol had been well acquainted with the activities of Guthrie. Lauder and Peebles were not a great distance from each other and from time to time they shared representatives to the Scottish Parliament and much else besides. In 1650 Guthrie was called to be minister of the Church of the Holy Rude at Stirling and by that time the seventeen-year-old James was experiencing the stir-rings of strong Protestantism, which was to become his guiding obsession. Guthrie encapsulated Covenanting Protestantism and had become its loudest voice. His time at Stirling had not been without problems, and not all of his flock embraced his extreme views. There had been sufficient dissention for the church at Stirling to be split into two congregations, with Guthrie as minister of one and his former assistant as minister of the other. Guthrie continued to argue for strict adherence to the Covenant and to deny that the King should have any power over the reli-gious conscience of the people.

In addition to his sermons, which attracted wide attention, Guthrie had written a number of tracts, most notably 'The Cause of the Lord's wrath against Scotland'. This brought him into conflict with authority. Although professing his continu-ing loyalty to the Crown, in it he spoke out against the claim of the King to have jurisdiction over the Church and the religious practice of the people. These views were regarded as treasonable and in due time copies of the tract were burned by the Public Hangman, an Act designed to signify official condemnation by the gov-ernment. To possess a copy was treason against the government and King. Guthrie had been arrested on a number of occasions, because of his denial of Charles as

Head of the Church. However, on each occasion he was released after a brief period of incarceration, but in spite of this he refused to moderate his views or the tenor of his sermons. In 1657 the General Assembly removed him from his position, exasperated by his continuing defiance. That same year he made his way to London where he met Cromwell. In spite of his opposition to control of the Church by the Crown, he nonetheless had remained loyal to it and actually argued for the return of the King. He had impressed Cromwell by his persistence and rigid adherence to his views, so much so that Cromwell had dubbed him 'the short man who could not bow'.

In August 1660 Guthrie met with a number of like-minded ministers near Parliament House in Edinburgh, where they had drawn up a petition to the King confirming their loyalty to him, but urging him to enforce the Covenant on England and Ireland and condemning the appointment of bishops and the use of the liturgy and Prayer Book. Aware that the meeting was taking place, the King's Commissioner, the newly ennobled Earl of Middleton, after several requests to the meeting to disperse, had sent a party of soldiers to arrest the participants. Guthrie and ten others were taken. Guthrie was imprisoned, first in Edinburgh Castle and then in Stirling Castle, where he remained for six months. He was charged with treason and twice appeared before the Privy Council in February and April 1661. In spite of a lengthy and stout defence and the misgivings of some of the Council, he was eventually condemned to die. There had been widespread dismay throughout Scotland when news of his condemnation became known. James Nicol was among those who thought it a travesty and an affront to decent Christian folk. Guthrie's steadfast defence of what he (and James) thought to be the only interpretation of the Word of God, and the denial of the right of the Crown to hold sway over the Church, now became deeply embedded in James's mind. Guthrie was noble, honourable and brave in adversity and this King Charles and his band of near-Papist cohorts were a disgrace to honest Christians. While perhaps not aspiring to the national notoriety and recognition accorded to Guthrie, James resolved to put his life in the hands of the Almighty, and as he would later say, 'if it be His will to witness to Him even unto death' – and, yes, martyrdom.

James has now reached Kingside Edge, the highest point on the road from Edinburgh to Peebles, and starts to make the long, gentle descent into the broad valley of Athelston Water, with its backdrop of the rolling southern hills, the Muirfoots and Birkscairn, Dunrig and the Hundleshope Heights in the far distance. Lying before him is Peebles, some 10 miles off. On this June day the sun shines and in the warm midday air the scents of bog myrtle, heather and heath waft across the moorland in the gentle breeze. The road ahead is deserted this day. There is no sound other than the occasional cry of the curlew and the bleating of sheep, but as he rides on, lost in thought, pondering the iniquities of recent days in Edinburgh, a new sound catches his ear. He pulls up his mount and listens. It is the sound of a lark starting to make its songful ascent into the sky. Higher and higher it rises as James watches. At that moment he recalls what he has been told of the last moments of James Guthrie before the hangman did his work. It was said that his last words had been 'I shall not die, but live. Now lettest thy servant depart in peace for mine eyes have seen thy salvation'. How honourable, courageous and sacrificial that death had been. 'I, too,' thinks James, 'would be prepared to die a martyr for my Lord and to witness to him if it be his will.' Would it not be a splendid thing to be called by God to lay down his life for Him and His glorious purpose? The lark climbs higher and higher singing on its way until it is lost to sight.

━━∘∘∘━━

17

Rullion Green

In days very different from those prior to the Union of the Crowns, when Peebles received the frequent attentions of the reigning monarch and had a role, albeit modest, in the national scene, the period following the Restoration was largely unremarkable. Parochial concerns predominated. The Town Council was exercised about the state of the weekly market, which the provost, bailies and Council considered 'is daillie more and more decaying' and that there was a risk of the meal market failing altogether. The problem was that those who should be buying and selling meal and corn were hoarding it for their own use, with the result that the price had risen to the considerable disadvantage of the poor and to the common good. As a remedy, the council 'in obedience of and conforme to divers and sundrie laudable acts of parliament' prohibited all those engaged in the meal and corn trade from holding more than was required to sustain themselves and their immediate family, in the burgh or elsewhere. Any quantity apart from that should be offered for sale at the weekly market at the current stated price, 'under panes conteaned in the saids actes of parliament'. Copies were to be made throughout the town, 'that none may pretend ignorance'. The magistrates were given the task of making regular inspections of the market and were, in particular, required to visit the meal and shoe markets and to check the weight of bread, which the provost reported was the normal practice in other burghs. The Council, somewhat doubtful of this, requested that the provost obtain written proof of this practice from the magistrates of Edinburgh. Law and order was a constant worry. In April 1662 the Council records note that 'the prophanite and lousnes' among young men and servants was a daily occurrence, often resulting in 'sad consequences' breaking out because of indiscipline and carelessness in the wearing and use of 'whingers[a]'. Their remedy was to prohibit both the young men and servants from wearing or carrying whingers. The penalty for failing to observe this order was to be 'five merks Scottes money' and the whinger would be forfeited.

On the wider Scottish stage weightier matters were afoot. In a letter dated 5 September 1661, the King had written to the Privy Council finally confirming his intention to have the Church of Scotland governed by bishops. This was proclaimed from the Mercat Cross of Edinburgh the next day and subsequently ratified by the Estates, but there was a problem. The passage of twenty-two years had broken the Apostolic Succession. Only the ancient Thomas Sydserf, formerly Bishop of Galloway and one time tutor of John Stuart, 1st Earl of Traquair, remained alive and new bishops had to be consecrated by three bishops. There was, however, a link with the English Episcopate and there had been an earlier precedent at the start of the first Scottish Episcopate. This allowed those destined for the Scottish bishoprics to be consecrated by their English counterparts. One of the principal architects of the restoration of Episcopacy was James Sharpe, the Minister of Crail in Fife. He had gone to London to represent the interest of the Resolutioners in their attempt to see the Presbyterian order retained. For whatever reason, in the course of his appointed mission Sharpe seems to have been persuaded to change his position and, although initially he did attempt to represent the Resolutioners' view, he came to accept Episcopacy. This is perhaps not entirely a surprise, as in former years he had leant in that direction. His reward was his appointment to Archbishop of St Andrews and Primate of Scotland. But his change of heart was to result in him becoming a figure of contempt and even hatred, at least as far as Protesters were concerned. In addition to Sharpe, twelve other ministers were consecrated as bishops. Andrew Fairfoul, Minister of Duns, became Archbishop of Glasgow. Of the remainder the most notable were: George Wishart, who had been Montrose's chaplain and was appointed to Edinburgh; David Mitchell, who was appointed to Aberdeen; and Robert Leighton, described as a saint of Presbyterianism and Episcopacy, who became Bishop of Dunblane. With their appointments confirmed the bishops also took their seats in the Estates, which met on 8 May 1662, and were confirmed in this return to the old order and restoration to 'their Antient places and vndoubted priviledges in Parliament'.¹ Thus was their spiritual authority once more combined with temporal power, but by the same token Parliament also confirmed the right of the King to exercise control over ecclesiastical jurisdiction. The King appointed the bishops. The bishops could control Parliament. The King ruled absolutely. Parliament now proceeded at his behest to ensure that the forces of the Covenant and Presbyterianism were severely circumscribed. On 11 June all ministers admitted to the Kirk since 1649 were suspended. Those suspended could, however, seek reinstatement under the new Episcopal regime provided they were lawfully put forward by a patron (usually the local laird), properly consecrated and admitted by their bishop. Parliament also enacted that anyone holding public office had to sign a declaration acknowledging the Covenants and any form of armed insurrection as unlawful. At its conclusion in September Parliament passed an Act of general amnesty, which set out 'that all seeds of future difference and remembrance of former proceedings may as well as his Maiestie as by his Subjects one towards another be forgotten'.[2] It was a forlorn hope. What happened in the years that immediately followed was characterised by a combination of a number of diverse factors, by overreaction on all sides, by rumour and suspicion, not least that a foreign power might intervene or at least seek to influence the course of events. All these were to result in a tide of events that would prove to be unfortunate to say the least. Introduced with enthusiasm by the High Commissioner, Middleton, the Act, which had suspended all clergy ordained since 1649, not only deprived those affected of their living, but also of the very roof over the heads of their family. Those clergy could, of course, conform and seek reinstatement under the new Episcopal order, and no doubt the threatened deprivations were intended as a powerful incentive for them to do so. Many did. They included John Hay, Minister of Peebles, no longer required to hide his Episcopal sympathies and who was thus sufficiently acceptable to the new order that he was also appointed as perpetual moderator of the Presbytery of Tweeddale by the archbishop.

In October 1662 the newly consecrated bishops summoned their respective Synods. Most accepted the new order, although some did so with a degree of reservation, particularly in relation to the forms of liturgy. In the west and south-west matters were very different. To the chagrin of Middleton and Archbishop Burnet, who had accepted Episcopacy with relish and was a 'hardliner' (he had succeeded Fairfoul who had recently died), only 32 members out of 240 attended the Synod in Glasgow; Rev. John Hay doubtless among them. In Galloway and Argyllshire there was a mass revolt and a refusal by most to accept the restoration of patronage. These clergy remained firmly in their charges, but ceased to provide the regular ordinances of religion. The primate persuaded the Council to extend the deadline for the recalcitrants to conform to 1 February 1663, but at the end of the day more than a fifth of the total clergy, around 200, resigned their parishes rather than conform. The parishes of the dissenting Protester clergy were given to the 'King's Curates', but as non-Covenanters had for years been denied access to the universities, there were few suitably qualified candidates and many of those appointed were lacking in the intellectual, spiritual and moral qualities possessed by those they replaced. As a result they gave little satisfaction to their new flocks. The saintly and moderate Bishop Leighton was later to observe that laxity in the selection of candidates and 'the negligent and indifferent throwing in upon them of any that came to hand was the great cause of all the disquiet … in those parts'.[3] As a consequence the dissenters had little difficulty in finding support from many of their former charges. A notable casualty was Middleton, whose heavy-handed approach lost him the sympathy of the King and he was replaced by Rothes. Much of the power of government, nonetheless, rested with Lauderdale, who increasingly demonstrated a lack of tolerance, which, had it been applied, might have avoided the anger and bloodshed that followed. In July he introduced an Act imposing fines on those who absented themselves from worship in the parish kirk on a regular basis, and in August further provisions were added. Dissenting clergy were to remove at least

20 miles from their former charges and not to live in any of the major centres of population. In practice these restrictions made it virtually impossible to live anywhere. Conventicles proliferated. The newly appointed curates reported those who failed to appear at the kirk. The collection of fines from those offenders was implemented, often by force. Ill feeling mounted. The Act became known as 'the Bishop's Dragnet' and merely hardened the resolve of those who refused to accept Episcopal rule. Mounting grievances gave ample ammunition to the rising number of fanatical Protester clergy. What they preached was not just freedom to practice their own form of Presbyterianism, but freedom to deny similar toleration to others. Their preaching was scriptural, but it was the scriptures of the Old Testament, with an emphasis on the destructive power of the Almighty against those who did not conform to his ways, or rather those deemed by them not to do so. The redemption of the New Testament rarely featured. Increasingly their ire was directed against those who were the cause of their distress and alienation: the government and the King.

In 1664 a force of military police, commanded by Sir James Turner and Sir Tam Dalziel of Binns, was raised on the proceeds of fines collected from kirk absentees. This force was now deployed in the south-west where the Protesters (who will from now on be referred to as 'Covenanters') were preaching armed rebellion. Fines were to be forcibly collected, or where payment was not possible soldiers were to be quartered in the households of the defaulters at their expense until the debt was satisfied. It was now that the international dimension came into play. England and Holland were at war and the Dutch saw advantage in lending support to the Covenanters, with whom they shared some religious affiliation and saw the militant elements among the Covenanters as at least an irritant to their English adversaries. The Scottish government viewed the possibility of material support for the Covenanters from the Dutch with alarm, although in actuality their alarm was misplaced. That support had more to do with rumour than reality, although the Covenanters were undoubtedly in touch with the Dutch authorities, who talked of supporting them with arms, ammunition and a sizeable subsidy if the Covenanters were to succeed in capturing the strategic centres of Stirling, Dumbarton and Edinburgh. In practice the Covenanters had nowhere near the resources necessary to achieve this, but the rhetoric of fanatical preachers raised the temperature and emotions of the common folk. The actions of the Privy Council in sending troops to the south-west provided further ammunition, while the incidence of the Great Plague of London in 1665, and the more recent Great Fire, were pounced upon as signs of divine retribution on a Godless nation and its equally Godless monarch. The situation in the south-west had become explosive. The fire of rebellion is so often ignited by incidents which on their own would be minor. On 13 November, at St John's Town of Dalry in Galloway, a party of Turner's soldiers threatened a prisoner who had refused to pay a fine. Violence followed and one of the soldiers was shot with a charge, which of all things contained broken pieces of pipe. Bizarre as this ammunition was, it proved to be the catalyst for what followed. For Turner this incident was too much, and an insult to the pride of the King's army. He determined to take action, but before he could do so, a party of fifty or so Covenanters rode into Dumfries, where Turner was quartered, and took him prisoner and thereafter advanced towards Edinburgh with him in their midst. At Brig O' Doon there was a gathering of some 700 Covenanters from Galloway, Clydesdale and Ayrshire. Most notable among the recruits was Colonel James Wallace. He was a soldier of some experience, having served in Ireland, and he had also been part of the Covenanter army at Kilsyth and Dunbar, and was able to instil some order and discipline into what was little more than a rabble. Exhorted by some preachers, the intention was to attack Glasgow, but Dalziel was barring the route and it was decided to make for Edinburgh instead, where, hopefully, contact might be made with a fleet of Dutch ships known to be lying off Dunbar. On 26 November they reached Lanark, by which time their number had grown to about 1,200, and there they once again swore allegiance to the Covenants. Their numbers failed to increase thereafter. Informal efforts were made to persuade the Covenanting army to disband, but, confident that the Dutch would come to their aid, they refused and, encouraged by preachers, who included the Rev. Alexander Peden, known as 'Peden the Profit',[4] they continued their march towards the capital. Having urged the faithful to fight for the true faith, Peden nonetheless felt it expedient to absent himself from the continuing march. Two days later they had reached Colinton on the outskirts of Edinburgh, but the capital was well guarded and Dalziel had followed them. They were forced to stand and fight at Rullion Green on the southern slopes of the Pentland Hills. A sharp action took place, which resulted in a heavy defeat. Fifty were killed and fifty more were captured; the rest fled. What was to become known as the 'Pentland Rising' had lasted no more than two weeks. The government reacted with brutality. The rebels were, in the main, simple, ignorant countrymen, badly armed and ill trained for warfare. They had believed the Old Testament rhetoric of Sandy Peden that 'the horses and chariots of Israel' would come to their aid. None did, and the government overreacted. Of the prisoners taken thirty-three were hanged, some after torture, in spite of the fact that quarter had been given to them on the field of battle. Some of the remainder were transported to Barbados.

In Peebles, just 12 miles away from the scene of the battle, news of the debacle would not take long to arrive, and the advance of the Covenanting army would have been known of as it progressed from Brig O' Doon towards Colinton by way of Lanark. No doubt the accounts of the battle, and not least its aftermath, also had a profound effect on James Nicol, raising him to anger and despair at the iniquity of what had been done to honest and God-fearing folk in the name of a Godless King and his 'Ba'al's priests'. It did nothing but harden his already strong resolve to support and if necessary fight for the true religion and the Covenants.

Chapter Note

a. type of dagger or knife.

—◦◦◦—

18

Awa, Whigs, Awa!

Our sad decay in church and State
Surpasses my descriving;
The Whigs came o'er us for a curse
And we ha'e done with thriving.
Awa, Whigs, awa!

Robert Burns[a]

The battle of Rullion Green swiftly brought to an end the Pentland Rising and the first Covenanters rebellion. In truth, in the greater scheme of things, it was a puny affair and in spite of the agitation of the government, it had posed little threat to national security. The real reason for that agitation was the knowledge that the forces of the Dutch Republic might have given support to the rebels. This produced a savage reaction in the treatment of the captured rebels that followed immediately after their ignominious defeat at Rullion Green. It was a reaction that a more thoughtful government might have avoided and where magnanimity might have produced a more worthwhile outcome. The Earl of Lauderdale and the members of his government had been severely shaken by the uprising and its implications, unrealistic as these proved to be, and it was fear for their own reputation which caused them to react with a short, sharp campaign of repression. It was a campaign which would not be forgotten and, far from extinguishing the flame of zeal for the Covenants, it merely stoked the fires of anger and resentment. The campaign of repression was an over-reaction. Many of the bishops, in response to the concerns of their clergy, tried to persuade the government to exercise restraint, but the Archbishops Sharpe and Burnet were strong in their support of the Privy Council. Perhaps the most distasteful aspect was the knowledge that many of the condemned had been tortured before suffering their final end at the hand of the hangman. Among those who suffered was a young minister, Hugh McKail. He had been severely tortured but refused to betray any of his colleagues. He was hanged at the Mercat Cross of Edinburgh on 22 December 1666. A brave man to the end, as were all those whose lives were ended on the gallows at this time, his final speech was most memorable and a fine statement of fortitude and faith:

> Farewell, sun moon, and stars. Farewell, kindred and friends. Farewell, world and time. Farewell, weak and frail body. Welcome, eternity. Welcome, angels and saints. Welcome, Saviour of the World, and welcome God the judge of all.[1]

The outcome, which in more sensible circumstances might have commanded general public approval, was in fact a wave of sympathy, to which the treatment of McKail in particular made no little contribution. As Agnes Mure MacKenzie puts it, 'the Government, having won the trifling war in the turn of a hand, and with the country's general approval, lost the peace, and heavily'.[2] Even the normally disinterested Charles, enjoying the pleasures of far-off London, seems to have been touched with concern when reports of the mounting public outcry reached his ears. It has been suggested that in a letter to Archbishop Sharpe he counselled tolerance and leniency, but that Sharpe suppressed the letter.

The situation of the government in Scotland was, to a considerable degree, influenced by what happened in England, where Edward Hyde, Earl of Clarendon was the King's chief minister. Hyde was a strong advocate of the repression of all dissenting religious factions, that is all except the Episcopalians. He was a strong supporter of Archbishop Sharpe and had great influence on Lauderdale. The storm of repression in Scotland owed a great deal to that influence. Hyde, however, now fell from grace, and with his fall the hard-line Sharpe, lacking his support, found his influence on the Scottish government severely curtailed. The ministry that followed Hyde was to become known as 'The Cabal' on account of the initials of its six members, who included Lauderdale representing the Scottish interest.

John Maitland, Earl of Lauderdale, has been described as 'coarse-fibred' and one to whom a 'cartful of oaths meant little'.[3] He became Commissioner and thus the King's representative in Scotland, which in the absence of the King made him the country's virtual ruler. Aware of the need to protect and preserve his own position, and aware of the disquiet which repression of the Covenanters had aroused, Lauderdale at this time adopted a more tolerant approach. In October 1667 an Act of Pardon and Indemnity was introduced, which sought to make some accommodation with those ministers whom previous Acts had dispossessed. The leader in the attempt to reach a compromise acceptable to the majority was Bishop Leighton. Although he was a strong Episcopalian, he believed that if a lasting peace was to be achieved, it could only be done by offering concessions. He proposed that the administrative powers of the bishops should be curtailed and, in particular, that they should revert to being constant moderators of their Synods, without a power of veto, just as they had been during the reign of James VI & I. Those ministers who accepted would be allowed to formally state that they only accepted the arrangement for the sake of peace and without compromising their basic beliefs. In spite of his recognised Godly influence, Leighton failed to convince either his fellow bishops or the government of the merits of his proposal. Lauderdale was concerned that the King would see it as an unacceptable dilution of Episcopacy, and that if he lent support his own position would be severely compromised in the eyes of the King. Nevertheless, Leighton continued to promote his ideas and might perhaps have made progress, but for an event which possibly produced a serious reaction against the factions of Presbyterianism and inadvertently did have a significant consequence in due course. This was an attempt to murder Archbishop Sharpe in July 1668 as he travelled through Edinburgh. The perpetrator was a preacher called James Mitchell, 'a youth of much zeal and piety'[4] who had taken part in the Pentland Rising. The shot that he fired missed its principal target, but his companion, the unfortunate Bishop of Orkney, was hit and crippled for life. Mitchell escaped, for the moment at least.

Regardless of this setback, Bishop Leighton continued his campaign and the government, for its part, continued to seek accommodation with the dissenting clergy. On 25 July 1669 an Indulgence was issued. This offered those clergy who had been dispossessed since 1662, and had lived peaceably and orderly since then, the right to return to their charges, including stipend, manse and glebe, provided they gave an undertaking to avoid 'seditious discourse' and to restrict themselves to activities in their own parish. The Indulgence was an attempt to create a clear separation between religious nonconformity and political dissent. In practice, although there had been no meeting of the General Assembly and bishops had been imposed, Synods, Presbyteries and Kirk Sessions continued to function much as before. There was no imposed liturgy and the form of worship practised varied widely. A few ministers used the English Prayer Book, but many others used extemporary prayers. Some 40 ministers accepted, in spite of maintaining a conscientious objection to Episcopacy, but 150 declined, because in their view the Solemn Covenant with God would be broken, and also because the link between civil and religious authority and the subordination of the Kirk to the Crown could be seen as a step back to Popery.

Thus the attempt at toleration largely failed. The ordinary folk of Whig persuasion had come to expect their preachers to combine and indeed dominate their preaching with politics, and those who came to listen to the 'Indulged' ministers were sadly disappointed to find that they now confined themselves solely to religion, which their hearers saw as 'a notable departing from those of divine assistance and called them "dumb dogs", the King's curates, worse than bishops'.[5] Nor were they alone. The Episcopalian establishment was equally disappointed. The Indulgence, which had been accompanied by an Asserting Act, appeared to allow the King to have the sole prerogative to establish whatever religion he wished. This had been introduced by the Crown unilaterally and without consultation with, or the approval of, the Kirk authorities. It provoked an outspoken protest from Archbishop Burnet of Glasgow; so outspoken that he was suspended from Parliament, but the sorely tried Bishop Leighton continued to seek an accommodation that would allow co-operation between Episcopalian authority and Presbyterianism, regardless of the lukewarm reception that his proposals had aroused. In reality the two were irreconcilable.

Parliament met in October 1669, and to further complicate an already complicated situation, Lauderdale, in his capacity as Royal Commissioner, attempted to introduce a scheme for the union of the kingdoms. This was something which met with the King's approval, much in the manner of his grandfather James VI & I, and was also supported by Scottish commercial interests, which had benefited from freedom of trade during the period of the Commonwealth, a benefit that had been lost at the Restoration. Although both Parliaments appointed commissioners, the scheme did not progress, in all probability because the Scottish body politic had no enthusiasm for closer ties with what they saw as an English body politic unsympathetic to the Scottish nation and its long-held Presbyterianism, even though this might now be in check.

The question of the Indulgences also took a prominent place in the parliamentary discussions. It was not so much the indulgence of dissenters that was the source of objection, but the question of ecclesiastical supremacy. Much to the surprise and consternation of the Council, the protest was led by none other than Archbishop Sharpe, denouncing not only the supremacy of the Pope and of the old General Assembly, but of the King himself. In response, the greatly displeased Council forced through an Act which declared:

> His Maiestie hath supream Authority and Supremacie over all persons and in all causes ecclesiasticall … the ordering and disposal of the Externall Government and policie of the Church doth propperlie belong to his Maiestie and his Successours As ane inherent right to the Croun.[6]

No doubt to save his own position (Parliament had now removed Archbishop Burnet from his see as well as from the Estates), Sharpe was persuaded to withdraw his opposition and, in turn, to persuade some of the bishops to follow him. The end result was that the Council had succeeded in upsetting almost every shade of opinion. Bishop Leighton, while refusing to accept the Archbishopric of Glasgow, was persuaded to take charge of the see as commendator while Burnet remained suspended. His first Synod was held in Glasgow and another later in the month in Peebles, the Royal Burgh once more emerging briefly into the national spotlight. Having dealt firmly with his own clergy and removed some who were unsuitable, he then tried to reach out to the 'Indulged' Presbyterians. Conferences were held, but no conclusion reached. In the absence of an accord he sent six of his most moderate Episcopal clergy to preach in the south-west. His honourable intentions were to no avail. However well-intentioned and moderate those clergy might have been, their mere identification with Episcopalianism was a red rag to a bull, provoking the attendance at their gatherings of the most extreme elements, who could see and accept no other path than the path of the Covenants.

Leighton still sought compromise by suggesting that a General Assembly should be the first arbiter in church affairs, but this was something that was unacceptable to many Episcopalians and was in danger of dividing them. At the end of the day the argument was not one about fundamental doctrine, but one of divine as opposed to secular authority over the Kirk. As so often in affairs ecclesiastical, it was politics which prevailed. Without any progress towards agreement on these issues, the voices of dissent and protest were beginning to be heard, not just in the south-west, but further afield. In Fife there was a field conventicle attended by large numbers and addressed by some of the fanatical itinerant preachers who were now emerging. In June 1670 another field conventicle was held at Hill of Beith, near Dunfermline. For the first time some of the congregation came equipped with arms and there was a small but violent confrontation with the local militia. It was an ominous portent. Not for the first time the news of these events created a climate of alarm, which was further exacerbated by a report that the congregation of the Scots Kirk in Rotterdam had given thanks for what they saw as a 'victory' at Hill of Beith. (Rotterdam and the Dutch Republic were to provide sanctuary for many of the dissenting clergy who had fled Scotland.) Once again fears were aroused of Dutch support for the Whigs and, when the Estates met in July, an Act was passed which effectively outlawed field conventicles. Dissenting ministers and laity were forbidden to preach at any meeting other than in their own house and to their family. The penalty for contravention was imprisonment, while hearers faced a fine. Preaching at a field conventicle was to be punishable by death and hearers would be fined twice the amount imposed for an indoor conventicle. Anyone accepting the ministrations of a non-Indulged minister would also suffer severe fines, as would those who failed to attend church on three successive Sundays. That these measures should be imposed by the civil authority is not so much evidence of religious fervour on its part, as a confirmation that the government was able to control the lives of the people by manipulating the Church.

In January 1671 Bishop Leighton met with the Presbyterians in a final effort to achieve a compromise solution. As he said, 'My sole object has been to procure peace, and to advance the interests of true religion ...' But what was 'true religion'? That was the problem. The Presbyterians could not accept any accommodation with Episcopacy or any acceptance of the authority of the Crown over the Kirk. Leighton's initiative finally collapsed and all attempts to unite the opposing factions were now at an end. As the decade progressed the rift grew wider and ever more polarised. The ripples of ferment, which had continued in the south-west, now began to roll out. Tolerance of the Indulged by the non-Indulged dissenters, never more than tenuous at best, evaporated amidst increasing acrimony and violence. At this point the King's brother, the Duke of York, 'came out' and announced his conversion to Catholicism. This was hardly a comforting message to send to repressed Presbyterians and naturally it raised suspicions that this might lead to the previously unthinkable Indulgence of Papists as well as Indulged Presbyterians. The spectre of universal tolerance (except, of course, of those who still adhered to the Covenants) was the final straw. This gave further impetus to the ranting of fanatical Covenanting preachers who now could cover the whole gamut of the damned to include that Antichrist, the Pope, prancing bishops and Ba'al's priests, and not least the King himself and his ministers who had promoted such an abhorrence. That said, the penal laws against the Church of Rome remained in place, although in practice, like the similar laws against Protesters, they were rarely applied. One exception was the case of the Countess of Traquair, widow of the 2nd earl, who was threatened with action because she had brought up her son in the Catholic faith (she herself had been Catholic at the time of her marriage, something which added to the tribulations of her father-in-law, John Stuart, in his fall from grace as the Commissioner of Charles I).

1673 Dec 3. At Holyrood House the Countess of Traquair compeared [ordered to appear] to exhibit her son the earl, in order to be educated in the reformed religion. The Council resolve he shall be sent to a good school, with a pedagogue and servants as the Archbishop of Glasgow shall name.[7]

In Peebles at this time, the days of royal visitations and patronage being long gone, there was little to suggest any great awareness of or involvement in the struggles for the mind and soul of Scotland. Yet, the Covenanting ferment was building up to a pitch of intensity not many miles away in the hills and glens of Dumfriesshire and Galloway, something of which the townsfolk could hardly have been unaware. A militia had been formed in the town in 1666, as in many others in the aftermath of the Pentland Rising. Its climax at Rullion Green had taken place just 12 miles distant from the Royal Burgh. In October 1668 a levy was made on the townsfolk to meet the cost of buying arms, which the Treasurer was sent to Edinburgh to purchase. There is no suggestion of any dissent in the Kirk. Another Mr John Hay, son-in-law of his predecessor of the same name, was peaceably admitted as Minister of Peebles. He had been long established in the Episcopal tradition and was to remain firm in that tradition for the next twenty years in Peebles. The town records of the time speak of much that is parochial, but loftier and more distant challenges, far from the struggle now developing on the borders of Tweeddale, do seem to have had a part, such as when, somewhat bizarrely, a collection was taken up in the Cross Kirk for the redemption of Christian captives who were suffering from slavery in distant Turkey. At a more mundane, but no doubt locally serious level, the personal behaviour of the citizens caused concern. Shortly after his admission, Rev. Hay is recorded as publicly rebuking two men 'for putting on women's clothes at a dancing; they engaged to more sober carriage in time coming'. In another recorded incident, Mr William Cock, the schoolmaster, fails to attend church for no good reason that is known and is dismissed by the Council as a consequence. In yet another, Rev. Hay seeks the advice of the Presbytery about the case of twin children, born to the wife of one Adam Russell, during the seventh month of their marriage. The Presbytery responded:

> The midwife and other honest women stated in the process before the kirk-session of Peebels that the children were not come to perfection, having neither hair or nails. Therefore the Presbytery judged the scandal to be removed, and advised the minister and kirk-session to desist from further process.[8]

In distant London, the seemingly perpetual shortage of money in the King's coffers at this time, so necessary to feed his pleasurable lifestyle, now brought about significant changes in foreign policy. The earlier confrontation with Holland had largely died down, and indeed Charles had reached an accommodation with both Sweden and Holland in an alliance against the ever more dominant France and its ambitious 'Sun King', Louis XIV. Nevertheless, sly as ever, Charles now allied himself to Louis, the Secret Treaty of Dover providing him with an annual subsidy from the French King of £120,000. In return, Charles was to renege on his alliance with Holland and to declare war against it once more. Charles also undertook to declare himself a Catholic at an appropriate time in the future. Devious to the last, the 'appropriate time' did not arrive until he lay on his deathbed.

A new Dutch war started in 1672, when, without prior declaration, an English fleet attacked a Dutch merchant fleet. This was followed by a joint invasion of the Netherlands by an English and French force, the former led by the young Duke of Monmouth, the eldest of Charles's many bastards. The invasion met with strong opposition from the Dutch forces, led by the twenty-one-year-old William of Orange, the Stadholder, who already at that tender age was a capable and experienced military commander. William would, in the course of time, become joint monarch of England, Wales and Scotland after the debacle of the short reign of James II, now Duke of York. Although not of direct concern to Scotland, as it was a purely English affair in theory, the Second Dutch War considerably alarmed the Scottish Privy Council, which still had memories of the possible threat that Holland had posed in its support of the Covenanters around the time of the Pentland Rising only six years earlier. William Carstares, a prominent Whig preacher and friend of William of Orange, who had fled the country some years before, now returned to Scotland from Amsterdam, and papers captured from him confirmed the Dutch intention of fomenting unrest once more.

In July 1673 a meeting of the Estates was called at which the Conventicle Act was extended for a further three years, and was extended so that only a parish minister could baptise children, while ordination of the clergy was restricted to those lawfully permitted to do so, that is to say the bishops.

In England, Catholicism was about to achieve short-lived legality. Regardless of what was done in his name in Scotland, Charles was at heart tolerant of religious belief. He recognised that in spite of the privations visited upon them, the Catholic community remained largely loyal to the Crown, while his brother, illegally but openly Catholic, undoubtedly sought to remove that burden of illegality from his fellow religionists. Earlier in the year the King had instructed the government to issue a Declaration of Indulgence which granted religious freedom to all in England. In September, prompted by this development, the Scottish Privy Council once again proffered an olive branch to dissenting ministers, and about eighty in parts of Lothian, Argyll and the south-west were offered the opportunity to recover their parishes and stipends, but on the same conditions as the first Indulgence, namely that they would behave themselves and avoid any political involvement. This move also brought the majority of the Presbyterian gentry back to the fold, as well as many of the more educated sort who had remained outside until now. In the south-west, however, the great mass of the Whigs once again declined to accept what was offered and steadfastly adhered to their demand that only acceptance of the Covenants throughout the length and breadth of the land could be tolerated. Ministers who accepted the new Indulgence soon found their kirks deserted and their flocks attending field conventicles for religious succour, where they were more likely to be inspired by wild and fanatical preachers whose sermons were as much about politics as about religion. They pointed out that if the King 'Indulged' those ministers, might he not also 'Indulge' Catholics in Scotland as well as England, something not to be contemplated by honest, Godly folk.

For the honourable and liberal-minded Robert Leighton, who had at last been persuaded to accept the Archbishopric of Glasgow, it was all too much. Deeply disillusioned he resigned his see and returned to live out his days in an English village where he died in 1684. A backlash was on its way and resentment of the Indulgence gained strength in both England and Scotland, so much so that Charles was forced by the English Parliament to withdraw it. In March 1673 Parliament introduced the infamous Test Act, which precluded anyone in England holding public office who did not subscribe to the oaths of supremacy and allegiance. Furthermore, it required them to partake of the Sacraments in accordance with the order of the Church of England and, more significantly, to deny the doctrine of transubstantiation, the central tenet of the Catholic Eucharist, which holds that the whole substance of the bread and wine becomes the whole substance of the Body and Blood of Christ. As a direct result, the Duke of York was forced to resign as head of the Admiralty. Regardless of his later political follies, which left such a legacy of failure, and to the demise of the Stuart dynasty, the duke had been an able naval commander, and the creation of a modern, professional navy was mainly his (aided in no little manner by the administrative skills of one Samuel Pepys). Although Charles had proved himself an able begetter of children, he had failed to do so with his Queen after ten years of marriage, and in the absence of a legitimate heir the Duke of York stood as Heir Apparent. His marriage to Maria d'Este further complicated matters as his father-in-law was like his daughter, staunchly Catholic and a close ally of Louis XIV of France.

In Scotland the rule of Lauderdale was under threat from Hamilton and also Tweeddale, who had the ear of the King to whom they reported Lauderdale's many failings. He had badly managed the whole religious issue and created trouble and strife, which might well have been avoided by a wiser leader. He was not assisted by his second marriage to his former mistress, the scheming, unscrupulous, but very attractive Lady Dysart. She was ambitious and well able to manipulate him to her will, and in reality was able to dictate the course of government, a course which was neither wise nor popular with his erstwhile colleagues or the people. By having her friends appointed or insinuated into positions of influence at every level, often to their and her personal enrichment, Lady Dysart pulled the levers of power. Realising in time that his position was highly vulnerable, Lauderdale countered the threat from the Hamilton/Tweeddale faction by proroguing the Estates. It would be 1681 before it met again. Although freed from parliamentary pressure, Lauderdale remained trapped by the opposing forces of Episcopacy and the Indulged moderates. The Episcopal Order was now firmly re-established and in the fourteen years since it was restored it had gained in strength and confidence and its bishops had become increasingly vocal. Although loyal to the Crown and the King, who had given them new life, they nonetheless resented any use of the royal prerogative that might interfere with what they considered was their sole right to set the agenda of Church government and worship. Several of the bishops demanded a National Synod, which they felt should devise a catechism, a liturgy and provide a firm definition of Church law. Lauderdale saw this as a challenge to his authority, but he had as his principal supporter the primate, Archbishop Sharpe, who sided with royal authority, as usual, no doubt as the best means of preserving his own position and power, both of which he sorely cherished. On the other side, the Indulged moderates found themselves under severe pressure from the more extreme Presbyterians and looked to the government for support. Field conventicles, in spite of their illegality, grew in number and in some parts of the country reached such a pitch of popularity that the common folk regarded them as the normal place of worship, rather than the parish kirks. Conventicles were fast becoming the equivalent of evangelist revival meetings, with emotions whipped up by fanatical, charismatic preachers, who were growing in number and, not unlike popular evangelists of later days, depended for their livelihood on the generosity of the great gatherings they commanded. Young men and women were especially attracted and attempts by roving militia to control or disperse these gatherings were met with a violent response. The Whig element was firmly under the control, or the spell, of the increasingly numerous itinerant preachers who competed with one another in their rhetoric; a rhetoric that was designed to raise their listeners to action, not least against those ministers and other followers who had committed the sin of accepting Indulgence. As the seventies progressed, conflict escalated. As a result, an Act of August 1675 issued Letters of Intercommuning against the most prominent of the non-Indulged ministers and their close supporters, some 100 in all. It was essentially a form of excommunication, debarring anyone from giving them food or lodging and was, as J.D. Mackie puts it, 'in effect a complete boycott against recalcitrants'.[9] Anyone who gave them support or harboured them was to be treated as offending in equal measure. Troops were despatched to the areas of wilder action and there were now frequent confrontations and violent skirmishes, often with fatal consequences on both sides. The south-west was descending into anarchy.

A proclamation of June 1674 had made it the duty of heritors and employers to ensure that their tenants and employees attended church and that they did not attend conventicles. Failure to do so resulted in heavy fines. As the anarchy grew, a proclamation of 1677 renewed the 1674 Act, but this merely served to aggravate the situation. On the one hand, it further alienated the Whigs, who rightly saw it as an attack on them. On the other hand it offended heritors and employers, who were threatened with fines for activities, not of their making, of which they disapproved, but in practice could not prevent. The pressures on Lauderdale and the Privy Council were enormous. Weakness on their part would be failure in the eyes of the King, but a heavy-handed response would further affront the extreme elements, who in any case needed little provocation. In this crisis anarchy could not be tolerated and it was the heavy hand that followed. Towards the end of the year the Privy Council summoned what troops it had at its immediate command, together with the various local militias that had been raised and the feudal clan armies of the north. In the spring of 1678 some 8,000 Highlanders were ordered into the south-west and remained there for six weeks. The local populace, which might have been expected to respond to this 'army of occupation' with force, did not do so, the wiser Whigs no doubt realising that acceptance of the 'occupation' was the best answer in the short term. All the same, the occupying troops were a sore burden on the ordinary folk who had little option but to give them food and quarters, which they demanded and took without recompense or consideration for the providers. Although for the most part held in check, there was rising resentment and when the Highland caterans eventually left, they treated their withdrawal as they might the lands of a defeated enemy, looting and pillaging whatever they could as had been their practice for centuries past in the many conflicts, great and small, in which they had been engaged. Looting was not confined to the produce of the countryside, but household goods and personal possessions were treated as fair game, leaving many destitute. That they were encouraged to do so by their commanders did little to abate the animosity of the people towards the government in Edinburgh, who had sent this plague upon them. The folly was that it was not just the wilder Whigs who were made to suffer, but the mass of the ordinary folk, who now, if not before, saw the King and his government as little more than callous oppressors.

Of those most closely associated with this inept and clumsy policy, Lauderdale was of course the primary target, but almost equally detested was Archbishop Sharpe, who, not for the first time, had committed an act of despicable and dishonourable conduct. In 1674 James Mitchell, the zealous young preacher who had attempted his murder some six years earlier, was apprehended. He confessed to his crime (although he later retracted) and was sent to the privations of captivity on the Bass Rock. While the Highland army was in occupation in the south-west, he was brought to trial in Edinburgh. He claimed that his confession had been made only on the promise from Sharpe that he would obtain a pardon. Sharpe denied that any such promise had been given and said that in any event his retraction had nullified it. Mitchell was duly condemned to death, but there were some who considered his trial to be less than fair. He might yet have been granted a reprieve, but Sharpe himself, in a final act of dishonour, insisted that he hang, which he duly did. The whole sorry affair did nothing other than make Mitchell a martyr and the archbishop little more than the Devil incarnate. The end result of these events was a worsening of the civil unrest in the south-west, which now began to spread to Fife, the Lothians and to parts of Perthshire. It was a fiasco for the prestige of King and government, and the policy of repression had done little other than to exacerbate an already volatile situation. Yet the lesson was not learned. Lauderdale, who was under even greater pressure, blundered again. He now sought to raise 1.8 million pounds Scots, supposedly to pay for a standing army, but also to impress the King. Regardless of whether or not Charles was impressed, this merely escalated resentment further. Many Whigs refused to pay the Cess[b] on grounds of conscience. Patrols of troops were sent to the south-west and quartered at the homes of those who refused to pay. Three troops of cavalry were despatched. The captains of the first two were the 5th Earl of Home and the 2nd Earl of Airlie, experienced soldiers both, while the captain of the third troop was a man whose name, rightly or wrongly, was to become infamous in the story of the Covenanters – John Graham of Claverhouse.

Chapter Notes

a. Whigs – the name given to the extreme Protester Covenanters, possibly deriving from West Country carters who used the word 'whiggam' to drive on their horses. Hence 'Whiggamore' in the Whiggamore Raid, which started in the west; **b**. the name given to tax assessment in Scotland.

—ᴕᴠᴕ—

The Deil of Dundee

Dundee he is mounted, he rides up the street,
The bells are rung backwards, the drums they are beat;
But the Provost, douce man, said 'Just e'en let him be,
The gude Town is well quit of that Deil of Dundee'.

With sour-featured Whigs the Grassmarket was pang'd[a]
As if half the West had set tryst to be hang'd;
There was spite in each look, there was fear in each e'e,
As they watched for the bonnets of Bonny Dundee.

From *Bonny Dundee* by Sir Walter Scott

John Graham of Claverhouse, later to be created Viscount Dundee, is one of those
historical figures whom legend has endowed with a romantic image. Yet he had a
darker side. There is the swashbuckling cavalier, loyal servant of the Stuart Kings
and gallant hero, and there is the savage represser of the Covenanters in south-
west Scotland, which earned him the name 'Bluidy Clavers'. It is probable that
both supporters and detractors have exaggerated his memory. His detractors are in
the main those who are apologists for the Covenanting cause. They have claimed
that the violent deaths of so many of the Covenanting martyrs are directly attributable to him, while supporters, including most recently Andrew Murray Scott,[1]
have claimed that only one death, that of John Brown of Priesthill, was by his
own hand, and that contrary to Covenanting legend, he was a man with a sense of
justice and not without compassion. The truth probably lies somewhere between
these two extremes, and if Claverhouse did not personally despatch more than
one Covenanter (apart from on the field of battle), then certainly those who
were under his command were responsible for many killings. These, if not actual
atrocities, were conducted often summarily, without compassion and contrary to

natural justice. The gravestones of some of the south-western martyrs bear tangible testimony, which leads to the unavoidable conclusion that he had a degree of responsibility at least for what happened. The headstone of Andrew Richmond in the kirkyard of Galston in Ayrshire records 'who was killed by bloody Graham of Claverhouse, June 1679', while that of Matthew MacIlwraith in Colmonell in south Ayrshire records 'By bloody Claverhouse I fell, who did command that I should die'.[2] 'Who did command', therein lies the crux, but Claverhouse himself was not responsible for the policy of repression, rather he was its instrument. The policy lay with the government of Lauderdale who had despatched him to the south-west with orders to track down and punish 'persons of disaffected and seditious principle', who were described as those 'who for disquiet and disturbance of the peace for divers years past deserted the public ordinances in their parish churches, haunted and frequented rebellious conventicles'.[3]

At the time of his appointment as troop commander Claverhouse was about thirty. He was a professional soldier and already had a distinguished career behind him, some of which was in the service of the Dutch Stadholder, William of Orange. From the many and varied accounts of him, both factual and fictional (Sir Walter Scott, as with many Scottish characters, was at the forefront in depicting him as the romantic hero), what emerges is a picture of a man of rigid military discipline, but a good leader of those under his immediate command, for whom he had a genuine concern. As a commander in the field he was less successful, as later events were to show, but there is no doubt that he was possessed of a strong personal integrity and sought to carry out the tasks assigned to him with firmness and fairness, whilst displaying a proper sense of justice. In this he may have been sorely tried. He was a strong Episcopalian and had a particular dislike for fanatical Whig preachers who, with their rabble-rousing rhetoric, exhorted poor country folk to disobey the law, this being the primary cause of unrest in the south-west, which he, along with others, was sent to quell. On 27 December 1678 he took up lodging at the Black Bull Inn in Moffat. What he found alarmed him. He wrote at length to his commander-in-chief, the Earl of Linlithgow, the following day:

> I am informed since I came that this country has been very loose. On Tuesday was eight days, and Sunday, there were great field conventicles just by here, with great contempt of the regular clergy; who complain extremely that I have no orders to apprehend anybody for past demeanours. And besides that, all the particular orders I have being contained in that order of quartering, every place where we quarter we must see them, which makes them fear less ... Besides that, my lord, they tell me that at the end of the bridge of Dumfries is in Galloway, and that they may hold conventicles at our nose.

Initially, Claverhouse had to confine his activities to Dumfries and Annandale, although in due course he was authorised to extend his remit into neighbouring

Galloway and Ayrshire. In those early days he had much to occupy him in an area where unrest was all too evident, with reports of increasing numbers of conventicles, many of them little more than cover for drilling and preparation for armed insurrection. Intimidation of those who attended the kirks of the Indulged or those who paid Cess was commonplace. Incitement to murder religionists other than those of Covenanting persuasion, be they Catholic, Episcopalian or even Indulged Presbyterian, was just as much a part of the sermonising of rabble-rousing preachers as the love and mercy of the Almighty, which they claimed was, in any case, reserved only for those who held to the Covenants.

Just at this time, when the fervour against the Indulged of every persuasion was reaching its height, south of the border, the country was thrown into turmoil by the 'Popish Plot'. The plot, 'uncovered' by the infamous Titus Oates, would have seen the murder of the King and a Catholic takeover of the State. In London it caused a wave of hysteria among the great and the good, who went in fear for their lives. Upwards of 2,000 Catholics were imprisoned. In Scotland the climate of fear did not pass by. All Catholics were ordered to disarm. Such priests as there were faced imprisonment, one on the Bass Rock, recently vacated by the unfortunate James Mitchell, the Whig zealot and assailant of Archbishop Sharpe. In the south-west news of the plot served to fan the flames of extremist rhetoric yet further and additional units of militia were sent there. In March 1679 Claverhouse and his deputy, Captain Andrew Bruce of Earshall, were appointed as Sheriff Deputes of Dumfries and Annandale, with increased powers to pursue and apprehend rebellious Covenanters and send them for trial. In April Claverhouse reported numerous preparations for an armed uprising. Various militias had been attacked and their arms seized. John Welsh, a prominent Covenanting preacher and a grandson of John Knox, was thought to be the leader. Like many of his kind he travelled the country with what was virtually a private army for his personal protection. The whole country from the south-west and through the Lothians to Fife was in a state of high alarm and at that moment an event happened that was to be the catalyst for the armed insurrection which followed.

Archbishop Sharpe had appointed William Carmichael as Sheriff Depute of Fife, charged with the task of rooting out Whig activists in that area. Carmichael had gone about his task with a will, harassing those who failed to attend the parish kirks. He was heavy handed and not averse to confiscating the property of his victims to his own benefit. On 3 May 1679 a group of prominent Covenanters led by David Hackston of Rathillet and John Balfour of Kinloch (Burley) were on the lookout for Carmichael hoping to settle matters with him, when they received intelligence that a far greater prize was heading towards them, none other than the hated, egocentric archbishop himself. They waited for him on Magnus Muir, near Ceres, and close to St Andrews, and there ambushed the coach in which Sharpe was travelling with his daughter. They followed alongside for some distance, first to ensure that it was indeed the archbishop and then, satisfied that it was, to bombard him with a catalogue of his crimes and the retribution of the Almighty which would fall upon him. Shots were fired. The coach stopped and Sharpe and his daughter alighted, whereupon the pursuing men fell on him and killed him, stabbing him sixteen times in the process. His daughter was also wounded, but her life was spared. With a fine degree of sensitivity, Hackston stood aside and declined to strike a blow, although, ironically, it was he alone who would be ultimately hanged for his part. With the murder complete the party withdrew to engage in a prayer of thanksgiving.

The murderers of the archbishop returned to the south-west and in the weeks that followed they embarked on a series of disturbances. The King's birthday was celebrated on 29 May, just three weeks after the murder of Sharpe. A party of Whigs led by Hamilton rode into Rutherglen, extinguishing the town's celebratory bonfire, burnt copies of the Accessary Act (which had established Episcopacy and outlawed the Covenants) and, in a further act of defiance, fixed a declaration and testimony to the market cross. Its authors were Hackston, Hamilton, John Speul, the town clerk of Glasgow, and Donald Cargill. The latter had come to prominence as a radical preacher some time before and, as early as 1662, when he was the minister of the Barony Church in Glasgow, he had provoked official wrath by preaching a sermon against the King, on the very day, 29 May, which was supposed to be a celebration of the monarch's birthday. He was ousted from his charge and became a regular preacher at conventicles. He became a wanted man and removed to the Netherlands, where he remained for several years, before returning to Scotland to become a prominent agitator once more. Having made this bold statement, Hamilton and his men retired to Loudoun Hill where a conventicle was to be held. News of this act of insurrection reached Claverhouse in Glasgow. He immediately set off with a party of dragoons, intent on disrupting the assembly, which he came upon on 1 June. Like most such gatherings this one was as much about preparation for war as for preaching, let alone worship. Reports of numbers vary, but there were probably about 400 present, including wives and children. About 50 mounted men and rather more than 200 on foot were armed. Claverhouse had about 150 mounted dragoons. Their approach had been forewarned and the preacher, Rev. Thomas Douglas, brought his sermon to a close with the words 'you have got the theory, now for the practice',[4] a clear indication that not all of his sermon had been about the love and mercy of God. Although some of the Covenanters had firearms, most had little more than homemade pikes and pitchforks. Claverhouse, no doubt confident of his ability to deal with the motley collection of apparently ill-armed rustics who faced him, took up position on the high ground of nearby Drumclog. The Covenanters, led by Sir Robert Hamilton, Hackston and Balfour, were now drawn up in formation. What Claverhouse did not know was that the ground lying between the two forces was a narrow bog. After an initial exchange of fire, Claverhouse ordered a general charge, which ground to a halt in the bog, where the Covenanters were able to set upon

the troopers, some of whom were killed, the remainder retiring in disarray, including Claverhouse whose horse had bolted as the result of a sharp jab in the belly
from a Covenanting pitchfork. As he later reported, 'they made such an opening
in my rone horse's belly, that his guts hung out half an elle, and yet he caryed me
aff an myl; which so discoraged our men, that they sustained not the shok, but
fell in disorder'.[5] As with many battles, numbers are disputed, estimates of losses
ranging from ten to thirty-six on Claverhouse's side, and those of the Covenanters
no more than a handful. In truth it was hardly a battle in the accepted sense, but
little more than a minor, though significant, skirmish. Minor or not, its effect was
electric. News of the Covenanting victory quickly spread, in the way of such
things, rampant rumour perhaps triumphing over sober truth. In any event, within
a matter of weeks the strength of the Covenanting army had grown rapidly and by
the beginning of June some 7,000 had gathered at Bothwell Brig in Lanarkshire, to
the alarm of the authorities. Such an upsurge in support came from far and wide.
The news, of course, reached Tweeddale, only a day's ride away.

Throughout the county there were stirrings of support for the Covenanters.
In Tweeddale Major Learmonth of Newholme gathered together 'a considerable
body of horse and foot'. In Peebles itself James Nicol was now resolved to action
and joined the force that Learmonth was assembling. Also in Peebles, the militia
of the shire was on the move in support of the government, having been ordered
out by the Privy Council, along with the militias of the shires of Haddington,
Berwick, Edinburgh and Linlithgow, as well as the more northerly shires of
Stirling, Fife, Perth and Forfar, to add to those of the Earl of Linlithgow. He had
a force of some 1,800 under his command in central Scotland. This, of course,
included the troops under the command of Claverhouse. In spite of the superior
quality of his troops, Linlithgow seems to have been greatly alarmed by reports of
the Covenanting army. He urgently besought the King to send troops to his aid:

> The numbers which flock to these rouges doe incress dayly, to the end his
> Majestie may send down such of his English forces as he shall think fitt, and
> make use of such other meanes for extinguishing this flam of rebellion as in his
> princly wisdome he shall judge convenient.

The King duly sent his illegitimate son, the Duke of Monmouth, north with
several battalions of dragoons. They reached Edinburgh on 11 June and a few days
later the whole government army, now assembled, set off towards Lanarkshire.
Charles, as ever, looked for compromise and had instructed Monmouth to treat
with the rebels if at all possible. It was not. Although offered a number of concessions, these were on condition that they disarmed immediately. This they
resolutely refused to do and the battle lines were now drawn.

The assembly of the Covenanting army, however, had not been a harmonious
affair. As so often in the past, the dominant ministers, which included Cargill, put

religious piety above military ability, and the usual wrangles had ensued about
who should command and what strategy should be adopted. There was no one
with real experience of military command. Sir Robert Hamilton, the 'victor'
of Drumclog, was a better student of the Bible than of the art of warfare, and
Hackston and Balfour, although adept at the minor skirmish or 'hit and run', also
lacked battlefield experience. The great mass of the army itself was, in truth, badly
trained, despite the many conventicles that were supposed to serve that purpose.
What they had imbibed in the rag tag army was a belief that the Almighty, against
whom none could prevail, was on their side, rather than the more prosaic arts of
armed combat. According to Wodrow:

> they were not only broken in their affections, but common soldiers were under
> no kind of discipline; their confusion increased, and numbers lessoned much,
> before the king's army came up … They wanted skilled officers; their arms were
> out of case; they had very little ammunition, their rising being without prior
> concert; they were in melancholy circumstances.

On 20 June John Welsh arrived from Galloway with a force of 1,000 of his followers, who were no better prepared for battle than their brethren already assembled.
The arrival of Welsh merely served to cause more debate and argument over the
selection of officers. Once more religious probity took precedence, even to the
point where any who had shown past support for the Indulged were deemed to
be unsuitable, regardless of experience and military ability, and while the dominant ministers continued to insist upon an army of purity and Godliness, many
lost patience and heart and began to drift away. By the time the government force
approached on 21 June, the Covenanting force had reduced to something over
4,000, while Monmouth had about 5,000 under his command. Although there
was no great numerical advantage on either side, the ill-trained Covenanters,
convinced of the support of 'God and his angels' as they might be, in reality stood
little chance against a well-trained and experienced adversary.

The actual conflict did not last long. It started early on the morning of 22 June.
The narrow bridge that crossed the Clyde at Bothwell was barricaded at its centre
and this was defended by a party led by Hackston, who had at his disposal one
small brass cannon as well as the muskets of his men. For his part, Monmouth
had a full complement of cannon and this provided an initial bombardment. The
Hackston force did defend their position with considerable resolution, despite
their more limited firepower, but lack of ammunition was their eventual downfall.
After a fierce firefight a party of dragoons was able to secure the bridge, which
opened the way for Monmouth's main force to cross and confront the remainder
of the Covenanting army, which was drawn up on the south side of the river
under the command of Hamilton. A wiser and more discerning commander
would have counter-attacked the emerging force, but remarkably, he held his men

back, allowing the government army to cross unchecked. There followed a rout. The disorganised Covenanters broke ranks and many, including Hamilton, fled the onslaught. The battle was over after only three hours. About 400 Covenanters were killed and in the aftermath a large number were taken prisoner. Those who escaped were scattered far and wide, seeking shelter and safety where they could in woodlands, ditches and barns, pursued by the government forces who now scoured the countryside in search of them. Some, like Major Learmonth of Tweeddale, managed to reach their homes. He was able to hide himself in an underground vault, which could be reached from inside his house, but it had an entry so well disguised that his place of concealment was not suspected. When danger approached he was able to take refuge, and this he did for several years before eventual discovery. He was tried and sentenced to death, but this was commuted to imprisonment on the Bass. He survived the revolution of 1688 and died in his own house of Newholme at the advanced age of eighty-seven. Among those wounded and left for dead was Cargill. However, injured as he was, he escaped and would shortly recover to become the effective leader of what was left of the rebels.

What of James Nicol? Nothing is known of his part in the battle. He clearly escaped the field and its aftermath and must have been able to make his way back to Peebles. As later events show, he did not go from the battle unrecognised. Thus the part he played must have had some prominence. He would eventually be apprehended, and at his trial he made no secret of his presence at the battle and his confirmation of this appears as a matter of pride. What is certain is that he was now an outlaw and was later to be included in a list of wanted men, having to suffer the indignity of being described in a royal proclamation as 'a fugitive and a vagabond'.

Chapter Note

a. crammed or packed.

20

Stones and Clouts

Men have lost their reason in nothing so much as their religion, wherein stones and clouts make martyrs.

Sir Thomas Browne

The treatment of those captured at Bothwell Brig or in its immediate aftermath was nothing short of shameful. Those not immediately apprehended made what escape they could, although many were wounded. Units of dragoons were sent to scour the countryside, tracking down those on the run to ensure that there was no possibility of a regrouping of the defeated army. In the two days following the battle, considerable numbers were rounded up and added to those taken on the field of battle, eventually totalling some 1,200. Monmouth had decreed that none were to be killed and now ordered their transfer to Edinburgh. The bedraggled company, whether fit or not, started on the long trek to the capital. Their lives may have been spared, but their treatment on the march and afterwards was appalling. Denied proper nourishment and any sort of treatment for the wounded, some did not survive the journey. An overnight stop at a farmyard near Lanark provided little relief as they were tied together in twos and threes and made to lie in the open air, while the guards enjoyed the comfort of fire and food. The next overnight stop on the bleak and exposed moorland of the Lang Whang, beyond Carnwath, was no better. Once again they were forced to lie in the open without fire and with precious little sustenance on a dark and rainy night. Meanwhile, Claverhouse and his fellow officers spent the night in Carnwath, enjoying the comfort and hospitality of the laird. It was a sorry, dispirited and broken band who reached the Grassmarket of Edinburgh next day, there to be herded into the Kirkyard of Greyfriars, where most were to remain in a state of abject misery until December.

A few days later Monmouth, accompanied by Claverhouse, returned to London. While certainly not condoning the rebellion or any of its participants, he was at least aware that much of the cause lay in the uncompromising attitude of the government. Field conventicles were a dangerous forum, but they had largely come about as a consequence of the penalties that had been imposed on those holding indoor conventicles, which, by their very nature, could not play host to the vast assemblies that field conventicles made possible, and which provided a fertile environment for rabble-rousing. King Charles, exercising a degree of understanding and wisdom, was persuaded by Monmouth to issue a third Indulgence which allowed the holding of indoor conventicles except in Edinburgh, Glasgow, Stirling and St Andrews, while continuing to outlaw those held outdoors. With some exceptions pardons were granted to everyone who undertook to live peaceably. As a result, about 800 of the Bothwell Brig prisoners were set free, but seven (including two ministers) were hanged; the ministers in Edinburgh and the others, symbolically, on Magnus Muir, the site of Sharpe's murder. The remainder, numbering now around 250, were to be shipped to the Plantations, but a worse fate awaited them as the ship carrying them to Barbados sank off the Orkneys and almost all perished. The second Covenanter rebellion was at an end.

It was not only the Covenanters that suffered. The events of 1679 heralded the final downfall of Lauderdale. In England, following the Popish Plot, the question as to whether or not James, Duke of York should be excluded from the succession on account of his rigid Catholicism was gaining momentum. To ease the pressure, Charles thought it prudent to remove his brother from the hot bed of London, and what better than to send him north to the cooler air of Scotland? On his arrival in Edinburgh it was clear to the duke, who himself had proved to be an able administrator, that all was not well and that Lauderdale was presiding over something of a shambles. He took a seat as a member of the Privy Council and there, allying himself to Lauderdale's enemies, engineered the departure of the unfortunate commissioner, who finally left the stage and ended his days in obscurity in 1682.

The disaster of Bothwell Brig had halted the Covenanting cause in its tracks, but the extreme Whig faction, licking its wounds, was far from quiescent. There was constant searching and harassment of the faithful by the King's dragoons. The principal leaders, such as Hackston and Cargill, were still at large and field conventicles still attracted huge numbers willing to risk the rigours of the law and worse. It was at this time that a new leader emerged. His name was Richard Cameron. He had been in Holland during the recent revolt. Originally a graduate of St Andrews, he had been ordained to the ministry there and had been sent back to Scotland to bolster flagging spirits. On reaching his homeland, he found that Cargill was now the lone voice of the extreme Whigs. Cameron set about reviving the civil war in his preaching, going so far as to advocate political assassination, which he viewed as having ample Biblical precedent. As Agnes Mure MacKenzie says, 'To preaching he added encouraging prophecy. The Lord would set up a sign against Anti-Christ, that starting in Scotland should go to the gates of Rome, wherefore blood should be their sign and their word No Quarter.'[1]

The extreme Whigs now came to be known as the 'Societies'[2] or 'Cameronians', and they set out to define their beliefs in a document known as the Queensferry Paper on account of an adherent of Cameron being found in possession of a copy at North Queensferry in Fife. It was a lengthy document, but the essentials were their belief that the Church of God must be established with true Presbyterian government, that Prelacy (and those who supported it) should be overthrown, and that God's judgement should be visited on all those who did not support those beliefs. On 22 June 1680, exactly one year after Bothwell Brig, some twenty mounted men led by Cameron and Cargill rode into the Dumfriesshire town of Sanquhar and, after fortifying themselves with psalm singing, pinned a declaration onto the market cross. This they called 'The Declaration and Testimony of the true Presbyterian, anti-Prelitic, anti-Erastian persecuted party in Scotland'. It was a declaration against King Charles and the Duke of York:

> a war with such a tyrant and usurper and all the men of his practice, and far more against such as would betray or deliver up our free and reformed motherkirk unto the bondage of Antichrist the Pope of Rome.

Agnes Mure MacKenzie comments, 'There is something rather magnificent about it: such casts of the gauntlet by a small resolute band have been not infrequent in our history ... nor have they always ended in swift collapse'.[3]

Once again the Privy Council was roused to a state of some alarm and more troops were sent to the south-west to put down what the Council perceived might be a renewal of rebellion. Just one month after the incident at Sanquhar, a mounted troop of 120, under the command of Bruce of Earshall, came upon Cameron and some of his followers as they rested on the open moorland of Airds Moss, between Muirkirk and Cumnock. Escape was impossible, but the Cameronians stood their ground and refused to surrender. The action was brief. Some, including Cameron, were killed and a further five who were badly injured were taken prisoner. These included Hackston of Rathillet. The head and hands of Cameron were cut off and taken to Edinburgh, where they were handed over by the officer in charge with the words, 'There are the head and hands of a man who lived praying and preaching, and who died praying and fighting'. So ended the brief but dramatic career of Richard Cameron, although his name would live on into the latter part of the twentieth century in the regiment that bore his name, and in the tradition that allowed the Cameronians to carry arms in church, the only British regiment to be allowed that privilege. Hackston, who had stood by at the murder of Sharpe, was executed in Edinburgh on 30 July after he had been drawn backwards on a hurdle to the Mercat Cross, where his hands were cut off before he was hanged, taken down while still alive and disembowelled. His head was severed and placed on a high pole alongside that of Cameron. In an age that was still violent, authority seems to have held the view that violence could only be deterred by more extreme violence.

These events left Cargill as the leader of the Cameronians and at his instigation pamphlets were widely distributed, which promoted further rebellion and justified the murder of those he judged to be the opponents of the true religion. At a conventicle at Torwood, near Falkirk, Cargill formally excommunicated the King, the Duke of York, Monmouth and leading members of the government, as well as Tam Dalziel of the Binns and Sir George Mackenzie of Rosehaugh, the latter two playing a prominent role in the rounding up, interrogation and condemnation of prisoners. Conventicles were held quarterly at Talla Linn near Tweedsmuir in upper Tweeddale, at which Cargill was a frequent preacher. There is a narrow valley nearby which is named after him and is known as 'Donald's Cleuch'. In June 1681 he preached at a conventicle at Holms Common near Broughton in Tweeddale, only 11 miles from Peebles itself. Originally it had been planned to meet further west, near Tinto in Lanarkshire, but the militia were alerted and had gone to the site of the proposed meeting, causing a rapid change of plan. News travelled fast and Cargill, and those who were with him, walked over the Culter Hills to Holms Common, some 8 miles away, where the faithful reassembled.[4] One month later, in July 1681, he was caught, maintaining before the Council that it was lawful for a man to kill another if called upon by God to do so. Cargill, like so many of his kind, was in no doubt that he had a direct line of communication with the Almighty. He was hanged on 27 July, leaving the Societies and Cameronians devoid of leadership – for the time being at least.

On the day following Cargill's execution, the Scottish Parliament met. The new High Commissioner was the Duke of York. In England the attempts to exclude him from the succession had failed and, at his behest, the Estates now passed an Act in which the right of succession to the Crown of Scotland by lineal descent could not be barred on religious grounds. Later in the month an Act was passed which required every holder of a public office to take an oath of loyalty to the King and Church, and to declare the Covenants to be unlawful. This was the infamous Test Act, which in time would be the cause of repression and the death of many. It caused a wave of protest, not least because it required acceptance of royal supremacy in all civil and Church affairs, in addition to acceptance of the Reformation Confession of 1560, and it made taking up arms against the government unlawful. The issue of royal supremacy was equally unacceptable to Episcopalians and Presbyterians. Several of the high officers of State, including the Lord President, Sir James Dalrymple, refused to take the oath. The Church, led by the normally quiescent Bishop Scougal of Aberdeen, sent a formal protest, which was supported by the dioceses of Dunkeld and the Isles. Some eighty Episcopalian ministers resigned their charges rather than take the oath. All shades of Presbyterians, both moderate and Whig, objected, as of course did the Catholics. To quote Agnes Mure MacKenzie again, 'Never in the history of Scotland has an Act of Parliament been so broadly disliked'. For once reflecting the general mood, the Cameronians ceremoniously burnt a copy of the Act at Lanark the following January.

Not only did the Test Act cause protest, it also caused confusion, and indeed the wording of the Act seemed to have many inconsistencies within it. Few, if any, were acquainted with the Reformation Confession, which had lain long years unused and unknown even by the scholars of the Church. Nowhere was confusion more evident than in Peebles. Such was the lack of understanding that the provost and magistrates felt obliged to present a petition to the Privy Council. This stated that the petitioners were anxious to take the Test, but as Peebles was a small, and in their words 'remote place', and the petitioners were 'ignorant and illiterate', they could find no one who could advise as to the difference between the Act of Parliament and the Act of Council. And as they did not have the Act of Parliament or the Confession of Faith that was referred to, they 'humbly' requested time to take advice. Because they could not be without magistrates, they had gone ahead with the annual election in the normal way and hoped that it would be time enough to take the Test in the January following. However, as soon as they were in a position to understand the Act of Parliament, they were perfectly willing to take the Test when and wherever the Privy Council might agree. They went on to affirm that they had always been very loyal and ready to serve the King on all occasions, and among other instances their 'care and diligence in the late rebellion' (the Battle of Bothwell Brig) had been noted by the Privy Council, 'who did the petitioners the honour to return them their particular thanks therefor'. What they now asked was that the provost and magistrates might take the Test in the presence of a member of the Privy Council and then be authorised, in turn, to administer the Test to the remaining magistrates and councillors before a date to be set. The Privy Council heard the petition and appointed one of its members to administer the Test to the provost, bailies and the treasurer, and agreed that these magistrates could deliver the Test to the remainder of the Council. They were to report back to the Privy Council before the third Thursday in December. The Test was duly administered to the provost, one of the bailies and the treasurer, and they then proffered it to the remainder of the Town Council, who met for the purpose in the Tolbooth of Peebles on 28 November 1681. Of the seventeen members of the Council, four declined. They were William Scott, who was then Dean of Guild, Alexander Jonkinson, James Grieve and Archibald Shiell. Strangely this does not seem to have affected their position, as all four appear on the list of councillors in office in October 1682, and of those four, Scott, Jonkinson and Grieve were all re-elected at that time, which is curious given that failure to take the Test was a bar to office. It could, of course, be that an initial act of courage crumbled under the pressure of threat and coercion, or that a moral standpoint was easily corrupted by the advantages and privileges of office.

What now of the loyalty of Peebles? In response to the second Covenanter rebellion a detachment of the local militia, equipped with arms supplied by the town, had responded to the government's call and had been present at Bothwell Brig, something for which they had received recognition and thanks. The petition to the Privy Council had been at pains to explain the collective willingness of the Town Council to take the Test (if they could understand it!) and its loyalty to the King, to serve him, and yet when it came to the point, that was clearly not a universally held view. The reality seems to be that once again Peebles was a town, if not divided, then certainly not of one mind. It was probably not very different from many communities in Scotland at the time, especially those influenced to a degree by rebellious activity not far off, and the knowledge of the response, which amounted to little more than atrocities committed in Edinburgh, which might be considered a step too far. Within the county there is certainly evidence of Covenanter activity, much to the concern of the Presbytery of Tweeddale, as the following minute confirms:

7th April 1680. This day, the Presbytery taking into consideration the frequent and rebellious meetings there are amongst them, where persons who have been intercommoned since the rebellion in the year 1665, now go publicly to other persons' houses, and take upon them to preach in the doors and entries of the houses where they are reset, at all which meetings there are several hundreds out of doors, who either have been at Bothwell Bridge themselves, or frequent the company of such; and their meetings being new-kindled fire in this place of the kingdom, where never any rebellious meeting of this nature formerly was, they humbly crave advice from the archbishop and Synod what to do in such cases.[5]

Even within the bounds of the Royal Burgh there were known Whig sympathisers, of whom, of course, James Nicol was the most prominent. However, in spite of the Presbytery's appeal, they seem to have remained unmolested.

In 1682 at a conventicle held at Talla Linn, not 15 miles from Peebles, a young man called James Renwick was chosen among others for the ministry by the United Societies, and was to be sent to study at the University of Groningen in Holland. In 1683 he would return and raise the banner of the Covenant once more.

———⟨✺⟩———

21

The Great Conventicle

James Nicol referred to the Presbytery by the kirk-session of Peebles as one who has a child long unbaptised, withdrawing himself also from the ordinances of the Church, keeps conventicles, and is disobedient to the kirk-session. He to be summoned pro secondo, and if he does not compear the Presbytery will summon before the archbishop and Synod.

Records of the Kirk Session of Peebles

It is 11 October 1682 and it is hardly yet light on this autumn morning, the twilight before the dawn. The moon still sheds its light as a silver sheen on the fast-running waters of the Tweed as it flows by Peebles. As it is not a time of great danger to the town, the West Port stands open, even at this early hour. A small party mounted on horseback makes its way through the still sleeping streets and out through the open gate, heading westwards towards Manor. The mounted group is James Nicol and his family, James himself riding on a good Border horse, as is his wife Jennet, while their children Jennet, John and James follow behind, although Jennet and John are hardly children now. Their destination is Talla Linn some 15 miles distant in the Tweedsmuir hills. Although the town at this early hour lies seemingly asleep, eyes are watching. Always eyes are watching these days. James Nicol makes no secret of his loyalty to the Covenants and it is known that he has been at Bothwell Brig. He is a marked man, although he is not without the sympathy and support of at least some of the townsfolk. He is one of those about whom the Presbytery has been concerned and who, as they have said, 'preach in the doors and entries of the houses' and frequently attend rebellious meetings. It is difficult for the little party to depart in silence. They turn south out of the West Port and across the old bridge over the Tweed, the sound of horses' hooves ringing out in the still, frosty air as they strike the cobbles of the bridge. Their route takes them past the Cowparks and on by the gait to Manor, up and over the Sware to ford the Manor Water close to its junction with the Tweed, and then along the Manor Valley, passing the tower of Castlehill and then the tower of Posso as they ride towards Manorhead, the hills rising ever more steeply on either side. The road itself now climbs steeply below the rocks of Bitch Craig and then by Redsike Head, reaching the summit at Black Rig before beginning the more gentle descent into Ettrick Forest and Megget. This is the self-same route taken by King James V on that fateful journey some 150 years earlier, which culminated in the demise of Cockburn of Henderland. Such thoughts have no place in the mind of James and his fellow travellers. Their route does not lie by Henderland, but follows the Megget Water to its source by Meggethead in the higher hills. It climbs on and up to the watershed, finally reaching the point where the Talla Burn plunges steeply down the Linn itself in a series of rushing cascades, which fall to the linnfoots and the valley of the Talla Water beyond. On either side of the Linns the hillsides climb steeply to Garelet and Garlavin Hills to the south, and the equally steep slopes of Fans Law and Muckle Side to the north. The eastern approach at the head of the Linns is guarded by pickets. These are numerous and armed, with their mounts tethered close by. Some are placed high on the rising ground on either side of the narrow valley, ready to descend if need be. All are ready to repel unwanted intruders. Claverhouse and units of his marauding militia are known to be in the vicinity. At the north of the valley, at the Linn foot, more pickets are similarly disposed, sufficient in number to cut off any intrusive attack from the valley beyond to the west. Indeed such is the nature of the terrain that any attack from east or west can be repelled. The pickets have a broad and distant view of any approach from Megget, while to the west there is a clear view for several miles down the valley toward Tweedsmuir. Even the sides of the valley are too steep to allow any attack from above. It is a place of almost perfect natural security for the vast congregation assembling from all around.

Since reaching Megget, James and his little party have been joined by many others coming from Selkirk, the Forest of Ettrick and Eskdale. On reaching the crest of the Linns they see that already there are many gathered on either side of the water. Rather more are heading up the valley from Tweedsmuir, many having travelled from Dumfries and the towns and villages, not to mention ferm touns, which lie between. There are folk from Lanark to the west and upper Tweeddale and the broad valleys to the north toward the Pentland Hills. It would be said later that upwards of 5,000 men, women and bairns were at Talla Linn that day. These are mainly country folk and their families, shepherds and labourers, with a sprinkling of minor lairds and burgesses such as James. All are there to hear what they believe to be the true message of the Almighty, spoken by men of fervent if fanatical passion. Apart from the preaching, which will form the lengthy centre-piece, there is business to be done. It is not just the watching pickets who have come armed. The majority of the menfolk carry some form of weaponry, if for nothing else than to show their determination to defend their beliefs by force if necessary. James, like many, is armed. The Town Council has ordered that as a burgess of Peebles it is his duty, and has been these several years past, to be fully armed and to provide and have in readiness sufficient arms, which they had specified should be a pick and a sword, or a musket and firelock. He had, of course, seen action at Bothwell Brig and it is perhaps ironic that in fulfilling his obligations to the Royal Burgh, he has equipped himself with the very weapons that had been used on that occasion and which, if used again, would be against the forces of the Crown, which Peebles for its part sought to support. Those who are best armed and horsed take up position on the outer edge of the assembled crowd. Many stand bridle in hand to make rapid defence, should the need arise.

With such a mighty gathering from all the airts, this is an opportunity for the leaders to discuss strategy and points of controversy, and such business as needs attention before the preaching begins. As a recognised supporter of the cause, and one who has been prepared to stand up for his beliefs in a town which was less than enthusiastic for the Covenants, and as one who had made himself prominent at Bothwell Brig, James is part of this inner circle. On this day James Renwick, later to become the last martyr to the Covenanting cause, has been chosen, along with William Boyd, John Nisbet and John Flint, for the ministry by the United Societies. They are to study at the University of Groningen in the Netherlands and here at Talla Linn they received the approval and blessing of their peers and lengthy admonition of their duty to preserve and fight for the Covenants. This conventicle will last three days, the day before the Sabbath being for assembly and preparation. On the Sabbath itself there will be much preaching, and what preaching and what a congregation! There will be many an empty kirk on this Sabbath. At places such as Tweedsmuir, close by and yet in Tweeddale, they are strong for the Covenants. There will be no public worship in the kirk of Tweedsmuir this day. It is said that all the elders are here at Talla Linn.

Early on the Sabbath morning, cold as it is this autumn day, the great congregation is called to worship and all round the narrow valley the sound of the psalms reverberate round the hills in a great wave of sound, so loud that the roar of the waters of the Linn are quite drowned out. The preacher has mounted a rocky eminence towards the top of the Linn, as is common on such occasions, from where he can be seen and not least heard above the babbling of the tumbling water. His voice is strong from much exercise in wild places. Even on a chilly autumn day, the power and eloquence of his preaching can warm the coldest spirit and inspire to zealotry. God had turned his face from all transgressors of this world, except, that is, his honest stalwart folk as are assembled here and their brethren of like mind. Christ stood by them, his wounds exposed, the man of sorrows. And were they not nearer to him here in this mountain sanctuary than in any prelate's kirk with its flummery and false priests? They were a remnant, a maligned and oppressed remnant of the Elect and God's faithful folk; but a remnant who, like the Israelites before them in Egypt and Canaan, had met the oppressors and had triumphed with the aid of God and his angels. They were now oppressed by gluttonous, perjured prelates, who rode about in much pomp and circumstance, and by Charles Stuart, who had been crowned at Scone in acceptance of the Covenants, but who now usurped kingship and claimed lordship of the Kirk, of which Christ only was the true head. And he was aided by evil, self-seeking ministers of State, who carried out a tyrannous oppression on his behalf. Worse still, his brother, the Duke of York, he who had been long suspected of Papacy, had the gall to openly flaunt his adherence to that abhorrence, the Church of Rome and its leader, that Antichrist, the Pope. It would not be long yet before now-skulking Papists would be Indulged and there would be toleration of all that should not be tolerated in this day. All these were the children of the Evil One, and Auld Nick would soon be peering out of the mouth of Hell, with hate in his heart, but laughter in his face. And yet all here assembled are the last bastion against the evil army, but in the fight to come, as come it would, they should be resolute and strong. God and His angels are with them. The horses and chariots of Israel will fight on their side.

Although the sermon was lengthy (approaching two hours in length), liberally littered with quotations from the Old Testament, dwelling long on the Book of Deuteronomy and the crushing of the opponents of Israel, the assembled faithful listen in rapt silence, none more so thari James. Here was the way. Here was righteousness. Here was power against the oppressor. Here was the promise of the Almighty. The preacher reaches his final peroration and at last falls silent, exhausted by his own oratory. For some moments a great silence grips the vast congregation and for a time the noise of the babbling water cascading down the Linns can be heard, and then a great sigh echoes round the valley. Whether it was the result of pent-up emotion or simple relief, it engulfs the assembled company. This is the 'holy groan', a phenomenon much reported from other similar gatherings.

Other preachers follow throughout the day. Their theme varies little, but their fanatical eloquence continues to stir the crowd. The day closes with a celebration of Holy Communion, not dispensed to all, for the doctrine of original sin of mankind and its continuing failure to achieve perfection dictates that only one half of those present are worthy of receiving the Sacrament, the remainder being judged sinners and not worthy to sup at the Lord's Table. The following morning, before the company disperses, there will be a service of thanksgiving, accompanied by further preaching before the faithful may make their way homeward, rejoicing in the cause of the Covenants and ready to meet any challenge to them. On this occasion, Claverhouse and his militia have been unable to intrude, although they are not far off.

1682, June – Claverhouse nearly captured at the Crook by hillmen returning from their quarterly convention at Talla Linns.

Extract from the Records of Tweedsmuir Parish Kirk

——∽∽∽——

22

A Fugitive and a Vagabond

By this conquer.

Inscription on one of the four communion cups of Peebles

The arrival on the Scottish scene of the King's Commissioner, James, Duke of York, precipitated a change in the administration. Gordon of Haddo became Chancellor and Queensberry became Treasurer. Both were closely allied to the duke and were fervent supporters of the Test and universal adherence to it. Like those whom they succeeded in office, they regarded all Presbyterians as being tarred with the same brush, and failed to appreciate that Cameronian Whigs were far removed from the more moderate body of their Presbyterian brethren, who were law abiding and opposed to rebellion, much as they disliked the present order. The south-west still remained a hot bed of extremist dissent, albeit much muted in the aftermath of Bothwell Brig. The government, having appointed Claverhouse as Sheriff of Wigtown, and Steward Depute of Dumfriesshire and the Stewartry of Kirkcudbright and Annandale, despatched him to the area again with orders to apprehend and punish all who attended conventicles rather than the Parish Church, and all who gave help and sanctuary to rebels. He was empowered to arrest and try offenders, although the power of sentencing was to remain with the Privy Council. Prior to his appointment, the Privy Council had issued a proclamation that required landowners and heritors to inform of any conventicle held on their land and heavy fines were to be imposed in the event of failure to do so. This was subsequently taken further when an Act for Securing The Peace of The Country was passed in August 1681, in which employers were to be made liable for fines imposed on servants, while heritors were to be liable for those imposed on tenants. To his credit, Claverhouse had a sense of justice and while a loyal servant of the Crown he carried out his duties with diligence; nonetheless, he made known his feelings about such extreme measures. To the Treasurer, Queensberry, he writes:

> It is unjust to desire of others what we would not do ourselves; I declare it a thing not to be desired that I should be forfeited and hanged if my tenant's wife, twenty miles from me, give meat and shelter to a fugitive.

The Commissioner and the Council, far removed from the sharp end of their policies, had little concern for the hardship and harsh treatment of the ordinary folk, which were their result. Claverhouse, at the sharp end, at least had concerns that the implementation of those policies was likely to exacerbate an already inflammatory situation rather than dampen the flames, even though he was a strong advocate of the proper execution of the law. Replying to a letter from Queensberry he writes:

> The way that I see taken in other places is to put lawes severely against great and small in execution; which is very just: but what effects does that produce but mor to exasperate and alienat the hearts of the wholl body of the people; for it renders three desparat wher it gains on[e]; and your lordship knous that in the greatest crymes it is thought wisest to pardon the multiud and punish the ringleaders.

In another letter he writes:

> It will be mor of consequences to punish on[e] considerable laird than a hundred little bodys. Beseids, it is juster, because these only sin by example of those.

Claverhouse pursued his instructions diligently and with as much justice as he was able. In practice his was a reign of terror, at least in the eyes of the beholders and in the inevitable hearsay and rumour which spread abroad to the rest of Scotland. In any event he was able to impose order once more, at least on the surface, and in March 1683 he felt able to advise the Council that the prospect of another rebellion had been extinguished. He now took leave of absence to spend some time in England. At this point, lacking his advice, the Privy Council decided upon a further turn of the screw, setting up a series of Circuit Courts, which were given the task of seeking out and punishing any sign of deviation from the prescribed order. Unlicensed preachers were a particular target and all ministers were to be scrutinised to ensure that they adhered to the strictures of the Indulgence, and that their sermons were strictly non-political. Travel was to be restricted and anyone travelling more than 3 miles required a pass, this being an attempt to control the movement of itinerant preachers, but it merely served to upset those who were going about their lawful business. Such was the nature of the countryside that it failed to deter those, like the Cameronian Whigs, who remained intent on pursuing their own agenda. It certainly did not deter the likes of James Nicol, who continued to travel the country in pursuit of his merchant enterprise.

The Test Act was extended to apply to anyone over the age of sixteen and this in itself became perhaps the most notorious and hated aspect of the policy. Poor country folk, in all probability ignorant of the implications, were challenged to say whether or not they accepted the required oath of affirmation. Any failure to confirm acceptance might and often did lead to dire consequences, which resulted in the years 1684–85 becoming known as 'the Killing Times'. Far from achieving the intended result, these policies served only to once again fan the flames of indignation and rebellion. In September 1683 James Renwick returned from his time of study in Holland and immediately set about reinvigorating the faithful. At a conventicle at Darmead, near Newmains in Lanarkshire, on 23 November he preached his inaugural sermon to a congregation of several hundred.

James Renwick was born in the Dumfriesshire village of Moniaive in 1662, the son of a weaver. In spite of their lowly background his parents were able to ensure that he had a good education, which allowed him to attend Edinburgh University. From an early age he had a vivid interest in the Bible and it was said that at the tender age of six he was able to read, understand and even question its content. University life was almost his undoing as its social life, as for many before and since, proved a greater draw than study, and at that time he even began to question his religious beliefs. It was the execution of Donald Cargill, which he witnessed, that changed all that and determined him to follow the Covenanting path, endorsed at the Talla Linn conventicle in October 1682, and his ordination to the ministry in Holland the following year. In the next few years he would become an outstanding leader of the Covenanting cause, eventually suffering martyrdom in 1688, the last to do so.

Violence and disorder was a feature of the times. Conflict with the 'Auld Enemy' might be over, but at a parochial, as well as a national level, personal hostility and violence was never far from the surface. At a time when wild preachers could advocate murder and mayhem it is little wonder that ordinary folk did not infrequently resort to physical settlement of disputes. The records of Peebles of the period are full of incidents of violent confrontation, which the Town Council and the Kirk Session sought to control. The Council exercised civil authority, while the Kirk Session set itself to uphold the moral fibre of the community, although neither was entirely successful. On the domestic front the Council exercised control over almost every aspect of daily life, be it markets, commodity prices, personal behaviour, cleansing of the streets, control of livestock, or who might work in the town and even who might live in it. Control of the price of comestibles did not escape the Council's attention. For example, everyone in the burgh who bought or sold eggs should do so 'in all tyme comeing for sextein pennies the dussone'. The penalty for contravention was a fine of 'fourtie schilling'. All ale was to be sold for 'sexteine pennies the pynt', while bakers and sellers of bread were to make sufficient loaves 'of ane pound, for tuelve pennies the piece'. The price of services was also a matter for its jurisdiction. Shoemakers were required to charge no more than 'eight pennies' for single soled work and not more than 'twelve pennies' for double soled. Price control is not new.

Personal discipline, especially in the area of personal morality, was largely the concern of the Kirk Session, but the Council had or took upon itself powers to order the behaviour of the citizens. In practice there was a degree of overlap between the two bodies and indeed some members of the Kirk Session were also members of the Council. The latter had a particular role in deciding who was fit (or unfit) to qualify for the status of burgess and freeman (there seem to have been no free women!). The councillors conferred this status but could also remove it, as sometimes they did. Who might or might not undertake trade in the town was a matter for Council approval. It also required their consent for anyone to take up residence in the burgh. 'Outland' men and woman were those who, as the name suggests, lived furth of the burgh. Their presence and activities in the burgh were regulated. One entry records that Thomas Rankine was licenced to take a house in Peebles provided that he 'always being serviceable in his calling and not to be burdensome', failing which he could be removed at the Council's pleasure.

Like many a town of the period, livestock and humanity were thrown together and animals could be a considerable problem when not properly controlled. Sometimes the Council had to take firm action in an attempt to remedy a somewhat intractable situation, which was compounded by the indiscriminate dumping of manure and ordure in the streets, blocking drains and gutters to the resigned discomfort of the townsfolk. Roving swine were a particular problem. Uncontrolled, they rootled in the ordure, spreading it further, and their presence in the narrow wynds could be a hazard to anyone passing on foot or even upended into the filth following contact with the lively animals. One order of the Council decreed that anyone in the town who had any pigs was required to keep them within 'cruives [pigsties] or houssis, and keep their neighbour skaithless [without damage]'. The penalty for the first offence was to be 'tuentie schilling' and 'so furth, doubland the samyn, toties quoties, over and above payment to the pairtie skaithed of the skaith'. In August 1678 a fine of ten pounds Scots was to be imposed on anyone permitting swine to go outwith their own home or close. This does not seem to have solved the problem and as time went by roving pigs had become a more general hazard to the townsfolk. The Council was obliged to take action again on 26 January 1680, following complaints made to the bailies and Council about the 'skaith[a]' done by swine within the burgh as a result of their going loose up and down the town. They ordered that anyone owning pigs must keep them within their own house or close, with a fine of half a crown as the penalty for failure to do so. Even poultry were the subject of orders by the Council. All who had 'any foulles to cause ather clog them or clip ane of their winkes'. More draconian measures were found necessary 'considering the predudice and wrong occasioned by the scraiping of foulles in the houssis and yairds', and the Council ordered that all who had 'henes or capons put and tye such weight of tymber to the foote of the saids foullis as will hinder them from flieing'. The penalty for failure was a fine of 'foure schilling Scotts' to be paid by the owner of each 'foulle going without that cloige'. Furthermore, if any person found a hen or capon 'without that cloige' then that person could take the offending bird and dispose of it as he or she thought fit, and without recompense to the owner. Two parts of the proceeds of these fines were to go to the public purse and the remaining third part was to be retained by the officers 'for thair paines'. If thereafter 'foulles' were found in their neighbours' 'cornes'[b], or upon their neighbours' houses, the owners of the 'cornes' were entitled to kill the offending poultry without need to recompense the owner, whilst the owners themselves would be required to pay a fine 'for each transgressions foure schilling for each foull so found transgressing'.

In March 1682 there was a riot in the town. It had nothing to do with the Covenanting troubles, but is certainly indicative of a volatile populace; and the government was well aware this was the case in a large part of the country. Any escalation could once more drive the authorities into a state of alarm. In this particular case, although the disturbance had an entirely local genesis, in due course it did involve the Privy Council. Its roots lay in a decision by the magistrates to let a small area of the town's common grazings by public roup[c]. Traditionally it was the right of the burgesses to graze their livestock on the common at no cost, although magistrates claimed the rent would be used to defray public costs and also to augment the Common Good fund, as, strictly, they were entitled to do. The good citizens thought otherwise and on 1 March an irate mob gathered and invaded the Tolbooth where the magistrates were sitting and threatened violence, not least to the provost who 'would be lyke proveist Dickisone who was sticted'. (Dickisone, a provost of an earlier era, had been beaten up and murdered in the High Street in 1572.) Two of the ringleaders were promptly arrested and imprisoned, but later in the day the mob returned and invaded the prison, releasing both, but no sooner had they done so than they were re-arrested along with their rescuers. The following day a group of women 'did in a most tumultuary and irregular way' manage to free the two ringleaders and their rescuers and the whole party proceeded to the town cross, where about 300 townsfolk were gathered and, amid considerable disorder and much to the consternation of the magistrates, drank to the health of the rioters as 'protectors of the liberties of the poor'. Some of the company even went so far as to gather stones at the cross, threatening to stone to death anyone who opposed them. The Council appealed to the Privy Council and the principal rioters were taken to Edinburgh to appear before the Privy Council, who committed them to the Tolbooth of

Edinburgh for an indefinite period. They also had their burgess rights removed. The magistrates were authorised to call 'the haill rest of the inhabitants that were accessory to the tumult and ryot libelled and to proceed against them therefore in fyning, imprisonment and ryveing[d] their burgess-tickets as they shall find cause'.[1] The 'hot heads' were immediately dealt with accordingly, but the ringleaders petitioned the Privy Council for their freedom, pleading that 'they were poore ignorant men, who did not think they could have given offence to the magistrates of Peebles, and are willing to undergo any censure'. They were freed on 31 March on giving caution for good behaviour and ordered to appear before the magistrates to 'acknowledge their fault and crave pardon'.[2] As a result of the riot some fifty-nine people, including a number of women, were fined for their part in what had clearly been a serious breach of public order.

Perhaps more significantly in the wider national context, and continuing the policy of suppression of any who might be deemed a rebel or a supporter of the rebel cause, the government had gathered a list of some 2,000 names of wanted men and women. A royal proclamation of May 1684 charged all these with rebellion and flight from justice. It went on to declare that if any should give themselves up before 1 August, and having proved that they had taken the Test, they would be given a free pardon. The list of fugitives who belonged to Peeblesshire contains twelve names. Most come from the smaller settlements and ferm touns of the shire, but among them is the name of James Nicol, described as 'vagabond in the said shire'. Although his own later testimony throws some light on his activities, this is the first official reference to him since 1665, when he was called before the Kirk Session for his Covenanting activities.

Shortly after the issue of the royal proclamation something occurred in Peebles for which there remains no relevant explanation. It should be borne in mind that while Episcopacy in its particular (and rather odd) Scottish form still held sway, not least in Peebles, there was a rising tide of dissatisfaction with the King and his government, which only the severest repression seemed able to hold in check. It was at this time that four new silver chalices or communion cups were presented to the Kirk of Peebles. Was this intended as a statement of support for the Episcopal order and for the King who had imposed it? Nothing is known of the reasons. Of the four cups, two were presented as a result of bequests by two gentlemen who were natives of Peebles, but who had gone on to achieve high office in the capital city of Edinburgh: one, Alexander Williamson, as provost of the city, and the second, John Govan, as Treasurer. Alexander Williamson was almost certainly a descendant of those Williamsons who had been provosts of Peebles and had played a prominent role during the period both before and after the Commonwealth. The third cup originally bore no inscription, but there is an entry in the minutes of the Town Council of Peebles for 14 July 1684, which records[3] that, 'The Councell now resolved to allow ane of the four communion cups, and ordain the Clerk to deal with Captain Cockburn therefor'. It has been long accepted that this third cup was indeed the gift of the Council, which must be a powerful endorsement, not only of the town's support for Episcopacy, but also of its loyalty to King Charles II, its instigator and defender in Scotland. The fourth cup bears the inscription (translated from Greek) 'By this conquer'. Conquer what or whom? It was presented by Mr John Hay, the Rector of Peebles and Manor. Mr Hay was, of course, a firm Episcopalian and the inscription on this cup gifted by him must surely also be interpreted as a bold statement of the power of King and Church. Taken together, these gifts show that whatever the ripples and rumbling that touched Peebles, as in so many parts of Scotland, the powers-that-be in the Royal Burgh were in no doubt of where they stood, even if some of their citizens might not agree. One who without doubt did not agree was James Nicol. Where had he been in the time following Bothwell Brig? It seems that in spite of being labelled a fugitive and a vagabond, he had in fact been able to go about his business as a merchant, travelling the country, not only in Scotland, but in England as well, much as he had done since the days of his youth. Edinburgh he had wisely avoided, and although in former times he seems to have regularly conducted business there and even had some sort of base in the city, he had not done so for several years. What business took him to the capital in August 1684 is not known. In view of his status as a marked and wanted man, it must have been of some importance, bearing in mind the risk of recognition and apprehension which he undoubtedly ran. Whatever it was, his days of freedom to live, work and worship as he pleased were about to end.

Chapter Notes

a. damage; **b**. grain; **c**. sale by public auction; **d**. robbing/taking away.

23

The Martyr of Peebles

Ye kine of Bashan, that are in the mountain of Samaria, which oppress the poor, which crush the needy.

Amos 4:1

It is 5 August 1684. In the Grassmarket of Edinburgh the usual throng of merchants, stall holders and townsfolk, who come here daily to buy and sell the basic commodities of life, is swelled by the curious and the voyeuristic, here to watch what has become an all too regular spectacle these days. The Grassmarket slopes gently down to the West Port, from where it is joined by the West Bow. Towards its upper end stands a platform with stout wooden, upright posts joined by a crossbar from which hang several ropes, each ending in a noose. Three ladders stand against the crossbar. It is a scaffold and as on so many other days in recent times, it awaits the arrival of its complement of those condemned to perish this day. As the hour of two o'clock approaches there is a stir in the crowd and heads are turned towards the West Bow, which falls steeply from the Land Market above. A cart is descending. Its occupants are three men bound and tethered. Although they sit with heads as high as they are able, they are emaciated and sickly of pallor. Blood seeps through their ragged clothing from untreated, festering gunshot wounds. Behind them, on guard, are two militia men armed with muskets. Although the condemned men have assisted recently in a great escape, for them there will be no escape. As the cart trundles on towards its grim destination there are many who watch, some from the elevation of the high buildings which border the route on either side. Some laugh, some jeer, but some look on with pity.

The three unfortunate men are Thomas Harkness, Andrew Clerk and Samuel MacEwan, farming folk from Nithsdale. They have been condemned for their part in one of the most audacious actions in the continuing conflict between the government and the Covenanters of the south-west. In early July, following their capture in Dumfriesshire, nine Covenanters, who included Alexander Gordon of Kinstuir, William Grierson of Lochmoor, James Welsh of Little Cluden and John Mackenzie, all active in the cause and wanted men, were tried in Dumfries and sentenced to be transported. They were to be taken to Edinburgh and sent off from Leith to the Americas. An escort of no less than twenty-eight soldiers commanded by Lieutenant Patrick Mulligan had been sent to collect them and convey them to the capital. Their route took them by way of Thornhill, where they halted overnight on 28 July. The next day the route that would lead them northwards was to be the old hill road, which led through the Enterkin Pass. Their planned route towards Edinburgh had become known and the brothers James and Thomas Harkness had gathered some thirty to forty sympathisers in an attempt to ambush the party and free the prisoners. The pass was a narrow defile and, using the classic ambush technique for such a location, the party had split in two and waited on the high ground above the pass. In the mist, which hung about the hills, they had waited undetected, and once the column had entered the pass they descended, blocking the way forward and any rearward retreat. Hostile action had not immediately followed, but the Covenanters made it clear that their intention was to free the prisoners. Lieutenant Mulligan had been injudicious enough to decline to release them and ordered his troops to fire a volley into the mist. Fire was returned by the Covenanters and in the melee that followed Mulligan and two of his men had been killed and most of the prisoners broke free and made their escape.

When news of the action reached the authorities there had been consternation, and on 31 July the government ordered a public inquiry. All men over fifteen years of age were to arm themselves and come to the aid of the militia in hunting down the attackers. Proclamations had been made from the pulpits of all the churches of the Nithsdale parishes, requiring anyone over fifteen to answer, on oath, any question put to them by militia men. Nithsdale suffered the backlash and there had been widespread arrests, followed by less than gentle interrogation of those arrested. It had not been long before Thomas Harkness, Andrew Clerk and Samuel MacEwan were apprehended. They had been sleeping rough and were in fields near Closeburn. Their treatment had been severe. They had suffered gunshot wounds, received when the soldiers had wakened them by discharging their muskets. The wounds were left untreated. Taken first to Dumfries, they had then been moved to Edinburgh, where they were duly tried for high treason and sentenced to death. That same morning, James Nicol, his business in Edinburgh concluded, made his way to the West Port, there to collect his horse and take his leave for Peebles. But, finding the saddle in need of repair, he delayed his departure so that the necessary repairs could be carried out. While he waited, news that three men had been condemned before the Justiciary that morning and would hang early in the afternoon had become the common talk of the Grassmarket. Having travelled recently in Nithsdale, James had of course heard of the successful ambush at Enterkin Pass and its aftermath. Curiosity and compassion compelled him to further delay his departure so that he might lend moral support to his Covenanting brethren at the time of their martyrdom. To do so was risky indeed. James, too, was a marked and wanted man, and had been these five years past since Bothwell Brig. While throughout those years he had somehow managed to continue his life as a travelling merchant, he was also a fugitive and even publicly named as a 'vagabond'. It was the very nature of his itinerant life and the loyalty of his family and friends that had thus far protected him. Perhaps the anonymity of that milling crowd in the Grassmarket would protect him now?

The last journey of the three condemned men is now at its end. The cart reaches the platform, where the lockman stands awaiting those he will soon des- patch into eternity. Having mounted the platform, each of the three men reads out a testimony, reaffirming their adherence to the Covenants and their faith in Divine Providence. One by one they climb the steps of the waiting ladder, paus- ing to commit themselves to God's mercy, before the lockman pitches them from the rungs and into the abyss. While such a scene was not uncommon to many, and while some there might applaud the end of these fanatical enemies of the King and his Kirk, the quiet and dignified end of these country folk, who had just sac- rificed their lives for their immoveable religious beliefs, provokes an awed silence as their inert bodies now swing in the breeze. As he stands anonymous among the crowd, James feels anger and despair rising within him at the barbarity of the event and its perpetrators. At last, unable to contain himself in the silence of the moment, he shouts out, 'A cow of Bashan has pushed three men to death at one push, contrary to their own base laws and in an inhumane way'. All eyes are now turned upon him. His time has come. This time there will be no escape. He knows that soon he will share the fate of those lately departed brethren, but first there will be a meeting with Sir George Mackenzie, 'Bluidy Mackenzie'.

A few days later, on 18 August 1684, James Nicol found himself before the mem- bers of the Privy Council, a rare privilege for someone of his humble origins and perhaps an indication of his greater significance than might otherwise seem to be the case in view of his apparent anonymity. The principal interrogator was Sir George Mackenzie. In his testimony James records that interrogation in his own words:[1]

First, I was interrogated by two in a room privately, thus:
Q. 'Were you at Bothwell Bridge?'
A. 'I am not bound to be my own accuser.'
'I am not,' said one of them, 'to desire you; but only say upon your honest word, that you were not there?'

A. 'I am not bound to satisfy you; but prove what you have to say against me, and especially you, till I come before my accusers.'

'Well,' said he, 'I am not one of them.' Then I answered, 'I was there'.

Q. 'How came you to rise in arms against the King?'

A. 'Because he has broken the Covenant of the Lord my God.'

Q. 'Was the Prelate's death murder?'

A. 'No, it was not murder.'

Q. 'Was Hackston's death murder?'

A. 'That it was, indeed.'

Q. 'How dare[a] you own the Covenant, seeing the King gave orders to burn it by the hand of the hangman?'

A. 'Yes, I dare own it; for although ye should escape the hand of men for so doing, yet ye shall all pay for it, ere all be done, and to purpose. As for me, I would not do it for all the earth.'

   ... Then I was interrogated by other two, who asked some frivolous questions which I baffled to silence.

   ... Then I was brought before the bloody crew.

   ... 'What now sir,' said they, 'Do ye own the King's authority?'

A. 'I own all things that the precious Word of God owns in less or more, and all faithful magistrates.'

Q. 'But do you not own King Charles also?'

A. 'I dare not for a world; because it is perjury; for he has unkinged himself in a high degree, and that in doing all things contrary to the Word of God, and Confession of Faith, and Catechisms Larger and Shorter.'

Q. 'Know you to whom ye are speaking?'

A. 'I know I am before men.'

   ... 'But,' said one of them, 'Ye are speaking to the Chancellor and members of Council, sir.'

   ... 'But,' said I, 'I have told you already that he has unkinged himself, and so you have degraded yourselves from being princes.'

Q. 'If the King were here, what would you say, sir.'

A. 'I know how I ought to speak to the King if he were King; "Sir", is ordinarily said to him, and so to let you know that I am no Quaker, or erroneous in any-thing, but a pure Presbyterian, and of a Gospel apostolic spirit, I call you "sirs", because ye are noblemen by birth, but not because ye are my judges.'

Q. 'Will ye not say, God bless the King's majesty?'

A. 'I dare not bless them whom God hath rejected: As it is written in the Second Letter of John at verse 10 "If any man bring another doctrine than ye have received, bid him not God-speed, nor receive him in your house," and in Psalm 16, near the beginning, says David, "Their drink-offerings will I not offer, nor take up their very names in my lips" (namely, them that hasten after other gods), and therefore I dare not pray for him.'

Q. 'And will ye not pray for him?'

A. 'If he belongs to the election of grace, he has part of my prayers. And also, if he were a king that had kept Covenant with God, I would give him double share, and make mention of his name; but he is apostate.'

... So my friends, they looked still one to another at every question and answer.

Q. 'How old are you, sir?'

A. 'I am fifty-one years.'

Q. 'How dare you own the Covenants, seeing we have burnt them by the hand of the hangman?'

A. 'I dare own them upon all perils whatsoever to the utmost of my power, all the days of my life.' And with that they smiled and laughed one to another, and to me, and said, 'My days were near an end.' I said, 'I am in your power, but if you take my blood, ye shall take innocent blood upon yourselves, as it is written in Jeremiah Chapter 26 verses 14 and 15, "As for me, I am in your hand; do with me as seemeth good and meet unto you; but know for certain, that if ye put me to death ye shall bring innocent blood upon yourselves, and on this city and the inhabitants thereof." And as for me, if ye take my blood, it is as innocent blood as ever ye did take, for I did never wrong any man to this day.'

Q. 'Do you go to church?'

A. 'I went aye to the church where I could get any faithful minister to go; but for your Prelates' kirks, and Baal's priests, I never heard any of them, nor ever intend to do, if I were to live an hundred years.'

... 'But (said they) ye shall not live long now, sir. How do ye prove by the Scripture what you say against Prelates?'

A. 'By many Scriptures, "The kings of the Gentiles exercise lordship over them, and they that exercise authority upon them are called benefactors; but it shall not be so among you: but he that is greatest among you, shall be servant of all;" not like your glutton, Epicurean, belly-god Prelates, who are riding in coaches in great pomp.'

But they would not suffer me to speak more, nor cite more places, but asked several questions which I have not got memory of; only this word I said, concerning the tyrant, 'He was brought home by Mr Livingstone and others, and put in a nobler estate than any king in the whole world, crowned a covenanted king with the eternal God to be for him, and to carry His work and cause, he and all the people; which if he had continued in, he would have been the greatest king in all the lands and nations in the world, and would have been a terror to all the kings in Europe; but now he hath made himself base, and a reproach to all the nations, so have all you; and another reason why I dare not own him nor you either is, because he and you have robbed Christ of His crown, although it be not in your power to do it.'

They bade take me away to the iron house, and to put irons on me, which they did on both my hands, that I could write none that day, till I got a mean to put them off the one hand.

Then they called me before them again, being the 19th day of this instant.

Q. 'What say you the day[b]? Do you adhere to all ye said yesterday?'

A. 'I adhere to all and haill[c] upon all perils whatsomever.'

Q. 'Do ye approve of Bothwell Bridge?'

A. 'Yes, I do.'

Q. 'Do you go to the kirk at Peebles?'

A. 'No, nor never intend to go there, nor no place else which pertains to the perjured Prelates.'

Q. 'Do you own the Covenants?'

A. 'I adhere to every point of them, because they are in short an obligation to the whole sum of Scripture, as the sum of the law is "to love the Lord our God with all our soul, and heart, and mind, and with our whole strength, and our neighbour as ourselves:" so it is the whole duty which the Lord requires of me and all men.'

Q. 'And how do you reject the King, seeing the Scripture commands you to obey him?'

A. 'Because the coronation sermon, and the coronation itself do openly declare, that the people make a king, and not the king a people, and he was received home, and crowned for no other thing nor end, but to maintain that interest to the utmost of his power; and no longer to be owned as king, than he did own that wherefore he was crowned; so that we were freely loosed from him, as soon as he played his base pranks, in taking malignants by the hand, and murdering a prince and a prophet, namely, Argyle, who set the crown upon his head, and Mr Guthrie, who was a godly reformer in our land.' Next I said, 'What thought they of Mr Douglas, who preached and gave him all his injunctions at Scone?'[2]

... 'They said to me, He should have been hanged for his pains.'

... 'But,' I said, 'God would be about[d] with them all for rejecting the Word of the Lord in these directions.'

Q. 'How do ye disown him, seeing the most part both of ministers and professors do pray for him?'

A. 'Because the General Assembly at the West Kirk disowned him altogether, till he made declaration of humiliation for his own sins and his father's. And the Parliament being then sitting at Edinburgh did ratify the Assembly's act, and disowned him till he should do that, which accordingly he did, and so we are loosed freely.'

Q. 'Do you own Airsmoss, Sanquhar, Rutherglen, and Lanark Declarations?'

A. 'Yes I do; because they are agreeable to the Covenants and work of Reformation.' And many more questions they asked, which I cannot now particularly remember, but I told them in general that I was against Popery, Prelacy, malignancy and profanity, and all that is against sound doctrine, discipline, worship and government; and all errors whatsomever, which are contrary to sound Presbyterian doctrine, be what they will; for there is none other right, but erroneous, how fair a face soever they have, which shall be found not agreeable to the Apostle's doctrine.

… And then they read something which I had said, and questioned if I would subscribe what I had said. I answered, 'No.'

Q. 'Can ye write?' 'Yes, I can write.' 'Then do it,' said they: But I said, I would not do it at all.

… Now, my friends, I say, these are part of my interrogations.

… Again, I was brought before the Justiciary (as they called themselves), on the 20th of this instant, and interrogated thus:

Q. 'What, now, sir, what think you of yourself the day?'

A. 'I praise my God I am the same as I was.'

Q. 'What think ye of what ye said yesterday before the Chancellor and the Council?'

A. 'I hold all, and decline nothing: No, not one ace.'

Q. 'Were ye at Bothwell Bridge?'

A. 'Yes, that I was.'

Q. 'Had ye arms?'

A. 'Yes, that I had.'

… One of them said, 'God help you.' And I said, 'I wot[e] not if ye can pray for yourself.' But, said he, 'I wish you better nor[f] ye do yourself.' But I said, 'No; for ye would have me disown my great Lord, the King of Zion, and obey men. Yea, base men, whose breath is in their nostrils, who give out laws and commandments contrary to His.'

Q. 'How dare ye rise in arms against the King?'

A. 'It is better to obey God than man, and he is an enemy to God.'

Q. 'Would ye rise in arms for the Covenants against the king's laws, if ye had occasion?'

A. 'Yes, that I would, say the contrary who will, upon all peril.'

Q. 'What think ye of yourself in spoiling the country of horse and arms, sir?'

A. 'Sir, I had not the worth of a spur whang[g] of any man's but was mounted of horse and arms of my own.'

Q. 'Where have ye been all this time?'

A. 'Sometimes here and there in England and Scotland.'

Q. 'Whom have ye conversed with?'

A. 'I was about my business, being a merchant.'

… They said, 'Ye have been about another business; for ye are found to be a fugitive and a vagabond.'

A. 'I have been a merchant from my youth.'

Q. 'But where had ye your chamber in this town?'

A. 'I had none these several years.'

Q. 'Where quarter ye in this town?'

A. 'I have not been much in it these seven or eight years.'

Q. 'But where were ye the night and the last night before the execution?'

A. 'I was not in town; I came but to the port just when the first cast was over.'

… Then they looked one to another, and whispered together. But they would fain have me wronging my landlords in all parts of the country, and in all burghs; but glory to my Lord, I have wronged none yet, nor yet hope to do, for it was aye my care, and prayer to God earnestly, that I might wrong no man, and that I had rather suffer before any were wronged by me, which He has kept me from to this day. Then they read what I had said.

Q. 'Will ye subscribe what ye have said?'

A. 'No, no.'

Q. 'Can ye write, sir?'

A. 'Yes, that I can.'

'Well,' said they, 'write down that he can, but will not.'

… They told me five or six times that my time should not be long and said to me, 'Will ye have a minister?'

'I will have none of your Baal's priests.'

If I could have gotten leave, I should have made them abominable to them, and also at every question I would have made them ashamed.

The interrogation was now at an end and on 22 August the indictment was delivered to him as he waited in prison. This told him that he would be taken before the Justiciary on 27 August and be taken immediately to the scaffold. A final message was added to his testimony:

… Now, my dear friends, I think all I have written is confused, because I could hardly get leave to write two lines, but was either put from it by the keepers, or called from it by one confusion or other, therefore ye must excuse me; but although it be not accurately written, yet there is no error in it. It is what I lay down my life for, and adhere to as testimony of a dying man, who must very shortly appear before my Lord, and give an account of all I have done and written. However, my friends, mistake me not, although it be confused, and ye find some things twice over; for there is no more fear on me now, than the quietest time ever I had, as to what man can do to me; although I be sad as to matters betwixt God and me, betwixt my glorious God and me, as good cause I have, who knew it as I do; but I hope, I shall get a glorious outgate[h] when His time comes, which I have always waited upon (and not mine) for which I bless Him this day.

These are the last words written by James Nicol, but the extract from *A Cloud of Witnesses* continues:

What further this martyr wrote in prison, cannot be published as it stands, in regard that, he being perpetually interrupted by the keepers, and having irons on his hands (as himself testifies) could not get it written with that composure which he would. Wherefore, take some of the more remarkable heads of it, mostly in his own words:

1. He declares his cheerfulness to lay down his life for the cause of Christ, and faith once delivered to the saints; admiring the riches of the free grace of God, in Christ's laying down His life for poor sinners, and blessing them with such a noble, precious and excellent blessing, as to be called the sons of God, which the angels cannot take up, though they have been a long time prying into it; and invites others to the same exercise of admiring and praising God's love, in making, through the blood of Christ, rebels and enemies, friends and servants.

2. He rejoices in his lot, of suffering, thus, 'Oh! But it be an excellent thing to be called of the Lord, to lay down my life for Him and His glorious interest! To me it is more than all the world: I cannot prize it. It has been my desire these twenty-four years to die a martyr for my Lord, and to witness for Him, if it be His will, and not else. I bless my lord for it, I have subscribed a blank, and put it in His hand, to do with me whatever is the determinate counsel of His will and decree, and not call myself.'

3. He blesses God, that though he would have got his life for doing what others, whom he calls better than himself, have done, yet the Lord had made it His glory, honour and crown, to hold fast till the Lord come, which he hoped would be quickly, to himself, and also to the land.

4. He testifies his assurance of God's love to him, and his children, whom he heartily and cheerfully gives away to God, as he had oft devoted them to Him in covenant; he exhorts them in the words of a dying father, to be for God in their generation, to live in love and unity, leaving them to the protection and provision of His God, charging them not to be moved for his sufferings, which he protests he would not exchange for the whole world.

5. He charges them all to be aware of wronging themselves by reproaching him anent the manner of his being apprehended, showing what a hand of divine Providence there was in it, and blessing God for it, and for the sweet peace he had in suffering.

6. He owns himself to have been the greatest sinner upon the earth, and hence takes occasion to magnify the redeeming love of Christ, in calling him effectually, and keeping him in the right way, and from the national sins and corruptions of the age.

7. He refers to a list of papers written by him, declarative of his judgement concerning the duty of the day, as a reason, among others, why he wrote no formal

testimony in the prison; save only that he testifies. First, generally against all things contrary to any point of truth in the Old and New Testament, or contrary to the Covenants and the work of Reformation; and more particularly, against the sinful silence of ministers in Britain and Ireland, at the command of a bloody, vile, adulterous, perjured tyrant and his underlings; against the indulgences and indemnities; against componing[i] and conforming either with a perjured tyrannical crew of statesmen, or with base, vile, filthy Prelatists, their blind guides, and Baal's priests; against backslidden ministers and professors, who condemned a poor young generation for adhering to truth, for slaying Christ in His members, for pleasing men, and displeasing a never enough exalted and glorious Lord; and finally, disowns all that is contrary to a Gospel and apostolic spirit.

8. He proceeds to warn and exhort all sorts of persons, and more especially the young generation, to repentance and amendment of life, enforcing his exhortation with the consideration of judgements and strokes come upon the land; upon which head he is exceeding large, founding his assertions upon the threatenings pronounced in the Word against these sins, wherein he demonstrates Scotland, England and Ireland to have been eminently guilty; interposing withal sweet and ravishing considerations of God's love, protesting, that he expects salvation not by merit, but of free grace, saying 'I have been beginning to pray and praise these thirty-six years, weakly as I could, but yet I am just to begin this night, both to praise and pray; for I lay no more stress upon all that I have said and done, believed and suffered, nor on a straw, God is my witness; so that I must have salvation upon Wednesday at three or four of the clock, as freely as the thief on the cross.' He winds up in imitation of David, with these words, 'And what can poor[j] James Nicol say more!' resuming again the consideration of God's wrath against the land, to stir up all ranks to repentance.

At about two o'clock on the afternoon of Wednesday 27 August 1684, James Nicol started his last journey from the Tolbooth of Edinburgh to the Grassmarket, there to meet with the hangman.

Chapter Notes

a. can; **b**. today; **c**. whole; **d**. deal with; **e**. know; **f**. than; **g**. thong or strap; **h**. deliverance; **I**. compounding or settling; **j**. feeble.

—◦◦◦—

24

The Happy Revolution

In the years that followed that August day of 1684, events moved quickly, as they often do at a time of great historic change. Persecution of the supporters of the Covenant continued unabated, and the harassment, torture and martyrdom of many occurred in the years 1684–85 – 'the Killing Times'. In October 1684 James Renwick, recently returned from Holland, published his manifesto, 'An Apologetical Declaration and Admonitory Vindication'. This restated the principles set out in the earlier Queensferry and Sanquhar declarations, and copies were posted on a number of market crosses and churches throughout the south-west. Although the murder of those who were not of Cameronian persuasion was something it claimed to 'detest and abhor', it went on to state unequivocally that 'whosoever stretcheth forth their hands against us' were 'enemies to God and punishable as such'. This included all soldiers and officers of the government, and not least 'all viperous and malicious bishops and curates'. The Cameronians would not be 'so slack handed in time coming to put matters in hand as heretofore we have been, seeing we are bound faithfully to maintain our Covenant and the cause of Christ'. To the depleted and dispirited Covenanters, who now wandered countrywide in constant fear for their lives, this was a renewed call to battle and a blueprint for murder. It was also a challenge to the government who had fresh reason to implement an even more ruthless campaign of repression. In response to the inevitable murders perpetrated by the Cameronians, the Privy Council introduced an Order which required anyone who might be apprehended on suspicion of treasonable activity to renounce the 'Apologetic Declaration'. Failure to do so was to be taken as an admission of treason, and anyone so failing was liable to be summarily shot without the formality of a trial. Claverhouse and his dragoons set to their work with a vengeance, with the wholehearted support of Sir George Mackenzie, the Lord Advocate and interrogator of James Nicol. These were indeed 'the Killing Times'.

Charles II died on 5 February 1685, little lamented in Scotland, a part of his realm he had not deigned to visit since his restoration, but upon which he had willingly or otherwise inflicted so much misery. He was succeeded by James VII & II, his brother, the Duke of York, an effective naval commander and administrator, but Catholic, obstinate and politically inept. It has been said that Charles, where he succeeded, did so through personal charm, which he had in abundance, but also by deviousness and a singular ability to obfuscate – all characteristics his brother lacked. At a time when anti-Catholic feeling was once again on the rise, his unabashed promotion of the Catholic cause could not have been more ill-judged, and by 1688 an exasperated nation had had enough.

James was proclaimed as King of Scots on 10 February 1685 and at the outset he was generally accepted by the great mass of the Scottish people, the only opposition coming from the Cameronians, who were but a tiny minority. Although he had had personal experience of Scotland as his brother's representative, he never returned and was never crowned as King of Scots. In England he declined to take the Coronation Oath to defend the Protestant faith. In an attempt to calm down the concerns, which the succession of a Catholic King had aroused in Scotland, he proclaimed an indemnity to all rebels with the exception of the Cameronians, and when the Estates met in April a new Act was passed which made adherence to the Covenants treasonable. Attendance at conventicles was to be punishable by death and the Test was reimposed. The Covenanters were 'the new sect from the dunghill, who kill by pretended inspiration, whose idol is that accursed Covenant'. A failed rising, led by Argyll in Scotland and by Monmouth in England, again sounded alarm bells and the King, now provided by Parliament with a standing army for the first time, sent his dragoons across the length and breadth of southern Scotland. In September 1685 the Earl of Balcarres, Lord Yester and William Hay of Drumelzier were appointed as justiciars for the shires of Roxburgh, Berwick, Selkirk and Peebles, with instructions to hunt down and punish rebels. Colonel James Douglas, the brother of Queensberry, was active on their behalf in Tweeddale, and in one incident near Tweedsmuir he attacked and dispersed a gathering of hill men at prayer. The men fled in different directions and Douglas and his small contingent could only go after a few, among whom was John Hunter, who they pursued for some miles over hill and heather before finally trapping him on the edge of the Devil's Beef Tub, where he was shot and his body thrown down the steep slope. Such an incident seems to have been all too typical. Hunter's body was retrieved and buried in the kirkyard of Tweedsmuir where his gravestone can still be seen. It carries the inscription:

when zion's King was robbed of his right
his witnesses in Scotland put to flight
when popish prelates & Indulgancie
combined 'gainst Christ to ruine presbytrie

all who would not unto their idols bow
they socht them out & whom they found they slew
for owning of Christ's cause I then did die
my blood for vengeance on his en'mies did cry.

While the government's focus seemed to be on the destruction of extreme Presbyterians, it was the attitude of James to his Catholic brethren which was to prove the catalyst for his final downfall. In France Louis XIV revoked the Edict of Nantes which for eighty years had granted toleration to Protestants. There was public protest in Edinburgh and Huguenot refugees crossed the water from France in considerable numbers. It was at this singularly inappropriate moment that James chose to embark on a campaign to grant toleration to Catholics. Seemingly oblivious to the consequences, or unheeding of them, he announced his intention to appoint Catholics to major offices of State, Test or no Test. When the English Parliament protested, he dissolved it. In Scotland the Earl of Perth was appointed Chancellor and his brother, the Earl of Melfort, Secretary of State. Both were recent converts to Catholicism. James asked Parliament to repeal the anti-Catholic laws, but when the Estates declined, he ordered the Privy Council to use the royal prerogative to annul the legislation. The Council also declined and found itself purged of dissenting members, including a number of the bishops. He further attempted to extend his influence at a more parochial level, and in September 1686 the annual election of Town Councils was suspended. The experience of Peebles may well have been typical. The provost received a letter from the Privy Council, which he produced at a meeting of the Council on 27 September, which authorised it to 'continow and exerce as magistrates and counsel until his Majesties all signify his further pleasur'.¹ Never before had the Council received such an instruction. Elections to the Council might be influenced or indeed manipulated by the local gentry, but never before had the central authority attempted to interfere with the age-old privileges of the Royal Burgh. The following year matters were taken a stage further. The Earl of Traquair, Catholic and a firm supporter of the King, attended a meeting of the Town Council on 5 February and submitted a list of magistrates and councillors whom the King wished to nominate. In Peebles, at least, the Council for its part seems to have accepted the situation in spite of this clear interference with their ancient rights. They were apparently content and 'accordingly entered upon the execution of their lawful offices'. This was the last time that the King's legislation would affect Peebles.

As a sop to the opponents of his policy of Catholic emancipation, James now issued fresh letters of Indulgence which were to grant toleration to all faiths to worship as they pleased, provided that they did not promote disloyalty to the Crown. Although clearly intended to aid Catholics, what the Indulgence did do was to legitimise the great body of moderate Presbyterians who had for so long lived and worshipped in a kind of no man's land between legitimacy and illegality.

In the face of changing public opinion, James Renwick remained the last bastion of the Covenanting extremists. He still commanded large congregations at field conventicles held throughout southern Scotland, but his days were numbered. The net was closing. On 29 December 1687 he was in Peebles, from where he wrote to Robert Hamilton:

> I have been at Peebles this week, and, through our Lord's providence, wonderfully escaped; our intended meeting near to the town, about nine of the clock at night, in the time of our gathering, being by strange providence discovered. It is a place I had not been before, and we had no armed men; there were four taken and imprisoned.[2]

He reports the incident in rather more detail in a letter to Alexander Shields dated 12 January 1688:

> I came forward to Peebles, where our meeting in the time of the gathering was discovered by a wonderful providence, namely, as I am informed, the pursuing of some for theft when people were observed to crowd out of the town; which made the clerk to enquire what they were, and whither they were going; the report whereof came unto me, being lodged in a most suspected house, I went forth and passed on towards the place of meeting until I came within speaking and hearing of the clerk and some with him, who were without all the town challenging people, and being in no capacity to resist, I turned again into the town, where there was some little uproar, and went forth of it another way, where I waited a considerable space for my horse, which was at length got into me with some difficulty; and finding that the meeting could not be kept I came away; but there were four persons taken. And since I came to this place I have lodged with Thomas and John, and lest I should trouble mine own spirit, I have not denied any to keep silent anent my being here, not reproved any for coming into my quarters, whatever the hazard might be; but left that to the providence of God, and people to their own discretion, and I find not the worse way.[3]

Shortly after, he preached for the last time at Riskenhope in Yarrow. According to James Hogg, the 'Ettrick Shepherd', 'When he prayed that day, few of his hearers cheeks were dry'. The following month he was captured in Edinburgh during a secret visit there. He was brought before the Privy Council and freely admitted to disowning the King's authority and encouraging his followers to attend conventicles and to carry arms. The inevitable execution took place on 17 February. On the scaffold he tried to address the crowd, but his words were drowned out by the drums of the assembled troops. He was the last Covenanting martyr.

So the long Covenanting struggle was effectively extinguished and moderate Presbyterianism began to recover its strength, not least as counter to the resurgence of Catholicism with which Episcopacy, although far removed from it, was inevitably associated in Presbyterian minds. Both north and south of the border James had continued his favour towards the Catholic community, against a rising tide of opposition. In April 1688 a further Indulgence was issued in England and was ordered to be read from all pulpits on the 20th of the month. Shortly before, seven of the bishops had protested to the King and were arrested for their trouble. On 11 June 1688 a son was born to the King. All his previous sons had died as infants but this, his fifth, showed every sign of robust good health. The succession of Catholic monarchy seemed assured. It was the last straw; the revolution quickly followed. In England, approaches had already been made to William of Orange, who agreed to mount an expedition for the purposes of establishing a free Parliament which would democratically settle all the current matters of dispute, both civil and religious. William also wrote to the Scottish Parliament offering to assist them in their struggle with James, but Episcopacy remained the State religion, and the Episcopalian element was still in control and was not enamoured with the idea of being led by a Dutch Calvinist. News came that William's expedition had been turned back by bad weather. This proved to be false and the Scottish bishops confirmed their loyalty to James. It was the last throw of the dice as support for the King was rapidly crumbling, and by the time William landed on the south coast of England in November, James had effectively lost his Scottish kingdom. As J.D. Mackie[4] has said, 'He had violated the fundamental but unspoken compact between the Crown and the nobles which formed the basis of the Restoration settlement in Scotland: he had challenged the right of the aristocracy to control Scottish society at local level.' A divided Privy Council was unable to suppress the rising opposition and local militias refused to act. James left London under cover of darkness on 23 December, scuttling off to France like a frightened rat, never to return again. In Edinburgh, even before news of his flight was known, the mob had attacked the Catholic chapel at Holyrood and ejected Perth, the Chancellor, and his hated brother, Lord Melfort.

No sooner had news of the King's flight become known, than the remnants of the Cameronians in the west began a campaign against the sitting curates. On Christmas day 1688, just days after the King's ignominious departure from London, they had gathered sufficient strength to be able to evict about 200 ministers and their households, who were ejected from their manses without consideration for the effects of mid-winter weather. A wider campaign was also directed against known Catholics. Clearly the Cameronian element was not without support in Peebles and Tweeddale, as the following extract from an Edinburgh publication of 1727, called *Vindication of Mr Richard Cameron* by Patrick Walker, suggests:[5]

In the end of 1688, at the happy Revolution, when ... the crown was vacant, in which time we had no King nor judicatories in the kingdom, the United Societies [as the Cameronians were also called] in their general correspondence, considering the surprising, unexpected, merciful step of the Lord's dispensation, thought it some way belonged to us in the interregnum to go to all popish houses and destroy their monuments of idolatry, with their priests' robes, and to apprehend and put to prison themselves; which was done at the cross of Dumfries and Peebles and other places. That honourable and worthy gentleman, Donald Ker of Kersland, having a considerable number of us with him, went to the House of Traquair in frost and snow, and found a great deal of popish wares there, but wanted the cradle, Mary and the Babe, and the priest.

After much searching they found two locked trunks, which they broke open to reveal in one a golden cradle, with Mary and the Babe, and in the other the priest's robes, the earl and his priest having fled. These items were taken to the cross of Peebles, 'with a great deal of popish books and many other things of great value, all Romish wares, and burned them there'.[6] At the same time they decided to approach 'all prelatic intruding curates' and warn them to remove with all their belongings, 'that we should call for the Church's goods, cups and basons, and also for the kirk-box, wherein was nothing but a few doits; likewise for the session book and kirk-door keys; and that we should deliver all to men of credit'.

What had effectively been the collapse of the Stuart dynasty[7] left the country in a state of limbo, but as early as March 1688, and therefore some time before this, it is clear that there were stirrings of a new order. This was certainly the case in Tweeddale. There is every sign that with the execution of James Renwick in February of that year the Covenanting cause, at least in its Cameronian form, was a spent force. At long last the government's campaign of repression and terror seems to have been at an end. Though as yet there had been no changes in the law, the more moderate Presbyterians were beginning to re-emerge and assert themselves. There is ample evidence that Presbyterian congregations were already being formed, presided over by Presbyterian ministers, some of whom had been supporters of the Covenants. Events in Tweeddale were doubtlessly not exceptional, and on 22 March 1688 a group of ministers met in a farmhouse at Stobo, which lies about 6 miles west of Peebles. Their leader was James Feithie, who is described as 'minister at Peebles'. The official (that is Episcopal) incumbent was, of course, still Rev. John Hay. Where Feithie emerged from is unknown, but he had studied at Edinburgh University, had been a supporter of the Covenants and was imprisoned for a time for holding conventicles, part of that time being on the Bass Rock, which was a common, if unpleasant location for religious dissidents. He was released in July 1679. It must be assumed that he was one of those ministers who benefited from the Indulgence of 1687, which had more or less permitted freedom of worship, and by November that year he had been admitted as Minister of Peebles. Thus there were two congregations in the town, one Episcopalian still worshipping in the parish kirk, and the other Presbyterian. The conclusion can only be that the support for Covenanted Presbyterianism in Peebles, as elsewhere, was stronger than might otherwise be supposed.

Following the hasty departure of James, William of Orange had arrived in London and at the request of a large body of the nobility and gentry, which included representatives from Scotland, he agreed to hold the reins of power until a decision could be made about the form of government that should follow. In this capacity he summoned a meeting of the Estates, but as there was no King when the Estates met in March 1689, it was as a convention rather than a Parliament. The Test was ignored and this was as near a 'free' Parliament as was possible. There was no Royal Commissioner, but the Duke of Hamilton was elected as president, although only by a small majority, and there was clearly a deep division between the supporters of William and those who would become known as the 'Jacobites'. By 11 April the Estates were able to issue a declaration, which included a Claim of Right. This followed the slightly earlier English precedent. Unlike its English equivalent, however, a long list of grievances against the departed King's rule included a statement: 'Prelacy and the superiority of any office in the Church above Presbyters, is and has been, a great and insupportable grievance and trouble to this nation ... and therefore should be abolished.'[8] In other words, the end of Episcopacy as the State religion. There was of course much more to it than that, which need not be of concern here. The Estates agreed that the Crown should be offered to the 'Prince and Princess of Orange', and on 11 April 1689 William III and Mary II were proclaimed from the Mercat Cross of Edinburgh as joint sovereigns. On 11 May William accepted the Claim of Right. He never visited Scotland and he was never crowned as King of Scots but he did take the Coronation Oath, to uphold the true religion as established and to defend it against its enemies. The 'established' religion was, of course, still Episcopalian, but by July, after much debate, an Act was passed which stated that 'the government of the Church' should be according to the way 'most agreeable to the people's inclinations'. The Acts which had imposed Episcopacy were revoked. It was the following year before the last chapter in the long process of reformation in Scotland was finally played out. The Estates met once more in April 1690 and on the 25th of that month an Act was passed which removed royal supremacy in Church affairs, and also restored to their charges all ministers who had been deprived of them since 1660. On 26 May the Estates declared the Westminster Confession to be the only doctrinal source of the new Kirk of Scotland. The Presbyterian courts, Synod, Presbytery and Kirk Session were restored in accordance with the Act of 1592. Bishops were no more. The Kirk of Scotland emerged as it has remained to this day established, Presbyterian and independent. From Wishart, by way of Knox, Melville, Jenny Geddes, Henderson, Guthrie, Cargill and Renwick, the reformation way had been long and often bloody. Lesser mortals had been caught up in the struggle and suffered for their beliefs, perhaps sometimes misguidedly, but rarely without courage. Often simple, ordinary folk, unsung, but who nonetheless were the driving force from which an improved, more tolerant order eventually emerged. Such a one was James Nicol.

Epilogue

The Revolution Settlement of 1690 marked the end of the long and painful journey which led to the final establishment of the Church of Scotland in the Presbyterian form in which it remains to this day. Naturally, the acceptance of the new order was not universal. There was still a substantial body of Episcopalians who wanted to have a part in the Established Church. Many did convert or revert to Presbyterianism, but those who did not were debarred, and when the first General Assembly since 1653 was called by King William in 1692, it expelled all Episcopalians.

The ousting of Episcopal ministers was also taking place at a local level. The situation in Peebles was probably not untypical. James Feithie, who re-established a Presbyterian congregation in the town, died in November 1689. John Hay had remained the Episcopal incumbent in the Parish Church, but seems to have been inactive by then. He died in 1690 and, in that year, his assistant Robert Knox was nominated as his successor by the Duke of Queensberry. The magistrates objected, declaring the church vacant, as patronage had by then been abolished. A call was given to William Veitch and, although this was resisted by the remaining Episcopalians who favoured Knox, in due course the Presbytery ordained Veitch as Minister of Peebles and Manor, clear evidence that Presbyterianism was in the ascendant. In addition, the choice indicates that the town was not unsympathetic to the more extreme elements, for William Veitch was a Covenanter of long standing. He had been at Rullion Green and had a long association with the south-western activists. He had been imprisoned for a time, some of it on the Bass Rock, and on his release in 1679 he had been banished from Scotland. Nevertheless, he managed to continue preaching at conventicles and went through a remarkable series of 'adventures' to avoid capture, including an escape to Holland, before he returned to preach openly, as he was eventually permitted to do by the Act of Indemnity introduced by James II. In this he was doubly fortunate, as at an earlier time he had been condemned to death for his activities. Thus this colourful character became the first Minister of Peebles under the restored Presbyterian order. His long allegiance to the Covenants would certainly have endeared him to James Nicol, had he survived.

The days of the Covenanters, as such, were over and from this time on they fade into the pages of history to become, for later generations, a romantic symbol of the struggle between good and evil, and the resistance by common folk against the forces of oppression. The National Covenant, which they espoused with such fervour, even to the point of death, stands together with the Declaration of Arbroath as one of the great statements defining Scottish nationhood. Although they were a spent force, and many of their number had felt able to join the newly established Kirk, there remained a small, hard core who declined to conform. Granted the tolerance they would have denied to others, they went their own way and it was not until 1876 that the majority of the remnant joined the Free Church of Scotland. How many gave their lives in defending and holding to the Covenants is not known, but certainly it ran to many thousands. There were those who died in battle at Dunbar, Inverlochy, Falkirk, Rullion Green, Bothwell Brig and its aftermath, and at Airds Moss, and countless minor skirmishes. There were those who suffered at the hands of the hangman, and the many others, often ordinary folk, who perished during 'the Killing Times'. Had their cause been in vain? Through all the vicissitudes of the half century since the signing of the National Covenant, they had remained steadfast, implacable and immoveable, but as J.D. Mackie relates:[1] 'It has been said "it was from the impact of Stuart steel upon Covenanting flint that our modern freedom of thought and belief was born". Scotland does not err in the revering of her martyrs.' As calmer days descended, albeit for a time disturbed by Jacobite rebellion, that freedom of thought was cherished and nurtured until it blossomed into the great period of the Scottish Enlightenment.

What of Peebles? Throughout the years from the start of the Reformation until the final establishment of the Church of Scotland, the town had taken part in its own parochial and perhaps not so parochial way in that great struggle. So much of what happened in the Royal Burgh mirrors the ebb and flow of the struggle that gripped all of Scotland for 170 years. Through all those years there runs a thread, at times tenuous, of loyalty to the Crown, but perhaps also a confusion about religious adherence. Was it a Covenanting town? Probably not in a strict sense, yet there is ample evidence that there were many who might have had more than a little sympathy for those who chose to challenge imposed Episcopacy. Apart from James Nicol himself there must have been those who were drawn to the great conventicles, many taking place in the west of the county at Tweedsmuir and Broughton and in the Pentland Hills, not far from the Royal Burgh. There had been 'a considerable body of horse from Tweeddale' at Bothwell Brig, the 'frequent and rebellious meetings … where persons … now go publicly to other persons' houses and take upon them to preach in the doors'. There were those brave councillors who, initially at least, declined to take the Test. Yet on the other side, throughout the long history of the town, loyalty to the sovereign of the day has exerted a strong pull, which has only been set aside in the most extreme of circumstances. A Royal Burgh indeed.

No records remain of the last days of Episcopacy in Peebles. The Kirk Session records for those years have been lost and only recommence after the final establishment of the Church of Scotland. Were they deliberately destroyed, perhaps by Presbyterian successors anxious to erase the memory of a time of Prelacy, which they wished to forget? Perhaps they were destroyed by former Episcopalians, anxious to remove all trace of an order they had themselves espoused, but from which they now wanted to be distanced? Did they want to dismiss from their minds their previous devotion, marked by rich silver chalices, to a King who had given them bishops, but also bloodshed? Perhaps the good folk of Peebles did not wish posterity to know that when their Presbyterian brothers were suffering the anguish of 'the Killing Times', they or their leaders were by such a gesture, honouring a tyrannical King and a religious order imposed by him.

What of James Nicol? Today his name and deeds are virtually unknown. The little that is known paints a picture of a man deeply versed in the scriptures, a man of courage, a man of deep conviction and unshakeable belief in an eternal life in the presence of God. In this he is not greatly different from so many Covenanting martyrs who, like him, gave their lives in the firm belief that their way, and their way only, was the true way, which would receive its reward in the hereafter. In this they did not greatly differ from martyrs of any generation. Like so many who suffered, he has no tangible memorial. What does remain in Peebles as a memorial of that time are the four communion cups, those presented for the edification and glory of absolute monarchy and a hierarchical Church, but still used today in the Church, which emerged from those distant days. Cups that are symbolic of the Blood of Christ, but perhaps also symbolic of the blood spilled by those martyrs, with one bearing the inscription 'In this conquer'.

In the Kirkyard of Greyfriars in Edinburgh stands the Martyrs Memorial erected in 1706. It was raised in memory of all those martyrs who have no marked grave. James Nicol is one of these. Its inscription reads:

> Halt passenger, take heed to what you see,
> This tomb doth shew, for what some men did die.
> Here lies interr'd the dust of those who stood
> 'gainst perjury, resisting unto blood,
> Adhering to the Covenants, and laws
> Establishing the same: which was the cause
> Their lives were sacrific'd unto the lust
> Of Prelatists abjur'd. Though here their dust

Lies mixt with murderers, and other crew,
Whom justice justly did to death pursue,
But as for them, no cause was to be found
Worthy of death, but only they were found,
Constant and steadfast, zealous, witnessing,
For the Prerogatives of CHRIST their KING,
Which truths were sealed by famous Guthrie's head,
And all along to Mr Renwick's blood.
They did endure the wrath of enemies,
Reproaches, torments, deaths and injuries,
But yet they're those who from such troubles came,
And now triumph in glory with the LAMB.

James Nicol –
Background Note

It is not known for certain when James Nicol was born. Although records of births, baptisms and marriages exist for the first half of the seventeenth century, registration did not become compulsory until 1855. A further complication is that the spelling of both surnames and Christian names was often not consistent. In the case of the records of the Parish of Peebles, the surname 'Nicol' appears in several forms as 'Nicoll', 'Nichol' and even 'Nicokell'. However, links can be found that make it reasonably certain the references which follow relate to the same person and his family.

It seems probable that James Nicol was the son of Walter Nicholl and Mergat Watsone, whose marriage is recorded as having taken place on 31 May 1632. The marriage of James Nicholl to Jennet Vaitche is recorded as 10 May 1654. It therefore seems likely he would have been born *circa* 1633, as indeed the 'Testimony' seems to confirm. This would have made him twenty-one years old at the time of his own marriage. He would also, in all probability, have been his parents' oldest son.

There is no further record or mention of his parents. However, as James is described in later years as a 'burgess of Peebles', it is likely that his father was also a burgess, and it was usual for a son to inherit that status, the principal qualification for which was the ownership of property (one rood of land) within the burgh. It is likely that the property would have passed from one generation to the next, and from father to eldest son.

It also seems likely that following their marriage, James and Jennet had a number of children. On 1 October 1660 the baptism of a girl, Jennet, the daughter of James Nicokell, is recorded. It is the only entry in the Register of a name of that spelling, but the coincidence of the name of the girl and the wife of James Nicol surely suggests that she is a child of their union. Later still, the baptism of a son, Johne, is recorded as having taken place on 3 May 1657, and the later baptism of another child, James, on 29 August 1669, is recorded as being the son of James Nicoll and Jonnet Veatch (again surely the same). All of these baptisms took place during periods when Covenanting Presbyterianism held sway, which is of interest in view of James's subsequent career and religious persuasion.

At a less happy time for him, during the Second Episcopacy, it is recorded that he was summoned to appear before the Kirk Session of Peebles on 5 October 1665 to explain his absence from the Kirk and his attendance at conventicles. It is noted that he also had a child 'long unbaptised', presumably born sometime after 1662 when Episcopacy was re-established. There would almost certainly have been other children of the marriage between 1665 and 1669, although their existence is unrecorded. A birth per year would have been nothing other than normal. Nevertheless, it is most unlikely that all would have survived. Whatever the circumstances, James Nicol was clearly a family man.

Glossary of Political and Religious Factions

The Estates	The Parliament of Scotland, comprising the landed nobility, representatives of the Church and of the burghs and counties presided over by the monarch.
The Tables	Representatives of the towns, nobility, the lairds and the Kirk, which met to counter the attempt by Charles I to impose Episcopacy, and which led in time to the National Covenant.
Presbyterianism	Form of Protestant church government by General Assembly, Synods and Presbyteries.
General Assembly	The supreme court of the Scottish National Church, comprising the representatives of the Synods and Presbyteries, first established in 1560.
Synod	Regional Kirk assembly, which equated to former bishopric or diocese.
Presbytery	Local ruling body, usually based on a county.
Covenanter	Broad term covering all those who supported the National Covenant. In time this evolved into the extreme fundamentalist Presbyterians who continued the struggle to impose the Covenant.
Independents	Puritan members of the English Parliament, ultimately led by Oliver Cromwell.
Engagers	Those who supported a policy of accommodation with Charles I, provided that he would agree to the re-establishment of Presbyterianism.
Malignants	Name given by their opponents to the Royalist party supporting Charles I.

Protesters	The party of the Kirk ministers opposed to the Engagers and to the support of Charles II, because they doubted his sincere support of the Covenant.
Resolutioners	Faction prepared to support an accommodation with Charles II in spite of his lukewarm support for the Covenant. They thought he would not try to re-impose Episcopacy in the light of his father's fate. They supported the broad principal of monarchy.
The Commonwealth	Government established by the English Parliament after the execution of Charles I, uniting England and Wales, Scotland and Ireland in a single State.
The New Model Army	Army established by the English Parliamentarians, under Oliver Cromwell.
Remonstrants	Those, formerly Protesters, who were of the Left, disowned the monarchy, sought dismissal from office of all who supported it and were prepared to treat with the English Parliament.
Whigs	Name given to the extreme Covenanters, based initially in the south-west of Scotland.
Cameronians	Extreme Whig faction, originally led by Richard Cameron, which became the mainstay of ultimate Covenanter resistance.
United Societies	Collective name adopted by Cameronians and the remainder of the extreme Whigs in the 1680s.

Notes and References

Part I

1. A Town of Kings

1 *The Works of Alexander Pennecuik* – Description of Tweeddale, p.282.
2 *Notes to the Works of Alexander Pennecuik*, 1815, p.283.
3 It stood where Veitch's Corner stands today. 'Cuinzie' or 'Cuinyie'; 'Coin' in Old Scots.
4 *Notes to the Works of Alexander Pennecuik*, 1815, p.283.
5 Ibid., p.285.
6 William Tytler, *The Poetical Remains of James the First, King of Scotland*, 1783.
7 Robert Chambers, *Picture of Scotland*, 1837, p.77.
8 Ibid., p.75.

2. 'The Guidman O' Ballengeich'

1 The assumption of full powers to rule following the years of minority.
2 The remains are still visible today.
3 *Wilson's Tales of the Border.*
4 *The Works of Alexander Pennecuik* – Description of Tweeddale, p.248.
5 A fragment of the 'True Cross' was allegedly found in Peebles in 1261 and was the cause of the founding of the Cross Kirk and the Monastery of the Trinity Friars.

3. A Rough Wooing

1 The Treaty of Greenwich.
2 A type of house with a stone-built vaulted ground floor and the upper floor built of timber and thatch connected by an outside stair. The entrance on the ground floor was protected by a very substantial door and the ground floor was thus a place of safety in times of strife.
3 Dr Clement Gunn, *The Book of the Peebles Church, AD 1195–1560*, p.126 (from an earlier source, Renwick).
4 De Termes was the commander of the French force which arrived in Scotland in 1549 to augment the already strong army which D'Esse had brought the previous year. Version of the text as recorded by Dr Gunn, *The Book of the Peebles Church, AD 1195–1560*, p.136.

5 The ruins remain today.
6 Dr Gunn, *The Book of the Peebles Church, AD 1195–1560*, p.137.
7 Ibid.
8 Ibid.

4. *Reformation*

1 The opening lines of the poem are quoted in both *Picture of Scotland* – Robert
   Chambers, 1837, and *History of Peeblesshire* – William Chambers, 1864. However, in
   several lines those versions appear to be in error. Some lines from the same poem appear
   in the *Etymological Dictionary of the Scottish Language* published by Edinburgh University
   in 1808, which differ from the two Chambers versions. One line in particular appears
   in the Chambers versions as: 'Thai lafit nocht with lady nor with lown, nor with
   trumpouris to travel throw the town.' In the *Dictionary* version these lines are: 'They lufit
   nocht with *Ladry* nor with lown.' Given the context of the lines the word 'Ladry' would
   seem to be more appropriate, meaning as it does 'idle lads', which sits better with 'lown'
   and 'trumpouris', which mean respectively, 'lazy wretches' and 'deceivers'. The version
   that has been used is therefore amended from Chambers, R & W, to correspond with
   the lines as they appear in the *Dictionary*.
2 Robert Chambers, *Picture of Scotland*.
3 Dr Gunn, *The Book of the Peebles Church, AD 1195–1560*.
4 Ibid., p.123.
5 Ibid.
6 Ibid.
7 Extract based on the version appearing in *The Book of the Peebles Church, AD 1195–1560* by
   Dr Gunn, but with some words amended to the versions in the *Etymological Dictionary of
   the Scottish Language*.
8 J.D. Mackie, *A History of Scotland*, 1964, p.147.
9 J.W. Buchan, *A History of Peeblesshire*, Vol. II, 1925, p.24.
10 Now Haystoun.
11 Where Dean Park and the Old Station are today.
12 Dr Gunn, *The Book of the Peebles Church, AD 1195–1560*, p.169.

5. *The Queen Returns*

1 Dr Gunn, *Book of the Cross Kirk, Peebles AD 1560–1690*, p.4.
2 Sir John Allan was a former priest and had been a chaplain in the Old Parish Church of
   St Andrews, and also a notary and the town clerk.
3 The first General Assembly of the fledgling Protestant Church of Scotland met in
   December 1560. In addition to other matters, it established the initial form of Church
   government. There were to be no bishops as such, but the country was to be split into
   nine regions, more or less conforming to the former Bishoprics. Each of these would
   have a superintendent.
4 A 'Reader and Exhorter' was in effect an assistant who, although not sufficiently
   qualified to be a minister, could speak prayers and conduct worship, but not the
   Sacraments. This does seem to lend credence to the reason for there being a request for
   him to be replaced.
5 As quoted in *The Works in Prose and Verse of Alexander Pennecuik, Esq. of New-Hall, M.D.*,
   Edition of 1815.
6 Alison Weir, *Mary Queen of Scots and the Murder of Lord Darnley*, 2003, p.92.
7 Dr Gunn, *The Book of the Cross Kirk, Peebles AD 1560–1690*.

6. *God's Sillie Vassal*

1 The crown, which is today on display in Edinburgh Castle as part of the 'Honours of Scotland', is the self-same crown and is largely in the original form as when made for James V. It is alleged to be the oldest crown in Europe with a continuous line of usage.
2 William Chambers, *History of Peeblesshire*, 1864, p.118.
3 Sir Anthony Weldon was an English courtier, who was among those who accompanied James when he returned to Scotland in 1617. He had nothing good to say about the country or its people and many years later, after the execution of Charles I, when the republic had been established, he published a viciously jaundiced account called 'The Court and Character of King James' in 1649. It is his descriptions of the appearance and character of the King that largely gave rise to the caricature image of him which prevailed until quite recent times, when a more objective view has come to prevail.
4 The ruin stands on the Perth/Stirling road west of Perth and is now known as Huntingtower.
5 A 'tulchan' is a calf skin stuffed with straw to look like a live calf and was put beside a cow to induce it to give milk.
6 J.W. Buchan, *A History of Peeblesshire*, Vol. II, p.27.
7 Ibid., p.29.
8 Ibid.
9 Ibid.
10 *The Book of the Cross Kirk, Peebles AD 1560–1690*, p.33.
11 Ibid.
12 J.W. Buchan, *A History of Peeblesshire*, Vol. II, p.31.
13 William Chambers, *History of Peeblesshire*, p.123.
14 Ibid.
15 Ibid., pp.123–4.
16 The original text of the Charter would have been in Latin. This is the translated version as it appears in Gunn.
17 J.W. Buchan, *A History of Peeblesshire*, Vol. II, p.35.
18 Ibid., p.36.
19 Ibid.

7. *Royal Supremacy*

1 The site was probably near to where Peebles Hydro stands today.
2 Dr Gunn, *The Book of the Cross Kirk, Peebles AD 1560–1690*, p.102.
3 J.W. Buchan, *A History of Peeblesshire*, Vol. II, p.43.

Part II

8. *Joshua Made a Covenant*

1 So called because it was made of timber baulks. Excavations in 1982, when the present bridge was rebuilt, unearthed several large pieces of oak dating from medieval times.
2 Now the Cross Keys Inn.

9. *Bishops' Wars*

1 A relic of this visit is an armorial panel in oak with the Queen's cipher, which can still be seen at Traquair House.
2 Papers of the Stewart Family, Earls of Traquair muniments.
3 Ibid.
4 Ibid.

5 Ibid.

6 J.W. Buchan, *A History of Peeblesshire*, Vol. II, p.46.

7 'The Long Parliament'.

8 Dr Gunn, *The Book of the Cross Kirk, Peebles AD 1560–1690*, p.123.

9 The Westminster Confession of Faith.

10 Dr Gunn, *The Book of the Cross Kirk, Peebles AD 1560–1690*, p.125.

11. Divine Retribution

1 The 'Wiggamore Raid'.

2 J.W. Buchan, *A History of Peeblesshire*, Vol. II, p.49.

12. Noble Neidpath

1 Modern-day Eddleston.

13. The Protectorate

1 Dr Gunn, *The Book of the Cross Kirk, Peebles AD 1560–1690*, pp.153–4.

2 J.W. Buchan, *A History of Peeblesshire*, Vol. II, p.53.

3 Ibid., pp.52–3.

15. The Merry Monarch

1 Later James VII & II.

2 Agnes Mure MacKenzie, *The Passing of the Stewarts*, p.175.

3 Ibid., p.178.

4 Ibid., p.195.

5 Testimony of James Nicol.

17. Rullion Green

1 Agnes Mure MacKenzie, *The Passing of the Stewarts*, p.189.

2 Ibid., p.190.

3 Ibid., p.198.

4 Rev. Alexander (Sandy) Peden was a prominent Covenanting preacher, who in spite of his encouragement of violent action, avoided martyrdom and died of natural causes in 1686.

18. Awa, Whigs, Awa!

1 Agnes Mure MacKenzie, *The Passing of the Stewarts*, p.208.

2 Ibid.

3 J.D. Mackie, *A History of Scotland*, p.236.

4 Agnes Mure MacKenzie, *The Passing of the Stewarts*, p.211, quoted from Rev. Robert Wodrow, *History of the Sufferings of the Church of Scotland*.

5 Agnes Mure MacKenzie, *The Passing of the Stewarts*, p.212.

6 Ibid., p.214.

7 William Chambers, *History of Peeblesshire*, p.190.

8 Dr Gunn, *The Book of the Cross Kirk, Peebles AD 1560–1690*, p.199.

9 J.D. Mackie, *A History of Scotland*, p.237.

19. The Deil of Dundee

1 Andrew Murray Scott, *Bonnie Dundee*, 2000.

2 Dane Love, *Scottish Covenanter Stories*.

3 Ibid.
4 Ibid., p.63.
5 Ibid., p.67.

20. *Stones and Clouts*

1 Agnes Mure MacKenzie, *The Passing of the Stewarts*, p.243.
2 Although the Covenanters were generally described as 'Whigs', there were various factions called 'Societies' and collectively the 'United Societies'.
3 Agnes Mure MacKenzie, *The Passing of the Stewarts*, p.244.
4 Dane Love, *Scottish Covenanter Stories*, p.132.
5 Dr Gunn, *The Book of the Cross Kirk, Peebles* AD *1560–1690*, p.220.

22. *A Fugitive and a Vagabond*

1 J.W. Buchan, *A History of Peeblesshire*, Vol. II, p.61.
2 Ibid.
3 Peebles Council Minutes, 1679–1714. NRAS ref. B58/13/3.

23. *The Martyr of Peebles*

1 These are as reprinted in *A Cloud of Witnesses*, published in 1871.
2 The coronation at which, according to Agnes Mure MacKenzie, 'there was much preaching' (*The Passing of the Stewarts*, p.146).

24. *The Happy Revolution*

1 J.W. Buchan, *A History of Peeblesshire*, Vol. II, p.62.
2 Dr Gunn, *The Book of the Cross Kirk, Peebles* AD *1560–1690*, pp.233–4.
3 Ibid.
4 J.D. Mackie, *A History of Scotland*, p.243.
5 Dr Gunn, *The Book of the Cross Kirk, Peebles* AD *1560–1690*, p.239.
6 Ibid., p.240.
7 James was strictly speaking not the last Stuart monarch, as his daughters, first Mary as joint monarch and then Anne, succeeded him.
8 Agnes Mure MacKenzie, *The Passing of the Stewarts*, p.289, and J.D. Mackie, *A History of Scotland*, p.244.

Epilogue

1 J.D. Mackie, *A History of Scotland*, p.248.

List of Sources

Aitchison, Peter and Cassell, Andrew, *The Lowland Clearances* (Tuckwell Press, East Lothian, 2003)

Brown, P. Hume, *A Short History of Scotland* (Oliver & Boyd, Edinburgh, 1908)

Buchan, J.W., *A History of Peeblesshire, Volume II* (Jackson, Wylie & Co., Glasgow, 1925)

Cameron, Jamie, *James V: The Personal Rule 1528–1542* (Tuckwell Press, East Lothian, 1998)

Chambers, Robert, *Picture of Scotland* (W & R Chambers, Edinburgh, 1837)

Chambers, William, *History of Peeblesshire* (W & R Chambers, Edinburgh, 1864)

Fraser, Antonia, *Cromwell Our Chief of Men* (Book Club Associates, London, 1974)

——, *King James I of England* (Book Club Associates, London, 1974)

——, *Mary Queen of Scots* (Weidenfeld & Nicolson, London, 1969)

Frieda, Leonie, *Catherine de Medici* (Weidenfeld & Nicolson, London, 2003)

Gifford, John, McWilliam, Colin and Walker, David, *Buildings of Scotland, Edinburgh* (Penguin Books Ltd, Harmsworth, 1984)

Gunn, Dr Clement, *The Ministry of the Presbytery of Peebles, 296–1910* (Allan Smyth, Neidpath Press, Peebles, 1910)

——, *The Book of Peebles Church – St Andrew's Collegiate Parish Church AD 1195–1560* (A. Walker & Sons, Galashiels and J.A. Anderson, Peebles, 1908)

——, *The Book of the Cross Kirk, Peebles AD 1560–1690* (Allan Smyth, Neidpath Press, Peebles, 1912)

Hermon, Arthur, *The Scottish Enlightenment* (Fourth Estate, London, 2001)

Love, Dane, *Scottish Covenanter Stories* (Neil Wilson Publishing, Glasgow, 2000)

MacFarlane, Rev. David C., *A Guide to the Old Parish Church of Peebles* (Kirk Session of Peebles: Old, Peebles, 1973)

MacKenzie, Agnes Mure, *The Passing of the Stewarts* (W & R Chambers, Edinburgh, 1937)

Mackie, J.D., *A History of Scotland* (Penguin Books Ltd, Harmsworth, 1964)

Macleod, John, *Dynasty: The Stuarts 1560–1807* (Hodder and Stoughton, London, 1999)

Pennecuick, Alexander, *Works of*, including *Description of Tweeddale* (Longman & Co., London, 1815)

Railton, Margaret (Compiler), *Andrew Lorimer's Life and Times in the Upper Tweed Valley* (Tuckwell Press, East Lothian, 2001)

Renwick, Robert, *Extracts from the Records of The Burgh of Peebles 1652–1714* (Scottish Burgh Records Society, Glasgow, 1910)

——, *Peebles Burgh and Parish* (A Repath, Peebles, 1903)

——, *The Burgh of Peebles: Gleanings from its Records* (Allan Smyth, Neidpath Press, Peebles, 1912)
Ross, Stewart, *Monarchs of Scotland* (Lochar Publishing, Moffat, 1990)
——, *The Stewart Dynasty* (Thomas & Lochar, Nairn, 1993)
Scott, Andrew Murray, *Bonnie Dundee* (John Donald Publishers, Edinburgh, 1989)
Scott, Ronald McNair, *Robert the Bruce, King of Scots* (Canongate Publishing Ltd, Edinburgh, 1993)
Stewart, Alan, *The Cradle King* (Chatto & Windus, London, 2003)
Tomalin, Claire, *Samuel Pepys, The Unqualified Self* (Penguin Books Ltd, London, 2003)
Weir, Alison, *Mary, Queen of Scots and the Murder of Lord Darnley* (Pimlico, London, 2003)
Whitley, Elizabeth, *Plain Mr. Knox* (Scottish Reformation Society, Edinburgh, 1960)

Internet Sources

European Institute of Protestant Studies, *Scottish Covenanters – James Guthrie*
Fire and Ice: *Puritan Sermons, James Guthrie*
Online Encyclopedia, *James Sharp (1618–1679)*
Reformed Presbyterian Church (Covenanted), Confession of Faith or The National Covenant
Scottish Covenanter Memorials Association, *Battle of Airds Moss*
Upholding the Testimony of the Covenanted Reformation, *A Cloud of Witnesses*
Wikipedia, *John Comyn, Earl of Buchan*
Wikipedia, *Battle of Bothwell Brig*
Wikipedia, *Battle of Rullion Green*

Additional Sources

National Archives of Scotland – Peebles Town Council Minutes, 1679–1714
Scottish Borders Council, Archives/Local History
Stewart Family, Earls of Traquair muniments

Index